GENDER UNCHAINED

NOTES FROM THE EQUITY FRONTIER

LORRAINE GREAVES & NANCY POOLE

Praise for
Gender Unchained - Notes from the Equity Frontier

"This is a must-read tour de force for women and men in all walks of life. It brings together, in a slim volume, a forensically argued case for justice and equity among genders. It not only provides 21st century reminders of the causes and costs of gender inequity across the globe, but provides us with the shared principles and tools for transformative action."

—Dr. Bobbie Jacobson OBE. Institute of Health Equity, University College, London, UK

"This book is brimming with provocative clarity on the big problems of the 21st Century. It offers compelling evidence of egregious gendered inequities in all regions of the world, that call out to our collective responsibilities as leaders, global citizens, students, politicians and advocates."

—Marilou McPhedran CM. Senator and human rights lawyer, Canada

"This is a fascinating wake-up call to feminists everywhere. Be prepared to be challenged. Be prepared to be inspired. Be prepared to rethink everything!"

—Constance Backhouse CM. Professor of Law. University of Ottawa

FriesenPress

Suite 300 - 990 Fort St
Victoria, BC, V8V 3K2
Canada

www.friesenpress.com

First Edition — 2017

GALVANIZING EQUITY
Insight for a Change

Galvanizing Equity is a company devoted to working alongside global partners to bring evidence to action, in order to improve health and social equity for all
www.galvanizingequity.com

The Boxing Bennett Sisters played a part in the long gendered history of women's boxing. From a glass negative from the Bain Collection, circa 1910. Library of Congress

ISBN
978-1-4602-9970-8 (Paperback)
978-1-4602-9971-5 (eBook)

1. SOCIAL SCIENCE, GENDER STUDIES

Distributed to the trade by The Ingram Book Company

GENDER UNCHAINED

NOTES FROM THE EQUITY FRONTIER

LORRAINE GREAVES & NANCY POOLE

TABLE OF CONTENTS

CHAPTER 1

Galvanising Equity

Equity. Equality. Fairness. The optimistic dream of progressive modern societies can be summed up as a yearning for equity and for all that accompanies equity – mutual acceptance, inclusion, opportunity, prosperity, and the related 'no one left behind' aspirational goals.

Amid increased anger and suffering attached to violence, poverty, terrorism, corporate representation, globalisation, environmental degradation, migration, climate calamities, and indigenous health and well-being, attention to gender disparities is still largely avoided. Over many centuries, feminists have highlighted, researched, activated, advocated, worked, struck, and died in the name of gender equity. But in fact, inequities persist for many women, especially in conservative families, regimes, and countries, and for some men as well. But despite this, and after all this, gender is still riding in the backseat of the vehicle of change for reasons that are as confounding and mysterious as they are serious.

Perhaps the idea of reaching equity for all is a pipe dream that just serves as motivation. Or perhaps it's a smokescreen for a range of 'isms' that persist in dividing and suppressing, such as sexism, racism, classism, heterosexism, nativism, or ableism. Perhaps it is just a benign rallying cry for change makers. Perhaps

GLOBAL SUFFERING

'Gender inequality is a pressing global issue with huge ramifications not just for the lives and livelihoods of girls and women but, more generally, for human development, labour markets, productivity, GDP growth, and inequality.'

"The Power of Parity: How advancing women's equality can add $12 trillion to global growth". McKinsey Global Institute, September 2015. www.mckinsey.com

calls for equity are just the hopeful, bright bungee cords linking together the many crucial issues of our time. For all progressives, whether activists, leaders, politicians, or indeed ordinary citizens, perhaps these calls are just reflexes, not reflexive.

Worse, calls for equity may be just dislocated, simplistic hopes for change, or as cynics and conservatives might say, 'hopey-changey' sentiments, easily smothered by disparagement. It is hard to say, because underneath all calls for equity is a desire for transformation unlikely to be reached unless all the various forms of comfort and benefit are addressed, dismantled, and reframed.

While equity must remain a laudable goal, it seems a state unlikely to be reached unless the most basic local and global gender inequities are resolved. It is hard to imagine a state of equity that has not resolved bodily autonomy, freedom of movement, access to power, and the universal scourge of violence against women and girls. It is hard to imagine that in any context: family or community, or in any country or regime or religious group. It is also hard to imagine that this can somehow be fixed, avoided, or nullified by just calling for the end to racism, classism, homophobia, or ableism. Or by hoping that in a racially, religiously, ethnically, ability, or class-based equal world, that gender won't still be playing a vital role in the inequity stakes. In fact, it's impossible to imagine.

This book corrects that possible misplaced assumption, or pitfall, by eliminating wilful ignorance and showing how men and women, leaders and citizens, can reverse any idea that equity can exist without gender equity, or that any optimistic future can emerge without ending sexism along with racism and classism and ableism. It posits that ending racism or classism or ableism cannot be done without addressing gender inequities within and among those social forces. In order to reverse direction and rebalance our

'THE MASTER'S TOOLS WILL NEVER DISMANTLE THE MASTER'S HOUSE.'

(AUDRE LORDE, POET)

'...gender [analysis] does not point to a hole or a gap in an otherwise intact "blanket" of sustainable climate policies. Instead it indicates entire needed reorientations...'

Ulrike Röhr, 2008 as cited in Seager, J. "Death by Degrees: Taking a feminist hard look at the 2° climate policy". Kvinder, Kön og Foraksning, 3-4 Special issue on climate change. (2009).

world, and to galvanise greater equity, a gender transformative approach is required.

In the complex and fast-moving world of the twenty-first century, we need to do many things at once, such as addressing issues like climate change, gendered decision-making, and land rights together, or globalisation and gendered labour force disruption together, or poverty reduction and caregiving responsibilities, or corporate representation and all forms of diversity, or indigenous well-being and violence against girls and women. Or you name it.

A gender transformative approach takes many things into account at once. These can be characteristics such as class, race, or ability, or can be several issues seeking perhaps common solutions. This enables us not only to see how gender operates at the root of many social and economic issues and problems, but also to confirm that the future of equity is comprised of multi-tasking. Taking action on transformative, gender-equitable change could move us past the pipe dream and into a new world order.

Generations of thinkers have highlighted class, race, and gender, often in turn, less often together, as key fault lines in society's armament. It is often suggested that thinking about them together, and attaching no automatic primacy to any is the best way to understand experiences. And it may be that one of these features has, at a point in time, more effect on an individual's opportunity, experience, or treatment.

But in acting on these issues, it seems clear that each of them benefits from being subdivided by gender, and that ignoring gender because race or class might be a key oppression, or casting gender into the wings, or leaving it until later, is folly. Indeed, addressing gender inequity *within* these other forces and groups makes us all confront the sexism among oppressed people as well, and the different roles and relegations assigned to women and girls within the margins of the margins.

LOST GIRL PRODUCTIVITY

If every Ethiopian girl finished school, it would add almost $4 billion US to the country's economy

Gable, S. "Girls and Income Growth in Ethiopia." Girl Effect Ethiopia, 2013. www.girleffect.org

Why Equity?

Many of us may quickly opt for equality between men and women where men and women get the same treatment, but equity is a far more elusive goal. Equity means opportunities are even and may mean special treatment, rules, laws, or programs for some. Equity is a more complex goal, one that ensures that girls get educated in a context where cultural prohibitions may subtly or overtly prevent attendance at school, even if technically, school is open to all.

Equity means that caregiving roles are taken into account when designing aid programs, or creating social assistance policies. It also forces us to think about how our traits and experiences mix and how sex-related factors such as bodily characteristics and processes, as well as gender-related factors, such as cultural, economic, and power issues, combine to generate equity, or not. It means that sex and gender are both recognised when funding health research or designing seat belts or testing drugs or planning cities. You get the idea – it is hard to name a circumstance, issue, object, ideology, policy, location, or yes, even an aspiration where gender and possibly sex are not crucial to the definition, design, implementation, allocation, recognition, or resolution. Try it. It's difficult to do.

LAND RIGHTS AND VIOLENCE

'...policy makers could reduce violence by elimination of gender bias in ownership rights and addressing norms that justify wife beating and male control of female behaviour.'

Heise, L. L., & Kotsadam, A. "Cross-national and multilevel correlates of partner violence: an analysis of data from population-based surveys." The Lancet Global Health 3, no. 6 (2015): e332-40.

There is something very important about gender, especially when we include sex along with it, as it marries the biological and sociological, and covers the individual experience from the corporeal to the societal. In other words, noticing gender means that we notice our bodies, and that others notice our bodies, and that our experiences inside our bodies matter in profound ways. Being noticed can fuel us, or it can instil heart-stopping fear. It can generate pleasure or absolute terror. It's about context.

Race and ability often, but not always, operate in the same way. Being black in America remains dangerous. But any race or ability identity also incorporates sex- and gender-based features, of whatever kind. So it's important to say that being a black male in America is particularly dangerous. Especially when near a police officer. Likewise, being a young, Indigenous girl in Canada is dangerous, especially when on a remote highway. Gender influences our social experiences in the world, especially if, like most, we cannot escape societal categories of men, women, boys, and girls.

Gender invokes all of us, whatever our gender identities or body structures, and demands a transdisciplinary look at our world. It includes all of us as our sex and gender attributes make fluid journeys through our lives, some more than others, by choice, design, experience, environment, or aging. So no one is without gender, although in some cases gender identity and gender experience are less easy to catalogue or measure, especially in circumstances where individuals reject, or do not appear to conform with mainstream conceptions of gender.

This importance forces us to grapple with facing gendered inequities, whether in the form of genital mutilation imposed by tradition and tribalism, or cosmetic genital surgery framed as 'choice' by girls and women in porn-infused cultures. Or in the form of reproductive, caregiving, and domestic work imbalances, whether biologically or socially imposed, where women across the world work double or triple the hours of men. Or in the form of relative poverty, whether politically or legally imposed, where girls and women simply make less money, or get paid less than equal for work of equal value, or when women-dominated work is devalued. Or in the form of power imbalances set by custom, culture, or law where few women are elected or in leadership positions. Or... well, you get the idea.

It's also critically revealing to look at specific issues. Climate change, for example, the pressure

WATER, WATER

'Worldwide, women and children spend 125 million hours *each day*, collecting water.' This is time spent not working for pay, caring for family members, or attending school.

"Facts about Children, Women and the Safe Water Crisis". www.tinyurl.com/zd5xk87

of our time; globally present, inequitably affecting, threatening our very existence, coming at some of us more quickly than others. Some of us are metaphorically on higher ground, some literally. How does gender play into this issue? Why aren't we discussing it more? Will women, the poorest in the world, be dislocated first? Will men need new jobs? Will women need new jobs? Will girls and women be vulnerable in light of climate chaos? Will women have a say in adaptation, relocation, sustainability, and renewal? What happens to women? What happens to men?

Let's also consider contagious disease, such as the pressures around the Zika virus on women, which are so obvious but not really addressed. Women who are pregnant are vulnerable to developing a foetus with brain malformations. So far, women in vulnerable regions have been exhorted to refrain from becoming pregnant. (Has no one heard of no access to birth control, illegality of abortion, unequal power in relationships, or the presence of coercive sex?) What are the advisors thinking? What about men? How about exhorting them to relinquish the focus on penetrative sex or to take responsibility for birth control? What about some sharing of reality?

HUGE NUMBERS

It is estimated that 60, 000 girls under the age of 15 are at risk of FGM in the UK, and that over 130 million girls and women worldwide have undergone FGM.

"FGM", FORWARD. www.forwarduk.org.uk/key-issues/fgm/

What about drinking or smoking? Substance use, in general, is influenced by biology and sociology, a perfect example of sex and gender at play. There is clarity about the effects of different amounts of drugs and alcohol on different types of bodies, depending on fat tissue, size, and metabolism, and genetics and influenced by reproductive roles and pressures. Generally, these are sex-based differences. But gender matters too. And gender inequity matters a lot as unequal power and gender relations, different patterns of trauma, and access to money and health care play into gendered substance use patterns. All of us would benefit by using this lens; as individuals and as a society. Again, what issues are there that are not affected by gender? Think of one!

Clearly, context matters. In some situations and locations, gender will matter most and more. In others, minority groups and ethnicities will confront added oppressions. In others, sexual orientation will sentence some to death and others to life, and in other situations, disability will render you without rights to dignity, comfort, or money, and in some contexts give you a silent, unnoticed death. In many cases, simple aging will render you an object of discrimination, invisibility, and control. But gender will come up in all of these situations, either first or later. And it will differentiate the experiences for those involved and for those reacting to those affected.

Are we winning or losing the gender war? Probably both at the same time. In 2017, we are feasting in many progressive countries and societies on an apparent resurgence of feminism, or more accurately, on a resurgence of the overt recognition of feminism and its importance. It could be fake and flawed or just a bandwagon. It could just be an increased willingness to use the word.

In any event, we are engulfed in more and more frank conversations about violence against women, globally and locally, as well as critical conversations about misogyny, sexual assault, and a range of global oppressions of women. We are seeing more men and male leaders take on the label of 'feminist' and engaged men, for what it's worth. After a decade of wondering why feminism was referred to as an 'F-word', we are now seeing more young women and girls declare themselves feminists, learning to fight back and claim spaces, on and off the Internet. We are, in some wonderful cases, seeing gender parity imposed or ramped-up pressures and regulations to see women leaders in politics and corporations. We are seeing women outnumber men in higher education in some countries but not necessarily reflected, yet, in positions of power and control in social, economic, or political circles.

LINGERING EFFECTS

'Since 2006, an extra quarter of a billion women have entered the labour force. And yet, the annual pay for women only now equals the amount men were earning TEN YEARS AGO.'

World Economic Forum. "The Global Gender Gap Report 2015": www.tinyurl.com/ja9bh2n

But simultaneously, in many societies, regimes, countries, and indeed families, there remains a situation of considerable oppression by gender and sex. This ranges from female genital mutilation by imposition or 'cosmetic' genital modification by 'choice,' forced marriages, child marriages, mass rapes, and violence against women in every country, caste, and class on the globe. There are still millions of women dying in childbirth and early maternity, or left permanently disfigured by the results of unattended childbirth in many countries. There are still widespread situations where the majority of the impoverished, malnourished, or illiterate are women and girls. There are multiple regimes that use women's inequality as a foundation for ideology and control, often through controlling or policing sexuality, dress, and independent movement.

RIGID GENDER NORMS ARE NOT HEALTHY

'Decades of the basic research has now found that when young men and women internalize rigid ideals for masculinity and femininity, they have markedly lower life outcomes in a cluster of related areas that can include: basic health, education outcomes, and partner violence.'

Wilchins, R. and M. Gilmer. "Addressing Masculine Norms to Improve Life Outcomes for Young Black Men: Why We Still Can't Wait." True Child. 2015. www.truechild.org/heinz

Almost incongruously, there are simultaneous debates focussed on the number or women in cabinets, or on corporate boards, or the pay differential in million-dollar executive compensation or movie star salaries. But this wide range of issues is, of course, all connected by gender. And unfortunately, the gender inequity in the world and indeed in our own families is still likely tipped against girls and women. And talking 'gender' implicates all of us: female, male, trans, as we are all connected to women. As American comedian Steve Lofstetter said in explaining his defence of women against a misogynist heckler: "My family is genetically related to women. My grandmother was a woman. My mother was a woman. So yes it does concern me".

There is no doubt that while we may be winning in some ways, there is plenty of evidence that sexism, misogyny, and gender-based violence are alive and well: disappeared girls; missing Indigenous women; mass rape in war; date rape on couches; domestic femicide; women's poverty mislabelled as 'child poverty'; anti-choice regimes that prefer foetuses to women; girls and women eating last and least and working more than their male family members; and an astonishingly rich global pornography industry and sex trafficking regime that focuses on violating, capturing, exploiting, traumatising, and profiteering from women and children.

These issues are not rare examples of cultural habits hanging on by threads in a few remaining regional pockets, particular to some social classes, countries, or ethnic/racial groups that are rooted in havens of remote, dwindling, autocratic religious patriarchies, but rather, they appear to be thriving around the world. So yes, we are winning and losing at the same time.

There are plenty of other problems to confront in modern society as well, as economies shift, political alliances shatter, the world heats up, and global migration is a given. The question of whether to blame others and retreat, or share resources and throw doors open to opportunity is as relevant in the twenty-first century as it ever was in the twentieth. Such pressures force the tensions between pluralism and liberalism to be stress-tested. Political leaders making decisions on immigration, trade, and cooperation are pressed to take positions on this, but this dilemma is present in our homes as well.

Can local and even familial decisions of sharing, caring, cooperation, and sustainable growth generate more equity? Or does the drawbridge need closing, to close out outside influences, protect land, nationhood, and tribalism and freeze-dry sexist cultural practices? Either way, and in any political context, it remains true that seeing all of these other problems with a gender lens is but the first step in understanding them better, solving them more effectively, and getting closer to equity in the world. Pipe dreams need plans too.

Root Causes

Politicians are sometimes mocked for wanting to address root causes, especially in times of crisis. Prior to becoming prime minister of Canada, in his reaction to a particular international terrorist attack, Justin Trudeau, then a rookie, suggested a look at root causes was necessary. Widely dismissed as inexperienced, juvenile, and unrealistic, Trudeau went on to win a majority government in Canada by espousing openness and sharing, a 'one world' view of politics that triumphed over hatred and closed borders.

Such 'root causes' discussions are consistently regarded as idealistic ruminations on deep-seated factors that may best be dealt with by sociologists or philosophers, at leisure and preferably in the future. In the moment, such ruminations are often dismissed as a legitimate focus for urgent, relevant, critical conversations.

But this is the policy equivalent of avoiding home maintenance until the pipes break or the roof caves in. Or on a global level, ignoring climate change until floods and rising sea levels drown us one by one. To ignore root causes, especially when surrounded by rubble or floods, leads only to knee-jerk responses and cover-up solutions. It leads to a practice of taping things together until the next event. But looking for underlying drivers is always a critical exercise, for it illuminates the termites gnawing away at the beams, or the pollution eating into our bodies.

Gender inequities have root causes too, all too often avoided in typical, everyday conversations. This is true even when discussing violence against women, surely the most emblematic, blatant, and universal scourge of gender inequity, and perhaps the great leveller among women across the globe.

In responding to violence against women, there is a tendency to focus on an event, or a situation, or a law, or a context, or the victim, as opposed to the basic

ACCUMULATED GENDERED EXPERIENCES

'We de-escalate. We are acutely aware of our vulnerability – that if he wanted to, that guy in the Home Depot parking lot could overpower us and do whatever he wants. **Guys, this is what it means to be a woman.** We are sexualized before we even understand what that means. We get stares and comments from adult men before we can process what they mean. We learn at an early age that to confront these situations could put us in danger. So we minimize and we de-escalate.'

Kelly, G. "This is how a lifetime of potentially dangerous situations affects every woman." In Upworthy, December 10, 2015. www.tinyurl.com/zv48e4e

drivers in society that create and maintain this phenomenon. This attention to detail often masks an ideological detour, shifting us away from the issue and indeed around it, so we can ignore it and carry on our way as usual. At our peril, we avoid the real drivers of violence against women, such as male child preference, female infanticide, misogyny, male entitlement, bystander inaction, sexist cultures, gender stereotypes, gender socialisation, official blindness, and cultural silences.

Indeed, most gendered inequities, whether violence, poverty, overwork, or lack of autonomy or bodily integrity, have root causes. Some of these are shared in deep-seated positions and attitudes about gendered roles, stereotypes, and gender relations, bolstered by tradition, religion, media, and cultural supports. To say these drivers need spotlights shone on them would be an understatement. All of these issues are up for scrutiny in a gender transformative world, and matter deeply to all the large issues confronting us in our modern world.

Root Solutions

Root solutions are less often discussed. But they too need more attention. No matter what the global issue we are confronting, there are some underlying factors that drive it, and they don't get any better by being ignored. Climate change and global warming have been disregarded for decades by many leaders around the world, to the rapidly escalating chagrin of both crusaders and victims. Economic inequity has also been ignored, to the annoyance of the one-percenters, Occupy movement leaders, and anti-Brexit leaders, among many others.

Similarly, gender inequity continues to be broadly ignored, relegated to the category of needing

MEN LEARNING

Promundo's Program H engages young men in critical reflection and dialogue about gender equality via participatory sessions in which they live, rehearse, and model gender-equitable and non-violent styles of interaction. Group education activities address caregiving, sexual and reproductive health, women's rights, gender-based violence, and violence among men.

www.promundoglobal.org

a deep think later, not now, and hopefully by those sociologists and philosophers. But even as we say that, new sectors are waking up. Justin Trudeau, the new prime minister of Canada, in creating his first cabinet, made it gender equal – fifty percent women and fifty percent men. When asked why, he famously and simply said, "Because it's 2015." What underpins that *GIF* is a notion that ultimately we have to recognise inequity and act on root causes by taking actions that leapfrog the conditions of our time, or of our lives, and make progress. And perhaps skip the interminable nit picking, encouraging, discussing, or even regulating and legislating and just do it – with some courage and clarity.

A leap to recognising root causes and solutions is not confined to parity in cabinet making. The equivalent in health care and research has been a forty-year discussion about the social determinants of health, with a lot of water under the bridge. In other words, recognition that poverty, class, education, culture, and yes, gender, are the main drivers of health or ill health. After the Brexit vote in 2016, mainstream science and medicine got into this debate in ways not often seen. *The Lancet*, the esteemed UK medical journal had this to say about next steps:

> The National Health Service is a core social institution that makes equity and altruism central values in our society. The response to Brexit from our scientific and medical leaders should be to widen the circumference of their concerns, not implicitly endorse a philosophy of competitive greed that some Leavers wish to foster. Instead, we should be strengthening our associations across society, encouraging a less selfish and more generous spirit in our public words, and promoting a more constructive internationalism that recognises that there is a slowly emerging world society,

one that will depend on our full participation and engagement.[1]

While all of this makes sense, digging up root causes forces us think in ways to which we are not accustomed. We are challenged to understand the details, history, and drivers of ongoing inequity and the political blindness that results. It also forces us to address our own privilege or lack thereof, our own comforts and expectations of others, and our own trajectories and responsibilities in making change. And most important, it forces us to consider root solutions and how they might feel.

How Difficult Can This Be?

Equity for all is the dream upheld by progressive politicians and community builders in twenty-first-century progressive countries. But this is by no means a universal dream or aspiration. Many countries, regimes, and systems, not to mention communities and families within progressive countries, do not share this aspiration. All too often, there is comfort with the status quo, a desire to retreat back to historical traditions, or to soak in the supposedly benign pleasures of benefitting from inequities.

There is certainly comfort in benefitting from the inequitable distribution of work and caregiving. Women work far more than men and girls more than boys, in countries around the globe. Women do more unpaid work and men, with rare exceptions, are not organising to change this. And it is consistently true that various groups of women in disadvantaged

LET'S CHANGE THE STORY

'Australia has a choice. We can change the story that currently sees a woman murdered every week by a current or former partner. We can choose a future where women and their children live free from violence. What our framework makes clear is that gender inequality is the core of the problem and it is the heart of the solution. An Australia free of violence against women and their children is an Australia where women are not only safe, but respected, valued and treated as equals in private and public life.'
Our Watch

www.ourwatch.org.au/

1 Horton, Richard. "The Meanings of Brexit." *The Lancet* 388, no. 10039 (2016). www.tinyurl.com/hhmuhwx

locations socially, economically, and geographically, work more and harder than others.

For many of us, it remains very easy to relax while someone else cooks a meal and washes the dishes. It appears comfortable for many to have 'others' metaphorically or actually haul firewood and water long distances over dusty tracks, or clean the house, or mind the children, or harvest the summer fruit. That this wide array of positioning on equity can exist at the same moment in time, or even within the same individual, is a signal of the complexity and dissonance involved. It speaks to the challenge of sharing the aspiration equally, let alone achieving equity for all. It is a complex, multidimensional task, best approached by multi-tasking and using all the human capital in the world.

CHAPTER 2

What is Gender?

So let's talk more about gender. The most common understanding of gender, still, is based on a gender binary that includes boys and girls and men and women, and relies on understanding maleness and femaleness, and masculinity and femininity, often as distinct from each other. This binary invokes categories for programming and policy-making, boxes on survey forms, and ultimately, differentiated toy aisles, clothing stores, sexual roles, career aspirations, and housekeeping responsibilities.

Like any fence, wall, or container, the gender binary requires a lot of work to maintain. It means we need to constantly corral and confine gender and all of its meanings and actions into these two groups. It means there is a very particular energy generated to deal with any outlier, or even any fluidity in gender diversity in any way, including dress, sexual orientation, language, movement among and through genders, gender diverse interpretations, intersex bodies, hormonal fluctuations, reproductive choices, or media representation. Outliers are often vulnerable, either seen as lost sheep, stray sheep, or black sheep, or more dangerously, as threats.

And it's not just the maintenance. Once you have walls and categories, it is also important to police gender as well. This ranges from manufacturing

THE POLICING OF INDIGENOUS GENDER

'In 1879, for example, the only surviving Hidatsa miati (male in a woman's role) was forcibly stripped of her/his female attire by the local government agent, who also dressed her/him in men's clothes and cut off her/his braids.'

Bowers 1985, as cited in Lang, S., "Native American men-women, lesbians, two-spirits: Contemporary and historical perspectives." Journal of Lesbian Studies, 20, no. 3-4 2016: 299-323.

pink and blue baby clothes, to schoolyard bullying, to police raids on gay bars, to mockery of transgender people, to stoning women adulterers, and yes, even routinely killing the outliers. Policing costs us. It requires rules, uniformity, and sometimes weapons. It often causes rifts or cements them. It undermines our morality. It threatens a shared humanity. It fuels clashes. Policing also wounds individuals who must suppress themselves to act in the name of policing, sometimes in the face of sexual harassment, gay-bashing, and racist putdowns.

This isn't new or straightforward. And it invades all behaviours. Colonialists and missionaries long ago focussed on removing or changing or adding to the costumes of those they oppressed. It was a particular obsession to shift women's clothing to costumes more 'suitable', 'modest', or 'better' as defined by the oppressors. British colonialists in India tried to change the sari, explorers through Africa tried to end female breast exposures and nudity, and Afghan women's blue burkas became a focal point for the West. These efforts sanctify imperialism in the name of liberation.

UNSCIENTIFIC SCIENCE

'The science that informs medicine—including the prevention, diagnosis, and treatment of disease—routinely fails to consider the crucial impact of sex and gender.'

Johnson, P.A. et al. "Sex-Specific Medical Research Why Women's Health Can't Wait." Brigham and Women's Hospital, 2014. www.tinyurl.com/p96q8ku

But in the moment, both the creation of the categories and the policing of the categories are upheld by a range of societal institutions on behalf of citizens. So medical practitioners assign sex at birth, governments issue documentation accordingly, educational institutions force compliance with these identities, closed communities shun, and families suffer, revile, or excommunicate, depending on how their members fit in.

Sometimes scientists generate research and ideas using and assuming these social categories, and media report on them. Religious institutions do their part in reifying gendered categories and behaviours, usually under the leadership and in the service of men. Mass media exploit and exaggerate gender categories for amusement, entertainment, profit, shaming, and mockery, and in the doing, set standards for masculinity and femininity that no one can reach. Educational institutions reinforce popular culture, and much less often set it or upend it. Politicians, who may be in or out of touch with gender categories, climb their ways through public readiness to shift definitions and treatments of gender and people in their jurisdictions, maybe, and after the fact. Gender is defined and policed, and then strengthened, in ways both benign and deadly.

But gender fluctuates and shifts over time. This is the best part, because it shows that change can come, and that people can break out of those two big containers. Not only that, whole cultures and societies can shift their rules, sometimes over remarkably short periods of time, and sometimes over life-threateningly long periods of time.

But such change making challenges the size and shape of the containers, if not their very existence, and rubs up against the policing. And then, when some brave outliers have staked out the way, it becomes up to all of us to understand and create the change we want. Where outliers live and are free and healthy, and yes, have rights to be educated (and to be research subjects) and yes, have freedom of movement and autonomy and pleasure and prospects and prosperity, well that's change. But this describes a utopian ideal for many, if not most, citizens of our world.

THE ARMED SERVICES VOCATIONAL APTITUDE BATTERY TEST

'Studies have found that women generally do not score well on... sections that test mechanical comprehension... Attitudes are mixed on the impact of this type of test. Some officials believe that if people have not had exposure to certain subject matter, they are most likely not interested in that field even if they have an aptitude for the subject matter. Others believe that people should be given a chance if they have an aptitude for the subject matter.'

"Trends in the Occupational Distribution of Military Women." In GAO Reports: US Government Accountability Office, Sept. 14, 1999. www.gao.gov/products/NSIAD-99-212

What About Sex?

Sex does matter. That is those biological characteristics that we are born with and live with, unless or until we opt to change some or all of them. This means that aspects of our anatomy and physiology, or our metabolism or body size or strength, form our bodies, state our category to the outside world, and define our experience. It means we have specific, expected roles in sex and reproduction, and different amounts of oestrogen or testosterone running through us (at different stages in our lives). Just because gender is a continuum that is cultural and social, and can be shifted accordingly, does not always erase the importance of these sex-related factors.

GIVING UP ON GENDER?

'I felt a dysphoria in my new trans-identity and I thought that it must be another failure on my part. When I retired from gender, it was because I came to the realization that the gender binary was what had been failing me all along. It's hard to imagine that any one person finds that their place on the binary fits them without some measure of discomfort. Since my "retirement" I have been striving to stop gendering things for myself and for other people.'

Rae Spoon in Spoon, R. and I.E Coyote. Gender Failure. Vancouver, BC: Arsenal Pulp Press, 2014: 17.

But to go further into the mud, sex exists on a continuum as well. We can have more or fewer of those hormones, and be bigger and stronger than some of the 'other' sex, or weaker or smaller than some of the 'other' sex, crossing over the average expectations of the 'other' sex. And, despite our sex characteristics, we may be unwilling or unable to fall into expected sex roles, even when we are forced to swim in heteronormative oceans.

So even when considering our sizes and shapes and inner workings, it's not two categories, but more like a long line or continuum that has various forms of expression, orientation, self-identity, objectification, experiences, and pleasures and pains. Even if these sex-related categories appear more obvious and maybe more easily measured, they are no less containing for us than gender categories.

All of these fluidities matter in real life. As much as most people continue to appear to gravitate into a heteronormative box and distinguish themselves as either men or women, it remains to be seen how many people would choose differently if there were less policing of and weaker fences around the containers.

And even if, for example, individuals assigned male at birth choose to be 'masculine' and identify as men, but choose to be sexually oriented to men, or women and men, they may still live a heteronormative existence. Indeed, in many countries and regimes, it is still the only safe way to be for such individuals. In many progressive countries, the container around sexual orientation is being broken open, with increased acceptance and expectation that there are many ways of living out our sex and gender and decreasing barriers to being openly diverse from a binary heterosexual existence as determined by our apparent sexual organs at birth. Certainly, the human possibilities are endless. It's only the political and social context that changes and allows elasticity, or not, in the interpretation and expression of our lives.

NON-BINARY LIVING

'Examples of individuals living comfortably outside of typical male/female expectations and/or identities are found in every region of the globe. The calabai, and calalai of Indonesia, two-spirit Native Americans, and the hijra of India all represent more complex understandings of gender than allowed for by a simplistic binary model.'

"Understanding Gender." GenderSpectrum www.tinyurl.com/qb3qhob

Gender + Equity

How do we marry the issues of equity and gender in order to make the leaps from practical to ideological, from discriminatory to freeing, for all? How do we begin to think about gender in new ways that implicitly invoke change and, at the same time, a responsibility for erasing negative stereotypes and engaging all of us, whatever gender category we claim or have been forced into? How can we reach solutions for the big issues of our time without harnessing the energy of all genders, increasing gendered freedoms, and making clear that gender is part of all of us? And that gender is intrinsically linked to a range of other factors affecting equity in crucial ways?

For there is little effect in fixing the products of gender inequity, such as universal violence against women, without making sure that we do it in a way that reflects root causes. After all, there is no conceivable way to end violence against women without engaging men and improving men's lives, and naming and eliminating the various drivers of violence. In other words, root solutions are needed. There is little effect in ending poverty without ending gendered poverty and being content with making relative progress only. There is little effect in slowing climate change if roughly half the world is left behind while it gets done. There is little long-lasting good in supporting migration unless gender equality is understood and respected by migrants and hosts alike. And clearly, there is little purchase in working for universal human rights unless men and women with disabilities have a say.

FLUIDITY IN HISTORY

Non binary gender roles have been reported in 131 Native American tribes. Among the Dine (Navajo) there traditionally existed four genders: women, men, women-men, and men-women. The latter two genders were called nadleeh.

Lang, S. "Native American men-women, lesbians, two-spirits: Contemporary and historical perspectives." Journal of Lesbian Studies 20, no.3-4 (2016): 299-323.

There are a couple of things we need to do to marry gender and equity in our actions and social and political lives. One is to reject the binary of gender (and sex) in everything that we do. Those of us who, for scientific or personal reasons, reject the binary, or even just reject the constraints of gender containment and policing, cannot respond by making new categories. Making new terms like 'cisgender', (which is meant to refer to those whose bodies at birth and gender identities match), while intended to be well meaning, is just creating another label and category. Declaring 'non-binary' a status reifies the binary. These new terms underline the binary and undermine the continuum on which we all sit and the fluidity of our gender identities, roles, and sex characteristics, which is the reality of everyday life. In other words, noting a 'third gender' as many before us have, is just adding another category.

So in rejecting the binary, we need to leap toward the embrace of a gender continuum. This leads us directly to toilets. And sports teams. And change rooms. In fact, anywhere that conformity of sex and gender is required in order to enter and stay. To challenge the binary, we have to embrace the ultimate mystery of gender and the range of possibilities in all of us, over our lives, over time, in some contexts, weighed, yes, by cultural constraint, but part of us nonetheless.

The fights over toilets and sports teams and change rooms are completely trivial to some and yet at the same time utterly crucial to others. And these fights are both. They represent the zone where sex and gender meet and where individuality and social constraints collide. They call up basic issues of vulnerability, fairness, and legality. They call up qualifications, legal questions, and gains and losses for all concerned. They call up the old and the new. They represent the crucible of change and the blasting of conformity. Somewhere in such fertile and volatile ground can be progress.

The second way is to adopt gender transformative thinking so we can consciously and overtly improve equity for all genders as we go about our lives, and jobs. It requires multi-tasking. It requires a conscious marrying of gender improvement goals along with equity goals. It means you don't do one without the other, no matter what your project is.

It means we don't launch a public health campaign to reduce Zika transmission without improving a range of other things at once, such as fixing broken mosquito screens and removing standing water from poor neighbourhoods. Offering free birth control to men and women in affected areas. Generating new laws to allow abortion and provide access to abortion for all women. And transforming what at first looks like a communicable disease problem requiring a few unrealistic, gendered admonitions, to a golden opportunity for improving reproductive rights for women and men with some anti-poverty action thrown in. That's gender transformative thinking.

Gender transformative thinking gives us the impetus for multi-tasking on big issues. It offers a blueprint for bringing the entire continuum of gender into all social change, and the plan for figuring out the details on the small steps required to progress. It is applicable to planning, policy-making, programme development, messaging, advertising, legislating, and researching absolutely anything. It can be done in families, communities, states, and countries, not to mention globally. In fact, global applications are growing for reasons that are as practical as they are earth shattering. It's a versatile tool and a levelling perspective, respecting root causes and providing root solutions, generating thinking and action for all. And best, it improves life for everyone. It capitalises

GENDER AND RACE

'Young Black men and boys face special challenges and barriers related to both their race and gender which can impact their health, achievement, and life outcomes... We still lack data to help explain gender differences, poorer life outcomes, and the values, beliefs and practices that are the basis for how Black males understand and enact manhood. '

Wilchins, R. and M. Gilmer. "Addressing Masculine Norms to Improve Life Outcomes for Young Black Men: Why We Still Can't Wait." True Child. 2015. www.truechild.org/heinz

GENDER INEQUITY IN COMMON

'The modern trans movement is redrawing the boundaries to show the depth and breadth of sex and gender oppression in this society. It is this common enemy that makes the women's and trans communities sister movements for social justice.'

Feinberg, L. Transgender Warriors. Boston: Beacon Press, 1996: 118

on human capital, which when you think about it, should be foremost in our minds if we are remotely interested in progress.

Mixed with a broad view of gender outside of the boxes, binaries, containers, and rules, you can see that gender transformative thinking includes everyone with no one left behind. And best of all, marrying gender and equity leads directly into thinking about race and class and ability and...everything else that affects our bodies, our lives, our futures, our families and communities. For what is the point of generating plans for gender transformative changes if they are not as flexible, tailored, non-categorical, and responsive as possible? This reflects the fact that, for example, violence against women is a particular experience for women with disabilities, who may be less able to defend themselves, more vulnerable and dependent on caregivers, or less able to report violence. This means that violence against girls as a concept or phenomenon has a unique meaning in cultural and religious contexts where female genital mutilation and child marriage are sought-after and revered practices. Or in societies where communications pivot on social media platforms, cloaked in anonymity or not.

WEB BASED BATTERY

All young female social media users, Sales contends, are assailed 'on a daily, sometimes hourly, basis' by misogynist jokes, pornographic images, and demeaning comments that 'are offensive and potentially damaging to their well-being and sense of self-esteem.'

Heller, Z. "'Hot' Sex & Young Girls." The New York Review of Books (August 18, 2016). www.tinyurl.com/zy4xlep (Review of Nancy Jo Sales book, American Girls: Social Media and the Secret Lives of Teenagers. New York: A.A. Knopf, 2016.)

This means that rape has its own meaning and feeling when you are a college student walking on a dark campus, or fending off sexual harassment from a professor or intense, drunken pressure from a date. Or when you are a minority within a minority, resisting sexual harassment in the military, the fire hall, or the boardroom. Or...well you get the idea. But none of this changes the fact that women are more likely to experience interpersonal violence than men in any and all of these situations, so while ability, race, culture, religion, social location, age, and socioeconomic status matter a lot, in this instance gender is the overarching category.

Being a victim of crime or being shot by the police offers another example. Being a black man and driving a car is an acutely vulnerable position in North America, where stereotypes turn into death, and automatic suspicions ignite police stops and tense police reactions. Gender and race provide an overwhelming and overarching theme in understanding such acts and their results. Again, gender matters a lot. Any man who is black is vulnerable, no matter what his income or education. Any man who is black in North America feels that, in a way that is visceral and consuming and leads to practising subservient, life-saving behaviour toward police in the moment, and different, more aggressive behaviour while protesting on the streets following yet another death. It leads to black mothers and fathers schooling their boys in how to react to police as a very early survival skill.

How Can This Be News?

Too much of history has been relegated or forgotten or dismissed. Too many insights and accomplishments of social justice movements have been lost or maligned. Feminism is no different. Feminism has provoked intense reactions in individuals, split families and relationships, ended friendships, marked out ideological camps, and created rude backlash and less than polite condescension. It has seen victory and defeat, been called for dead numerous times, policed, lost, found, and celebrated. It has rescued many women, focussed many men, protected a lot of children, and earned rights, votes, and property.

It has caused strikes, pushed for abolition and abortion, marched, paraded, and walked on silently. It has inspired poetry, art, music, prose, scholarship, and drama, and created both fiction and facts. Feminism has crossed a lot of boundaries, offering a haven for gender outliers, blending energy and leadership with those fighting race discrimination and civil rights

MARKET LOSERS

'...women have almost universally been on the down side of global marketization and structurally constrained to be so; when the basis for sustaining life and livelihoods is commodified, everyone will be losers, but women are especially disadvantaged. A willful confusion of market policy and social policy as in "what's good for markets is good for people/environment" has never been good for women.'

Seager, J. "Death by Degrees: Taking a feminist hard look at the 2° climate policy." Kvinder, Kön og Foraksning, 3-4. Special issue on climate change (2009).

challenges, pushing for franchise for all, leading strikes and movements for workers' rights, and instigating child protection systems.

Some of what has happened has excluded men and boys and left them outside without a ready-made, comfortable place in feminism. Allies and self-organised feminist men's groups have sprung up in some cases. More often men have reacted, resisted, and in some cases, generated a set of men's rights to create conflict and express resentment or malaise. Or just to hold onto privilege. In the worst-case scenarios, women and girls have been revictimised, kidnapped, banned from schools, contained, kept inside like domestic animals, set on fire, raped, killed, traded as payback, or have received acid in the face. It takes courage to be a feminist, whether male or female, and clarity to understand feminism for its many gifts.

FREE TO BE

'We don't often talk about men being imprisoned by gender stereotypes, but I can see that that they are and that when they are free, things will change for women as a natural consequence... Both men and women should feel free to be sensitive. Both men and women should feel free to be strong... It is time that we all perceive gender on a spectrum not as two sets of opposing ideals.'

Watson, Emma. "Gender Equality is your Issue Too." HeforShe speech at the United Nations, 2014. www.tinyurl.com/nuypn4g

Progress on improving the status of women and girls is being made in some contexts. But there is plenty of evidence that the progress is spotty, temporal, choosy, and easily reversed. There is also evidence that precepts of feminism such as choice, freedom, and rights can be perverted, misread, misused, and destroyed in the name of feminism. So the question is, how can gender inequity be reduced? How can the world's women and girls be lifted up, so that all other tasks and issues and calamities befalling the human race can be addressed by all of us? How can the 'gender war' become an antique characterization? How can everyone, whether regarded as female, male, transgender, or other, see that the gender equity issue is theirs, too? How can gender be seen as a unifier? For that is a requirement and one that is more pressing than ever, as binaries disappear and yet equity is still so elusive. Gender transformative thinking could be a unifier.

Part of this is about identities and appealing to a wide range of them. But another part is about grafting gender equity goals into all other projects, like a golden rule. Whether addressing climate change, pollution, saving the species, creating democracy, or smaller tasks such as fixing your own house, caring for your kids, generating food and water for your family, or even more close in, fixing your body, keeping healthy, or staying sane. Issues of gender equity fit into each and every one of these and are essential moving parts in figuring out how to proceed.

Gender Blindness is a Common Condition

Gender blindness is an affliction that many individuals and larger entities such as families, communities, and social institutions often suffer from. Or more precisely, those living with gender inequity suffer from it. Gender blindness is a wonderful thing when you have it as only your peripheral vision is limited, and the rest is clear as crystal. It can be rectified with special lenses, but you have to want to wear them, and more, you have to be able to interpret what you see with them on.

We often do not know what we do not know. And that's a problem. If we don't know what we don't know, how can we learn it, identify how to find out, or suggest how it might be useful? It often happens that individuals with a particular experience, insight, or observation are trying to tell us, or are willing to tell us, but don't get heard. Racism, sexism, and every other preconceived assumption or stereotype will get in the way, acting like locked gates on the road to progress.

When research scientists meet to determine new research questions, and when their peers judge their proposals for funding, the blindness of not knowing what they don't know has profound consequences. What evidence is there to suggest that sex and gender and other characteristics matter to our knowledge

CHOICE IS NOT FREE

'We cannot frame "choice" as political while simultaneously depoliticising and decontextualising the choices women make in a capitalist patriarchy. We cannot confront rape culture while normalising the very ideas that found it: male entitlement, sexualised violence, and gender roles that are rooted in domination and subordination (i.e. masculinity and femininity).'

Murphy, M. "Defining the F Word: Why We Need to Be Radical with Feminism." In i-D, March 8, 2016. www.tinyurl.com/zhjw3sz

base? That was the scientific rallying cry twenty years ago in North America. A tautology of ignorance, kept so by those already funded, already in power, and making the decisions. When those who are blind also have power, the result is a threat to progress. As James Baldwin said,

> It is certain, in any case, that ignorance, allied with power, is the most ferocious enemy justice can have.[2]

MEN, WITH BENEFITS

'We believe that, whatever any of us think about the label, the ideas of feminism are still relevant. More than that, we figure that these ideas are relevant not only to women, but very much to men. And in a good way... Even if bits of it might make us uneasy, it holds out the promise of better relationships, better lives for the women we love, and better lives for ourselves.'

Kaufman, M., and M. Kimmel. The Guy's Guide to Feminism. Berkeley: Seal Press, 2011.

The 'right not to know' about gender and racial inequity or any other inequity is another form of ignorance that is a benefit of privilege. In the context of gender inequitable institutions, men exercise this right about women and sexism, and thus contribute to the maintenance of gender inequity. Similarly, white people often exercise this right about racism and its effects. Exercising this right can insulate a person or institution from feeling discomfort or taking action or inviting redress.

The 'right not to know' can be extended to those with any power at all such as able-bodied people regarding disability or heterosexuals regarding homosexuality. It is excellent insulation. Not only does it provide protection and warmth, but it also keeps a lot of other elements from creeping in. However, when politicians, or CEOs, or administrators of social institutions use it, the results can be heartbreaking and destructive. Think faith institutions ignoring decades, or indeed centuries of child sexual abuse by their religious leaders, or think CEOs of industries spewing mercury pollution into rivers upstream of Indigenous people's settlements for decades, or think decades of police inaction in the face of selectively arresting black men and ignoring woman abusers,

---

2 From Brainy Quote www.tinyurl.com/zqeyz3n

or think years of silence about restraints and abuses of developmentally disabled people institutionalised against their wishes, etc. In fact, these acts of ignoring take lives and health and prosperity and mental health away from many. They add trauma and hurt and lost health. The 'right not to know' is a vile and catastrophic form of ignorance that is as good as any weapon of war.

Nancy Tuana[3] offers a typology classifying various forms of ignoring, ignorance, and being ignored, all linked to prevailing values and power structures. In focusing on women's health, she elaborates on the unknown knowledge about the structure and function of the clitoris, and how this knowledge is very, very, new. That is formal knowledge, scientific knowledge, and certainly not experiential knowledge. It seems that in women's lived experience, the clitoris is *the* sexual organ, despite the misguided and untrue penis-accommodating wisdom that the vagina renders orgasms.

It seems very clear that in removing the clitoris of a girl in situations deemed 'cultural', there is a great implicit underlying awareness of the power of the clitoris, despite there being few research articles about the subject in major medical journals. Tuana also discusses the lack of innovation in male birth control and links it to a range of assumptions about men, virility, and power, which has now persisted for years.

Tuana identifies those many instances when many were kept ignorant on purpose of the impact of smoking cigarettes or of new drugs, or the effect of environmental pollution on cancer. For example, the drug Diethylstilbestrol (DES) was used for decades after evidence began to filter in that it was ineffective

DECADES OF DAMAGE

DES is considered to be one of the worst drug disasters in human history. It should be noted that the transgenerational effects of endocrine disrupting drugs seem to intensify with each generation, and people suffering from infertility, cancer, reproductive abnormalities, hormonal abnormalities, or autoimmune disorders should look in their family history for DES use.

Bloomquist, L. "One of the Worst Pharmaceutical Disasters in History Is Still Relevant Today." Collective Evolution, August 21, 2016. www.tinyurl.com/jtsk3pf

3 Tuana, Nancy. "The Speculum of Ignorance: The Women's Health Movement and Epistemologies of Ignorance." *Hypatia* 21, no. 3 (2006): 1-19.

in preventing miscarriage. Over the course of several decades, the damage was done, not only affecting the users of DES but their daughters, who developed cancer. Some research on DES sons has asked whether prenatal exposure to DES in males may be linked to sex and gender effects such as gender dysphoria or intersex conditions.

These forms of public ignorance are imposed upon us, or on specific powerless groups, on purpose to feed and support profits, greed, or reputations. It is often a conscious act to keep others ignorant. These acts can range from monumental to inconsequential, but they always cause damage and dislocation. Hiding war crimes or misrepresenting research data can produce serious reverberations for generations and cause cynical and misinformed tides of opinion to proliferate.

LOST AND FOUND?

'In one way, this "discovery" was one giant leap for womankind. In another, however, the fact that this seemingly basic bit of anatomy was still being elucidated so recently was an unsettling reminder of how little effort society has made to understand women's body parts when the parts in question aren't crucial for making babies.'

Sarah Barmak on the "discovery" in 2009 of the extent of the clitoral structure. From Closer: Notes from the Orgasmic Frontier of Female Sexuality Toronto: Coach House, 2016.

Being kept in the dark about a family secret or the source of your family income may be of lesser scale but equally damaging in the long run. Cultivating ignorance is an important skill, as many individuals and institutions illustrate. Churches and medicine ignored incest for decades, if not centuries, in spite of repeated evidence. Police and courts ignored domestic violence and rape in marriage for centuries, by refusing to call it what it was. This ability is linked squarely to the cultivation of ignorance and the wearing of gender blinders.

Ignorance in some form underpins all gender blindness. While some clever thinkers may try to argue that gender blind = gender neutral and gender neutral = fair, don't be convinced. Gender blindness is a conscious decision to be ignorant, and a callous refusal to investigate gender and sexism in the context of everyday life. The very same has been said about the stance of many white people about black people. A conscious rejection of thinking about facts, evidence, benefits, costs, comfort, discomfort, history, fairness, cruelty, injustice, and pain is involved. It requires constant and conscious self-deception. It's actually quite a lot of work to be ignorant.

What is the State of Your Consciousness?

Being conscious is a deliberate and political act. To be conscious we must be aware of a wide range of history, shared and unshared experiences, the differences as well as the similarities among us, and the responsibility of affecting our human existence in whatever small or large ways. Being conscious means knowing what is happening to those very different from us in locations far away from ours. It reflects our own personal experience as it becomes political.

Becoming conscious is a time-honoured tradition in progressive politics. Not surprisingly, consciousness-raising (CR) is a technique to generate solidarity, work out the meaning of our individual experiences, and re-form them into a collective experience. CR brings us out of the shadows of our own lives, and into the courtyard of shared experience. CR is the process that many have followed as they find themselves and their comrades.

Consciousness-raising has a bad rap. It is sometimes perceived as participating in group think, relegating your old life to the ashes, and taking on new meaning that often renders you foreign to your family, partner, friends, and co-workers. It's true that CR can render you different, but it's not to be avoided because of what others think of you. CR was a tool of the women's liberation movement of the 1960s and 1970s in North America. Contemporary groups such as the USA National Women's Liberation, still use it:

> We use consciousness-raising (CR) to compare and contrast our experiences, and draw conclusions to get closer to the truth of our

EXERCISING OURSELVES

'The approach itself is based on the radical democratic practice of feminist consciousness-raising... The process includes... sharing experiences related to a theme in a way that pays close attention to the national, racial, and class and other relevant contexts and histories in which the experiences being articulated are being played out; examining the experiences with an eye for the multiple relations of oppression and resistance at play; and exploring the barriers to, and possibilities for, coalitional action with regard to the experiences.'

Keating, C. "Building Coalitional Consciousness." NWSA Journal 17, no. 2 (2005): 86-103.

> condition. We can gain a clearer understanding of our lives as women by using our feelings and experience as data. As it was originally formulated, and as we use it, CR is not a way to develop listening skills or speaking skills; it's not a way to give advice to women to solve their problems—if individual solutions were that easy to come up with we wouldn't need to organize politically. It's not a way to get something off your chest, or to feel good in an all-woman space, though sometimes that's an unintended result. The purpose of hearing women's feelings and experiences is not to be therapeutic, but to be scientific in our analysis of our condition as women.[4]

CR was also used in the civil rights movement in the USA during the 1950s and 1960s. It was a tool for bringing together activists and ordinary people to give stories broader life and turn them into political actions. Race-based movements have used CR, even within feminism, to sort out their own collective experiences and name the many forms of oppression to be confronted. Without CR, many movements would be bereft of material and energy. CR is still a construct, fuelling the Occupy movement of 2011, and generating energy in a range of workers' rights, democracy groups, climate change, and anti-capitalist causes.

> Like consciousness-raising, Occupy Wall Street started with small groups of oppressed people who spoke to one another about their personal struggles, and in doing so learned they weren't alone or insane or weak or lazy, the way Those In Charge suggested. That

CRITICAL THINKING FOR EVERYONE

Program H engages young men in critical reflection and dialogue about gender equality via participatory sessions in which they live, rehearse, and model gender-equitable and non-violent styles of interaction. Program M was developed to work specifically with young women, ages 15 to 24, and seeks to promote their health and empowerment through similar critical reflections about gender, rights, and health. Program D promotes respect for sexual diversity and challenges homophobia by promoting critical reflections on gender stereotypes and sexual behaviors among both young men and women.

www.promundo.org

4 "National Women's Liberation: What We Want, What We Believe." www.tinyurl.com/hjotkbf

> discovery gave them the strength to channel the individual anger and suffering they experienced into a larger collective call to action.[5]

Many members of the Occupy movement were inspired by or victims of the economic meltdown of the USA in 2008, forcing job losses, housing insecurity, and mortgage foreclosures. But that too is gendered:

> And women suffer disproportionately in the current economic climate, which means that a protest for economic equality is a feminist protest—whether it admits it or not. A majority of the nation's poor and unemployed are women, especially women of color and single mothers.[5]

A key bedrock of CR came out of the traditions of the pedagogy of the oppressed, popularised by Paulo Freire. He identified the process of conscientization or the achievement of becoming conscious of one's own oppression, as a key liberation issue. It meant that both internal and external oppressions needed to be named and dealt with, and that habits of critical thinking and inward analysis go along with assessing the oppressor's interests in forming plans and actions for liberation. Liberation theology and other offshoots became the theme and theory of various peoples' liberation movements in the past century. These principles are derived from Marxist principles, and have been adopted by poor, displaced, homeless, landless workers and citizens in many countries around the globe. Liberation politics took on class

POSSIBILITIES FOR LIBERATION

'Feminist action research recognises and works with the evident possibility that individuals can be creative and imaginative, even when confronted by oppressive regimes and cultures of regulation, and that the role of feminist action is to move beyond the resistant and defensive.'

Weiner, G. "Critical Action Research and Third Wave Feminism: A Meeting of Paradigms." Educational Action Research 12, no. 4 (2004): 640.

5 Rogers, S. "What Occupy Wall Street Owes to Feminist Consciousness-Raising." In *Ms. blog*: Ms Magazine, December 13, 2011 www.tinyurl.com/jgeevds

and dispossession, using techniques that reflect in feminism and civil rights movements.

Men's CR was a much more limited phenomenon in the latter part of the twentieth century. It may be that men had many situations in which to do CR, in all-male boardrooms, sports events, or work settings. It may be that those were engaging situations for both internal and external rumination and work, and that essential male privilege meant that there was less urgency in those settings to make political plans that were designed to upend the status quo.

When CR did take place among men, it engaged groups of pro-feminist men interested in generating brotherhood for progressive politics, and to create a supportive place to share. Similar to the CR groups of feminists in the sixties and seventies, but on a much smaller scale, these groups offered a haven for the isolating role of being a pro-feminist man, and generated plans for parallel political activities.

Now, CR often happens online. It is a new and wild and wonderful opportunity and far more efficient, albeit maybe less personal. It's a way to generate a wide circle of communication and support and generate collective action on line, sometimes globally, and sometimes in minutes or hours, using blogs, social media, and a rich depository of history and current events on the Internet.

Online connecting and consciousness-raising among progressive people can also be risky. Trolls, bullies, and 'haters' abound in modern day online media, and often gang up on those who have edgy, radical political goals, or who express that they are fed up with the status quo of inequity. This arena can be clearly sexist and racist, and not easily tamed or explored.

But the possibilities for CR remain intense and accelerated. In all of these examples, however, there is a theme: taking responsibility for making sense of your own life and experiences, and linking those to

EQUAL OPPORTUNITY CHANGE

'The African Transformation toolkit is designed regionally to engage both women and men in a similar process around critical analysis, dialogue, and action. "What we do through these interactive tools is create safe spaces that provide disruption, enabling people to think about things differently and critically reflect on how gender beliefs and practices are operating in their lives."'

Jane Brown, Johns Hopkins Center for Communication Programs As cited in Schwartz, E. "Exploring Gender Transformative Approaches to SBCC." In Solutions Centre: NETHOPE, Oct. 19, 2015. www.tinyurl.com/zxojoqo

others' in order to gain insight, empathy, and solidarity. This is the basis for any change. CR is a prerequisite for decision-making about gender transformation. It means that women matter, that all kinds of women matter equally, that it takes effort to cross those lines of understanding, that men can contribute, and that all kinds of men are essential to the liberation of humanity. CR calls us to take responsibility for our own lives as well as those of others, and to resist those who erect barriers.

So self-knowledge is a requirement for moving forward on gender transformation. And courage. Courage to reject the binary in one's own life and in society in general. Caring. Caring about others so that the world gets reconstructed in a more positive and fair way. And clarity. Clarity to analyse circumstances, injustices, solutions, and one's own benefits. All of these elements matter as we journey forward.

CHAPTER 3

Principles and Action

Talk is cheap. Aspirations can be undeniably ephemeral. Goals like fairness and equality are elusive, dismissible as 'feel-good' and all too commonly unmet. If we really want to achieve something, improve gender equity at the same time, and ensure some kind of long-term positive effect, then there are some bedrock decisions to make. Ideally, these bedrock decisions should be based on a set of ethics. We couldn't really go wrong if ethics underpinned our decisions in reducing inequity.

Ethics are often understood as the high bars in life, not necessarily and obviously linked to our everyday assessment of our politics or the structures of our collective well being. But they are intrinsically related to the way we do things and the outcomes we might see. They include things like: respect for persons and their autonomy; vulnerability; ability to consent; concern for the welfare of both individuals and groups, taking into account risks and benefits and justice or fairness.

Ultimately, which ethical paths we choose reflect our values. But once we can express our ethical principles and our values, it's much easier to defend them and convince others to join us. But that means we have to think things through a bit, long before we act. The ethics involved in shattering the binary of gender

CHORE WARS

'The precise figures for OECD countries are 273 minutes of housework per day for women compared to 141 minutes for men... A study by Janeen Baxter and Belinda Hewitt found that when women earn more than men they actually increase, rather than decrease, the amount of housework they do. Similarly, the less men earn, the less housework they do. The authors suggest that these baffling patterns are about couples conspiring to restore the gender order. Chores are a "means of reasserting gender identity." To avoid emasculating their partners, women sweep and mop their way back into submission.'

Simmonds, A. "The Chore Wars." womankind, no. 8: jackal (July 27, 2016). www.tinyurl.com/hd8ly92

and adopting gender transformative thinking revolve around the basics of consent, autonomy, concern for others' welfare, and justice.

The key principles guiding medicine overlap somewhat and include autonomy, beneficence, and justice. But there's a lot in these principles that apply to any field or endeavour. Autonomy means that the individual or group has a chance to be informed and make decisions, and this implies that they have full information. It's hard to conceive of many situations when people have all the information available or even enough, and it's easy to think of many where people have virtually none.

Across the world, the education and information gap is crucial: between countries, between social classes, between girls and boys, men and women, across castes and classes, and between governors and the governed. The ongoing challenge of our work in equity is to make information as available as possible. This can mean everything from opening up access to existing information, including research results, which the Internet has accelerated tremendously in the past twenty-five years, to engaging people in research, to increasing literacy and education in places where it is lacking. After all, how can a campaign to eliminate female genital mutilation or to reduce environmental degradation or to tackle voter registration or create more affordable housing actually work if there is no way to share existing information, gather new information, and make sense of it together? And further, how would you know if progress was being made if there was no shared and easy access to existing information and research?

In engaging community members in research and training peer researchers, the FORWARD peer research program in Sierra Leone generated information and created camaraderie around the issues of obstetric fistula among girls and women. Obstetric fistulae result from damage to tissues and organs during

HOW TO MEASURE WHAT?

McKinsey Global Institute has mapped 15 gender equality indicators for 95 countries. The indicators fall into four categories:

1. equality in work,
2. essential services and enablers of economic opportunity,
3. legal protection and political voice
4. physical security and autonomy.

Woetzel, J. et al. "The Power of Parity: How Advancing Women's Equality Can Add $12 Trillion to Global Growth." McKinsey Global Institute, 2015. www.tinyurl.com/hrn4qtf

childbirth that can cause considerable and lifelong faecal and urinary incontinence. This condition, in turn, results in social marginalisation and loss of opportunities. While the immediate cause of fistula is obstructed and prolonged labour and unattended birth, particularly in girls, the solutions garnered from the peer-driven, community-based research were not about health care improvements.

Rather, the research formed the basis of gender transformative solutions that focus on keeping girls in school, and on teaching communities to end child marriage, delay sexual activity, and generate poverty reduction to prevent girls from engaging in transactional sex. Just as important and empowering, the research training created peer groups and skill building for girls and women who had been ostracised by this disabling and stigmatising condition.

Justice, the next principle, is about fairness, and often involves thinking through what everyone wants out of something. It is a pretty important concept underpinning equity, as it helps us figure out how to redistribute things or resources and how to get a feel for what would be fair to people. And, critically, to figure out what people actually need or want. Despite its apparent simplicity, there are various forms of justice, some of which focus on consequences for the whole society and some on redistributive effects for individual people or groups. Clearly, justice has political underpinnings, making it a key contested principle.

But it's hard to determine what's fair and just unless you hear from those on the ground. Sometimes, it is about redistributing resources such as money, housing, jobs, or food, through taxation, charities, policies, or regulation. But other times, it's about destroying stereotypes, systemic racism, sexism, or homophobia, or dealing with stigma and marginalisation and blasting out old attitudes that presume fairness is operating when it's not.

'DISORDERLY' INJUSTICE

Australian government data show that 34% of the Australian woman prisoner population are Indigenous women (yet they represent only 2.2% of Australian women). In Western Australia, their most frequent offences are disorderly conduct, driving while a licence is suspended, common assault, bail act offences, and exceeding the PCA limit (traffic offence related to drinking).
From The Indigenous Justice Clearinghouse

www.indigenousjustice.gov.au

You need only look at the preponderance of Indigenous people in the correctional system in Canada, or at the preponderance of black people in prisons in the USA to see that official 'justice' is meted out to particular people in particular ways and reflects larger injustices in society. You need only look at the tiny, tiny, tiny proportion of rapes and sexual assaults that get prosecuted, let alone rendered convictions. These forms of 'justice' form indelible harms to entire groups of people in our societies, whether direct victims or not.

The principle of beneficence refers to the practice of doing some good while you roll out your treatment, intervention, policy, or program, while at the same time, preventing harm. Doing some good is a lot more complex than preventing harm, as it calls up the question of making a positive difference that addresses, hopefully, some of those root causes. And root causes such as child marriage may be the key problem when it comes to solving obstetric fistula. And a root cause of child marriage might be misogyny or boy child preference or extreme poverty.

Or all of those. Poverty, unemployment, and racism are the key issues when it comes to solving disproportionate incarceration rates in North America. The root causes of racism and poverty in North America are residual and untamed histories of slavery, colonisation, ownership, and power, lingering on and on and on without honest dialogue. It's easy to figure out root causes when given a few minutes to think, but it's way harder to deal with them and extremely difficult, it seems, to have an honest conversation about them.

William Ryan, an American psychologist and social justice activist, wrote a pivotal book in 1971 called *Blaming the Victim*. It argued that race and class were pivotal to explaining poverty in the USA, and criticised the focus on individual or exceptionalistic solutions, such as teaching health literacy or sex

SANITATION AND TRANSFORMATION

In Bangladesh, the Nijera project used community-led sanitation work to forge new relationships between men and women, poor and elite, to facilitate discussions on gender, power, and rights. By implementing the community-led sanitation initiative, CARE identified 'natural leaders' among participants and trained them in analysis, facilitation, and negotiation, equipping them to lead groups, mobilize communities, and give voice to the economically and socially marginalised.

From CARE. "Strategic Impact Inquiry: Women's Empowerment." 2014. www.tinyurl.com/gru9uov

education or re-forming the black family from matriarchal to nuclear. Rather, Ryan offered a different analysis, presaging the one-per-centers by forty years, and arguing that the majority of us were potential victims of poverty at the hands of the few who owned the most of the resources and levers of power.

Root solutions for Ryan were universalistic and structural in nature, meaning that the principles of equity and redistribution needed to prevail. For example, he suggested that creating fair and even public school quality across neighbourhoods and cities would do a lot more to erase poverty than blaming the victim. Ryan's book was explosive and radical in 1971. But, like most of his compatriots, he ignored gender completely as a basis for analysing relative inequity and poverty. His book did not discuss sexism at all, even though it is a virtual exposé on racism in the USA. His attention to women was in explicating his theory using the example of poor, black 'unwed' mothers or connecting the history of slavery and racism to matriarchal black families. This gender-blind attempt to explain and solve poverty missed half of the population and the majority of the poor in the US. Ryan was not alone in this.

Preventing Harm and Doing Good

Almost no one wants to do harm, but it needs saying that harm can easily get done unless we think critically and think far enough ahead. Reaching for gender and equity at the same time requires a number of skills. But first it has to be based on some principles. 'Do no harm' is a familiar one for almost anyone working with people, or trying to better people's lives. Usually, this means that we try our hardest to avoid introducing a negative effect on someone's life, or to leave people worse off after our encounter or intervention.

PREVENTING MORE HARM

'Abuse and other trauma are about violation: of our bodies, our minds, our basic human needs, our choices... Rights are about who gets to exercise power and control over a person or group... Abuse and other trauma inevitably involve events out of one's own control, and service providers need to be aware of how their services can be experienced by those coming for help as another traumatizing experience and yet another context where control is not in their hands.'

Chambers, J. "What Do Client Rights Have to Do with Trauma-Informed Care?". Chap. 25 In Becoming Trauma Informed, edited by N. Poole and L. Greaves, 317-25. Toronto, ON: Centre for Addiction and Mental Health 2012.

This principle is, we might think, somewhat obvious, but its reassertion has been constantly needed after too many examples of research experimentation done without informed consent, and drugs introduced to entire populations with dire consequences.

Harm can also hide in the shadows and be a bit harder to spot. It can manifest in various ways such as when a policy might be introduced to improve the greater good and yet some of its consequences could be negative for some. For example, bringing in smoke-free zones to rid public spaces and children's spaces of tobacco smoke has been included in what are called 'denormalisation' policies in the field of tobacco control. These policies are aimed at spreading the idea that tobacco smoking is increasingly a minority practice (at least in many high-income countries); and making smoking less acceptable in a range of locations is a key strategy to achieving that. It's a policy that is intended to denormalise smoking, not the smoker, but as it turned out that's not the way it is felt on the ground.

Indeed, for those who might be seen smoking, are known to be smokers, or smell like smokers, there is a growing stigma. This stigma can prevent people from seeking treatment for smoking, or can actually lead to them being harassed on the streets. This stigma is amplified by gender. For example, for pregnant women smoking in public, or for young fathers caring for children, this can sometimes involve interference. This is all because the more smoking is denormalised, the more smokers stand out, and the majority becomes more emboldened, and acquires a right to say something.

So doing harm is not just a straight line, but can result from not thinking through all of the unintended consequences. Thinking through these is a critical dimension of seeking gender equity, or improving someone's lot. Without critical thinking about impacts, blunders can be made that may be delayed

GENDERED VICTIM BLAMING

'...if staff in schools are really worried about boys viewing girls as sexual objects, they should be giving those boys lessons in how to respect women, rather than training girls in the art of dressing like a nun.'

Moss, R. "Sending Schoolgirls Home for Wearing 'Short Skirts' Is Where Victim Blaming Begins." Huffington Post (April 15, 2016). www.tinyurl.com/grwl5ea

or less obvious, but can be equivalent to introducing a drug to people without testing it.

Gender transformative thinking combines doing good with doing no harm and incorporates an analysis of gender along with the problem at hand. Think about that. *It is a tall order.* It requires multi-tasking and deep thinking, critical research, consciousness, and the desire to uncover the desires and goals of ordinary people.

Done right, gender transformative thinking actually makes the two principles of preventing harm and doing good into concurrent and explicit goals, and generates multitasking skills among all of us as we address the big issues in our global context.

As much as William Ryan was a ground breaker, a progressive activist, a change maker, and an amazingly insightful, courageous, and influential thinker, he missed the main event. While the term 'blaming the victim' has shown incredible longevity, it is little wonder that most examples of 'blaming the victim' in contemporary times are about girls and women, transgender people, and gays and lesbians who are victims of violence, sexual assault, rape, murder, war crimes, acid attacks, stoning, shunning, or excommunicating; all for simply being guilty of breaking out of gender roles.

POWERING THE GIRL EFFECT

'Deeply rooted in our theory of change, our unique approach to social norm change uses the latest ideas in media, technology and girl-centred community engagement to challenge discriminatory gender norms and start conversations about how girls are viewed in society.'

"Our Purpose." Girl Effect. www.girleffect.org/our-purpose/

How to Move Forward?

Well, so what? We can name a few key principles to serve as guiding lights, like buoys in the harbour of a social maelstrom. But how do we move from that into action? It is work. But generating efforts with principles and multi-tasking in mind is work that is long overdue. There is way too much theorising about change in academic circles, and way too much well-meant unfounded action in programs and policy among those on the ground. How many academic articles pose arguments for better living and never speak in everyday language or get shared much past a few argumentative colleagues who read scholarly journals? How many program managers and policy makers lurch headlong into action because something has to be done now, or yesterday even, and often without evidence or evaluation?

But acting from each of these positions also has its pluses. Theorising in academia allows the mind to wander and to generate ideas for change, but only if the thinker is inspired. Theorising is only as good as the thinker behind it all. When it is inspired, theorising offers a grand diving board, launching a whole body of thought high above the lagoons and bays of confusion and murkiness, and it offers all of us the clarity and promise of a deep dive. But some theories are better; more permanent or more useful than others.

Practice also has its benefits (even when done without the benefit of theory, data collection, evaluation, or testing...). What wisdom evolves from experiences with real people on real solid ground! What elegant kernels of truth come bursting out of messing around and doing things differently. What growth emerges, almost naturally. What engagement and ownership grows when all kinds of collectivities get involved. Programs evolve and policies fail and get rewritten, often without the benefit of theory. And that's not always bad.

For practice can lead to theory, and theory can lead to practice. In our work with groups across many sectors and jurisdictions, the links between theory and practice are often blurred or non-existent. But despite advances in sharing information and some considerable democratisation of thinking and writing and learning in recent years, there are still distinctions drawn between theory and practice that assume they are discrete activities.

GENDER INEQUITY IS DEADLY

'The difference in the impact of natural and man-made disasters on women, girls, men, and boys can be shocking... 90% of the nearly 140,000 deaths reported in the 1991 Bangladesh cyclone were women. Women and girls consistently suffer greater loss of life in crises, not only in poor low-income countries but also in high-income countries.' Despite the clear benefits of engaging women and girls – and the broad consensus around doing so, those voices struggle to be heard, and women are not given sufficient opportunity to make decisions that could save themselves and their communities during disasters.

Sprechmann, S., and B. Jackson. "CARE Issues Report on Empowering Women and Girls in Crises." May 2016 www.tinyurl.com/jdeffqy

Making this link can be hampered by academic positioning and what seems like deliberately obfuscating language, or by academics who have yet to leave the 'ivory tower.' On the other hand, practitioners can exhibit rampant anti-intellectualism and superiority linked to 'doing' and 'acting' and 'knowing' while policy makers can revel in being needed to act 'in the moment'. The inherent relevance of these actions is presumed to be high when compared to mulling over the theory that might apply. All of these positions have problems, and prevent a considered look at either root problems or root solutions, and they certainly detract from gender transformative skill building.

Thank goodness for those who can build these bridges between big picture and everyday action – between thinking and doing. And who can do so with courage and utter and complete, straightforward, brutal clarity. Surely Stephen Lewis, the renowned Canadian human rights activist, qualifies as the king of verbal disarmament for rendering into jelly those who support inequity, gender inequity, violence against women, and AIDS by inaction or action. There are too few of him, but lessons can be learned for all of us who seek to bring our thinking in line with our practices, and to do so with apparent ease and no time to lose.

In 2006, Stephen Lewis addressed the International AIDS Conference and said, among other nuggets: 'Gender inequality is driving the pandemic, and we will never subdue the gruesome force of AIDS until the rights of women become paramount.' 'Women's rights are human rights...it's never been made real and so long as men control the levers and bastions of power, it never will be real.' Or, 'The demeaning diminution of women is everywhere evident...freedom from sexual violence, the right to sexual autonomy, to sexual and reproductive health, social and economic independence, and even the whiff of gender equality are barely approximated. It's a ghastly deadly

STRAIGHT TALK

'Gender inequality is driving the pandemic, and we will never subdue the gruesome force of AIDS until the rights of women become paramount.'

Stephen Lewis 2006 at the 16th International AIDS Conference

'The real reason we haven't beaten this epidemic boils down to one simple fact: We value some lives more than others. We value men more than women. Straight love more than gay love. White skin more than black skin. The rich more than the poor. And adults more than adolescents.'

Charlize Theron 2016 at the 21st International AIDS conference

business, this untrammelled oppression of women in so many countries on the planet.' www.youtube.com/watch?v=_EkIQBmJ_VM

At the 2016 AIDS conference, a full ten years later, Charlize Theron, an actor and an AIDS activist, made similar leaps when she bluntly said, 'AIDS is transmitted by sexism, racism, and homophobia' www.youtube.com/watch?v=4sJQ7RfQbyo.

Such uninhibited linkages between theory and practice, root causes, and solutions are incredibly rare in social and political discourse. Such direct, head-on implications of gender and processes of sexism, racism, and homophobia are often avoided by leaders. Without more of this thinking and acting, how can the rest of us make headway, instead of mucking around, repeating errors, causing new problems, stabbing in the dark at solutions and problems, avoiding the real issues, arguing with each other, and failing everyone?

Scaffolding

It's important to be secure. It's not enough to pay allegiance to the few principles named above, or to cover ourselves with an ethics review, or to treat our values and principles as a checklist. It's not even enough to name the underlying issues and carry on from there, in the faint hope that the verbal linkages and the blunt force of rhetoric will serve the purpose of channelling action into productive results. That is never enough, as history proves. No, it seems essential that we build a scaffold of principles, so that we can see it, climb it, and use it to get from one position to another, all the while leaving a track and an assist to those who follow. This takes planning, and consciousness about our own values, principles, and approaches. It also takes some dogged construction.

So let's think about drugs for a minute. Far from Nancy Reagan's war on drugs is Vancouver's Insite gallery where trained medical personnel oversee people injecting illegal drugs. Harm reduction in action, this setup is meant to prevent deaths, overdoses, and transmission of diseases such as AIDS and hepatitis C, all in a blame-free environment. In fact, that's about as far as you can get from Nancy Reagan's war on drugs, where the guiding force was the message: 'Just Say No!' Her message was the epitome of the individualization of the drug problem, the poster for a Ryanesque example of 'blaming the victim', and the blind ignoring of structural factors that might prevent saying 'no' and indeed, which might then cause death and disease.

The principle of harm reduction is an illustrative fundament to underpinning and building that scaffold. It embodies the meaning of do no harm and doing good at the same time. How does a supervised injection site do good, you might wonder? Well, it saves lives, reduces disease, treats drug addicts as human beings with a right to health care, and possibly keeps neighbourhoods safer and cleaner. What is there not to like about that? It blends the principles of beneficence (do good) and maleficence (do no harm) into a smoothie of public health policy and practice, inspired primarily by on the ground wisdom and practicality, not moralism.

To say it's a long way from the general public's impulsive understanding of how to treat drug addiction is an understatement. Of course it is, but deriving principles and putting them into practice in the name of equity is, so far, rather alien to public policy and discourse. So it's no wonder that the average person has not considered harm reduction as a first principle. It is the responsibility of change makers to soften that ground, articulate these principles, and make the examples sing. Then, within a flash, public opinion might change, quickly followed by political opinion and policy.

Evidence

Building the scaffold also requires evidence. Do we need to say any more about evidence? Probably, yes. Making decisions for programs or policies without evidence is a time-honoured practice. Getting evaluations of practice done to produce evidence is often hit and miss. But this is where academia and practice can collide and create new stars. This is where the co-development of an evidence base about inspired ideas and how they work on the ground is a useful role for academic thinkers or researchers in hospitals, governments, or institutions, in concert with communities. Thankfully, there are more and more examples.

GLOBAL TO LOCAL KNOW HOW

Gender transformative practice has benefitted from multiple forms of evidence: from research capturing country level data such as that conducted by the McKinsey Global Institute, to the wisdom of young men and women about their local USA context found in the Black Youth Project survey described by TrueChild

"The Power of Parity: How Advancing Women's Equality can add $12 Trillion to Global Growth." 2016. www.mckinsey.com

"Addressing Masculine Norms to Improve Life Outcomes for Young Black Men: Why We Still Can't Wait." 2015. www.truechild.org/

But don't be misled into thinking that any and all evidence is going to serve as a strong enough foundation. Producing evidence is not a straightforward path. Evidence is produced and often presented as ready for our digestion, and future evidence is generated to build on past evidence. But evidence is not objective or similarly understood or experienced by everyone.

In particular, evidence that has been understood as formal, official, or not debatable, has historically emerged from institutions run by men. Think the university, the church, the mosque, the media, the government, or fields such as sport, medicine, law, or education... It is very, very, recent history that these sources of information, evidence, decree, treatment, exposure, curricula or polity have been infiltrated by women and other marginalised groups.

On the other hand, women have often historically generated unofficial evidence or wisdom pertaining to issues such as homeopathy, medicine, wellbeing, childbirth, illness, spirituality, animal care, husbandry, horticulture, food, stories, and folklore. Much of this evidence has been unofficial for a reason. Without access to formal institutions, education, publishers, or pulpits, women did not have the controls to drive the building of evidence – formal evidence, that is.

So whose evidence is real? That depends on your position, your vantage point, your experience, your opportunities, and the wideness of your worldview. Your ability to read, write, or talk, and the theories you claim, or your methods for generating evidence. The questions you ask, the people you canvass, the assumptions you make. And those depend on who may be funding you or guiding you or hoping for answers from you. And, well, you get the idea; there are so many ifs, ands, and buts in evidence that it's really hard to accept that there is one hunk of evidence out there that matters. It cannot be true, and it likely isn't.

Health research is a prime example. It has been conducted and controlled by medicine for centuries. While medicine is extremely important, it is not all there is to health. Medicine is a discipline and profession that has been controlled by men, and like many professions has been licensed, regulated, and jargonized to protect itself. Medical research has been based on seeking objectivity and minimising subjectivity. Medical researchers have been trained by other, older medical researchers. Certain methods are deemed to produce evidence that is superior to other forms of evidence. For example, the 'hierarchy' of evidence assumes that randomised control trials (large studies where part of the sample does not get the intervention and part does, and where the groups are assigned using random methods, meaning everyone has an equal chance of being assigned to either) produce the best form of evidence.

Way, way, down at the bottom are qualitative studies that produce deep insights from a few people

EXPECTING GOOD EVIDENCE

Forty years into the use of crash test dummies for automobile safety testing, dummies modeling women's bodies were required, but not dummies modeling pregnant women. Despite the development of a pregnant crash test dummy in 1996, as of 2012, pregnant crash test dummies were not yet used in government-mandated auto safety testing in the US or Europe. Women on average tend to sit closer to the steering wheel to compensate for shorter stature, which puts them at greater risk for internal injury in frontal automobile collisions. The traditional three-point seatbelt can harm a fetus.

"Pregnant Crash Test Dummies: Rethinking Standards and Reference Models." Gendered Innovations. www.tinyurl.com/z67vugr

SPACES FOR NEW EVIDENCE

The Homeless Hub in Canada has reworked the traditional hierarchy of evidence to include the following three levels of practices:

1. emerging practices
2. promising practices
3. best practices

www.tinyurl.com/za5v3r9

using more direct contact as part of the method. Such studies may offer us deep meaning, unearth wisdom, generate new ideas, illuminate life, or respect lived experiences, but are deemed less important in that hierarchy of evidence. There are also observational studies that rely on data collection and recording by a researcher and anecdotal evidence, often relayed as an important starting point for action or further research.

Missing from medical research in the past century has been consideration that sex and gender might make a difference to research, medicine, health, treatment, getting diagnosed, or getting better. Unbelievable as this is, most countries are still conducting research without considering the fact that cells, animals, and humans all have sex-related characteristics, genetic patterns, and biological qualities that affect or even determine health or illness and responses to drugs and treatment. Equally, most are still ignoring gender-related factors as well. The kaleidoscope of gendered expressions, identities, practices, relations, and power distributions seems lost on much traditional health research. As a result, we do not have a comprehensive understanding of how such everyday practices and experiences influence how health is acquired, lost, maintained, or ignored.

EVIDENCE OF OMISSIONS

'Transgender people and their needs remain little understood, not only by health-care providers but also more generally in society. An absence of appropriate information together with misinformation, breeds stigma and prejudice, leading to discrimination, harassment, and abuse, with alarming consequences for transgender people's health and wellbeing.'

Winter, S, et al. "Synergies in Health and Human Rights: A Call to Action to Improve Transgender Health." The Lancet 388, no. 10042: 318-21. www.tinyurl.com/zf5d8eu

Even in the handful of progressive countries that are reluctantly taking on the issue and gently forcing the inclusion of sex and gender in health research, such as Canada, the United States, and some European countries, this is so recent that many researchers can still live with their heads in the sand on these factors, or deftly resist by degrading any attempt to change their methods, analyses, samples, or reporting practices. The only upside is that the regulatory nooses will tighten or these particular ostriches will die off in due course before any more damage to people's health gets done.

So evidence, as you can see is not only contested, personal, changing, partial, limited, and gendered, it is also controlled, diminished, ignored, and stamped on when it suits. Attempts to change the means of production of knowledge are often met with disdain and contempt and resisted by those with privilege and tradition on their side, until ultimately the tide turns. Progress occurs, but never in a straight line. And definitely, when it comes to producing official evidence about health and many other human conditions, women and other marginalised groups have stormed the barricades so recently there is still shock in the institutions and considerable resistance among the keepers of these keys.

Yes, evidence is essential to stabilising and building your scaffold. It is essential to doing gender transformative thinking and creating effective gender transformative interventions, but make no mistake, it's gendered, moving, blinkered, and limited. We must, as part of gender transformative practice, develop evidence bases that matter, that reflect varied realities, that conjoin wisdom and facts, that draw on all kinds of perspectives and positions, and that emerge as transitional, iterative, and always changing. This is the evidence we need, and all of us have to care about this often-invisible activity as much as the above-the-surface activities we call life.

Gender Transformation

So now we have identified some ethical principles, reflected on our values, sorted out some ways to do good as well as do no harm in our own neck of the woods, and critically produced, curated, or reviewed the evidence. Now what? Doing gender transformative practice requires that you internalise that gender is no longer binary, and that it is possible to reduce gender inequity in every move you make if you give it enough thought and plan accordingly.

CULTIVATING AND SIFTING THE EVIDENCE

The Bill and Melinda Gates Foundation has a goal of building evidence for its programs that is grounded in women's experience:

'We work to ensure that program objectives include women's active involvement and that progress be evaluated in terms of women's successes as well as household successes. Programs should collect feedback, measure results, and adjust their design to ensure that women are participating and benefiting.'

In a program with women farmers, 'through its data collection and analysis, P4P is working to **know** women farmers and understand how the initiative might affect women and men in both intended and unintended ways. It is **designing** measures to reach women more effectively, and it is ensuring **accountability** by conducting gender-disaggregated monitoring of all program activities.'

"What We Do, Gender-Responsive Agricultural Development Programs." Bill & Melinda Gates Foundation, www.tinyurl.com/nbpdqm9

RIGHTS TO RIDE

A display at the Canadian Museum for Human Rights includes a bicycle helmet and jersey from Mountain2Mountain, a group working in Afghanistan to promote women's rights and acceptance of their cycling. 'Recognizing the vital role sports can play to foster equality, conflict resolution, fairness, and inclusion, many organizations use sport programs to advance human rights around the world.'

"Year of Sport." Canadian Museum for Human Rights, www.tinyurl.com/zluloj2

But sorting out how to erect that scaffold, and making it strong, requires everyone. Gender transformative work is not solely a 'women's issue,' nor can it be left to women to inspire it and maintain it, lead it, or publicise it. Rather, everyone has gender – absolutely everyone. And those understandings and experiences of gender are not contained in two neat little categories anymore. And whatever your identity or container, it's not static anymore. More and more people are agents in changing their gender, as emerging practices and some courageous individuals illustrate. In fact, the esteemed medical journal, *Lancet*, estimates that there are, to date, twenty-five million transgender people in the world. And even they are on it, wondering how to shape health care accordingly, and musing that this, indeed, is a human rights and equity issue!

Men, women, transgender people all matter. And those experiencing poverty, racism, violence, homophobia, discrimination, terror, assault, shunning, or marginalisation matter more acutely and immediately. For those emerging from centuries of injustice and hurt, invisibility or trauma, or who are trying to emerge, the need is utterly acute. So yes, some matter more than others. This is always the way with inequity. The agenda gets set for us if we are paying attention. The path forward depends on our strength, our values, and our scaffolding.

CHAPTER 4

We All Matter Somehow at Some Point

In recent years, men have been exhorted to subscribe to feminism. This has been portrayed as a key act of personal growth signalling solidarity with women and a commitment to power sharing and progressive social change. It has been particularly fundamental to the launching of men's anti-violence movements and related organisations. Recently, there have been men in positions of power or political leadership in several countries who have come out as feminists because it seems like the right thing to do. Or because some genuinely feminist men have been models for this and they feel pressured to fall in. But largely, exhortations and social pressures, or a few male leaders adopting feminist identities have not really worked to turn the tide or to turn men and boys into gender equity comrades. Indeed, in the scheme of things only a relatively few progressive, self-described feminist men have really lived this out in their daily lives.

But for all its dispiriting track record it now seems a pointless and rather dated request. Asking men to recognise gender issues and inequity for the good of women and in the name of feminism or social justice

MEN, FALL IN

'I have been involved with White Ribbon now for a number of years. I'm an ambassador for White Ribbon. I feel deeply that I have at least a voice in reminding Australians, particularly Australian men, particularly white Australian men such as myself who have never been discriminated against in their lives, that they can't be bystanders here. They may not perpetrate any violence against women, they may not distribute foul images, but if they know about them, if they know about violence, if they don't do something about it, if they're bystanders, then through their actions they need to be held to account, in my view.'

David Morrison, "Army Chief Calls on All Australians to End 'Terrible Statistics of Violence against Women'." Australian Broadcasting Corporation, www.tinyurl.com/oeo7dxk

was a call for some kind of compassionate shifting over, or presented as a selfless sidestep so that women and girls could have some space and power. In retrospect, it seems like a silly stunt, akin to calling for help while dog-paddling in a giant wave of expert surfers. It called upon men's finer natures to stop their own trajectories, or to at least slow down to avoid obliterating those trying to surface and join the swim.

More fundamentally, it assumed a world of finite power, a binary of gender, a direct link between the body and power, and an essential competition. At root, it hoped that a revolutionary but quiet consciousness would overcome men in general, and white men in particular. There's a lot in that request, and it's no wonder it didn't really graft itself onto modern life.

So this raises questions about what strategy has to do with gender and gender transformative thinking. If rejecting the binary is a key step in moving forward in reducing gender equity, then the old notions of 'the battle of the sexes' or the 'gender wars' must surely be put down once and for all. Wouldn't that be a relief? If we exhort men to mine their own compassionate feelings in order to enhance the lot of women, we may fall well short of a transformative revolution. His-story provides few role models for this kind of act. If we exhort white people to do that to enhance the lot of people of colour, or typical people to enhance the lot of people with disabilities, we will find similar results. Again, the seeds of change and revolution will have depended on a few selfless change makers.

Back to the Future

The evolution of modern transgenderism is a welcome advance and assist in this revolution. Its very existence helps in dispatching the battalions of the so-called 'battles' and creating the potential for a less divisive world. More than a 'third sex,' transgender, gender questioning, and gender diverse people offer to push the door open to a smashing and splintering of gender categories, well past binaries and well past trinaries. The ancient Hijra in India have been recognising gender diversity for over 4,000 years, including intersex, transgender, and eunuchs, except for a brutal period of criminalization and erasure by British rulers in the 1800s. Hijra incorporated the outliers of the gender binary and unified them under one banner. In 2014, they were recognised by the Supreme Court of India as a 'third gender' worthy of noting on official forms.

Indigenous 'two-spirited people' across North America cover a wide range of gender variant, diverse, and transgender expressions, and also include gay, lesbian, and bisexual people. This term is complex in that it differentiates between dimensions of gender roles, such as jobs and sexual orientation, and further, carries with it some fluidity, recognising that within one person may be several forms of gender expression and orientation, and that this can change, even from day to day. Known as man-woman or woman-man, two-spirited people were usually revered and respected prior to colonisation. This all ended with the imposition of homophobic mentalities amid Christian conversions that resulted in the eradication of such roles and identities by Spanish and other colonisers.

The fluidity inherent in two-spiritedness is its key attribute and is utterly far-reaching in its contributions to today's struggle with gender. The reclaiming of two-spirited people and identities over the past two decades is not only a pushing back against colonisation, which it is, but is also against the imposition of static binaries on a people. It's an example of how modern life can reclaim, offer illustration, and radically alter the future all at the same time. It's as if now we are finally reconceptualising and reclaiming

WHAT IF?

'Gender is socially constructed all the way through, an externally imposed hierarchy, with two classes, occupying two value positions: male over female, man over woman, masculinity over femininity... The solution is not to reify gender by insisting on ever more gender categories that define the complexity of human personality in rigid and essentialist ways... The solution to an oppressive system that puts people into pink and blue boxes is not to create more and more boxes that are any colour but blue or pink. The solution is to tear down the boxes altogether.'

Reilly-Cooper, R. "Gender Is Not a Spectrum." Aeon (June 28, 2016). www.tinyurl.com/zvgsjjg

gender from its historical oppressions, usually by colonisers intent on spreading rigid ideas. Such fluidity about gender is at the heart of transformation. Indeed, as Sabine Lang says:

> Their ambiguity reflects general patterns found in Native American world views, which appreciate and emphasize transformation, ambiguity, and change [6]

As in India, however, 'explorers' colonising North America regarded two-spirited people with disdain and brutalised them into isolation or shame. Stories of agents naming such groups 'berdache', a derogatory term indicating femaleness, femininity, prostitution, and passive sexual partner, replaced a variety of indigenous terms. Colonisers executed strong policing of gender where individuals were forced to wear gender congruent clothing and erase signs of their two-spiritedness. Now, within many North American Indigenous societies, a range of gender qualities in one person is again being reclaimed and recognised and often carries with it pride and the implication of special roles and powers.

Is the total erasure of gender categories a clear solution? At risk or under pressure are the safe and promising spaces for human expression and development. For example, women's sports teams are a very recent phenomenon in the world's history, but are at risk of being defined out of existence if the category of 'women's sport' is erased in favour of ability-based participation. The Paralympics and Olympics are designed as separate events, but arguments for

THE NEW LESBIAN?

Millennials are the backbone of Henrietta Hudson's [lesbian bar in New York] clientele. '28 years of age, educated, out to their families, confident, got their act together.' It offers decent drinks, good DJs, good music, karaoke, clever hosts, burlesque, drag kings, speed dating parties, bachelor(ette) parties, *The L Word* trivia... 'We create an experience that's interactive, where you don't just go order a drink and stand around...' Bar co-owner Lisa Cannistraci in *Curve* Magazine

Johns, M. "Viva Henrietta! Long Live This Lesbian Bar." Curve Magazine (July 26, 2016). www.tinyurl.com/hsssnbx

---

6 Lang, S. "Native American Men-Women, Lesbians, Two-Spirits: Contemporary and Historical Perspectives." *Journal of Lesbian Studies* 20, no. 3-4 (2016): 305.

and against merging them expose the importance of identity.

Reclaiming the Spirit of Sexual Orientation

Sexual orientation refers to one's mode of sexual attraction: heterosexual, homosexual, bisexual, asexual, men who have sex with men, pansexual, etc. This quality can be hidden or silenced, and often has been in many societies and situations where the gender binary brings with it compulsory heterosexuality. Indeed, many people around the world play out heterosexual roles and build heterosexual public lives while maintaining other sexual orientations in private.

Pushing for rights or recognition for sexual orientation in repressive regimes requires courage, radical thinking, and risk taking. As societies or countries become more accepting, and gay rights are set in place, there is much less to lose in living out a public version of one's sexual orientation. Indeed, pushing for gay rights has generated massive social movements extolling 'Pride' and numerous social and legal changes in increasing numbers of countries.

But mining the energy and generating gender transformative acuity in the contemporary lesbian, gay, and bisexual community may be a bit more difficult. The understandings of gender identity among Hijra and two-spirited people go where homosexuality and its categories of gay men, lesbians, and bisexuals typically do not. Further, transgender players within the gay rights movements have been on the forefront of confrontation on occasions such as the Stonewall Riot in New York City.

Being homosexual does not free one from living through a gender binary. Often it's the contrary. Gay

THE RISK OF BEING OTHER

An American man is facing a capital murder charge after killing in cold blood, a Kenyan gay man in Texas. The victim is said to have posted a same-sex advertisement online. The murderer reportedly asked for a meeting to discuss the advert and during their meeting, opened fire on the deceased. Initial investigations revealed that the murderer is a pornographic Internet sensation, who has 38,000 people followers on his X-rated Twitter account and another 5,000 people on Facebook. He had been targeting men who post same-sex personal adverts online.

Baraka, J. "Kenyan Gay Man Murdered in US after Posting Same-Sex Advert." ZIPO (June 9, 2016). www.tinyurl.com/zrorefa/

men often self-describe as various forms of masculine or feminine, as do lesbians, as butch or femme. Such self-assigned or group-assigned attributes may reflect personal, physical, or cultural characteristics and serve to cohere elements of the larger community of gay men and lesbians. These cultural attributes are not all negative in their effect. Indeed, they have been sources of great pride, comfort, and identity, and clearly create and recognise diversity within groups of lesbians and gay men.

MISOGYNY, AN ENDLESS HATE CRIME

Two women behind a campaign for police to record misogyny as a hate crime were subjected to abuse. The two women led research into hate crime in Nottingham UK that resulted in the city's police becoming the first in the country to recognise street harassment as a hate crime. Both were then subjected to personal threats and claims they were "not attractive enough" to talk about street harassment. One of the two said that she was told she "looked like a man, a 12 year old boy, one of the Proclaimers, Michael Gove, a 'bull dyke' and pretty much anything other than a woman that they'd want to sleep with."

Ridley, L. "Women Who Helped Make Wolf Whistling a Hate Crime Have Now Been Bombarded with Sexist Abuse." Huffington Post (July 26, 2016). www.tinyurl.com/zbxlm2t

But they are in no way a guarantee of progressive thinking about gender. Gay men do not automatically or even particularly understand or care about women, much less women's rights or gender inequity and can just as easily exhibit misogyny as straight men. Some elements of gay male culture illustrate this, taking up masculine privilege and disparaging woman in the name of humour, or theatre, or slang. More benignly, for some gay men, women just don't exist. This is often made easier as gay men, especially white gay men, enjoy elements of male privilege such as higher incomes and better jobs, and hence easier access to a range of resources, powers, and comforts. Gay-bashing, for men, is usually at the hands of men.

For lesbians, however, it is less likely that they can cease to notice men, gay or otherwise, in living in a gender inequitable world. Lesbians may still be consistently vulnerable to sexual assault, sexual harassment, or sexist remarks, especially when they do not conform to typical heterosexist modes of dress, behaviour, or presentation. But just being lesbian does not necessarily make one care about, analyse, or understand the constraints of being feminine or female, or automatically take up feminism to counteract gender injustice.

The gender binary brings a number of accoutrements with it. These are very wide ranging. They affect all of our lives, our bodies, our futures, our incomes, our opportunities, and our safety. They range from dress codes, to job roles to division of labour, to leadership and policy of major institutions held sacred by heterosexual and patriarchal forces. In this context, the widespread contemporary push among gays and lesbians for marriage rights as the emblem of equality stands out as an essentialist anomaly. Without a lot of critique, the historical, heterosexual, state-defined, imbalanced framework of marriage has been acritically adopted among mainstream gay rights movements in many countries. And with increasing and considerable success.

Masses of cross-cultural history regarding 'marriage resistance' among free-thinking feminists and progressives have been seemingly obliterated. Despite the fundamentally threatening spectre of sharing marriage with 'same sex' couples to, well, fundamentalists, the larger community sees this as indicative of similarity. 'If gays and lesbians want so desperately to get married and have children, perhaps they are really just like us?' they may be asking. If so, what's to fear? Really.

Longstanding feminist critiques of marriage and its political and institutional characteristics such as joint finances, reciprocal wills, intrusive tax laws, and patriarchal assumptions about name changes, children's names, family structures, coupledom, roles, and monogamy have been drowned in a sea of cries for marriage 'equality.' So social movements also have mainstreams and diversions, as can be seen in the case of gays embracing marriage equality.

In contrast, the social movements that finally achieved recognition for people such as Hijra, two-spirited, or gender diverse individuals are key elements of erasing rigid ideas about gender for heterosexual, gay, lesbian, and bisexual people. These movements potentially *render gender atomized*, crushing the binary into not only trinaries but also paving the way for multiple manifestations of experience and understanding, and more importantly, gender

THE WORKAROUND

In the Kurya tribe in Tanzania, women are allowed to marry under a local tradition called *nyumba ntobhu* ('house of women'). By Kurya tribal law, only men can inherit property, but under *nyumba ntobhu*, if a woman without sons is widowed or her husband leaves her, she is allowed to marry a younger woman who can take a male lover and have children whom they can raise together. Cultural experts note that while the tradition is a longstanding one, it is having a revival as it provides women stability and freedom (including the ability to choose male sexual partners), and equitable division of work and finances within the relationship, while it reduces risk of domestic abuse, child marriage, and female genital mutilation.

Haworth, A. "Why Straight Women are Marrying Each Other" Marie Claire. July 25, 2016. www.tinyurl.com/jxb62t4

transformative thinking. Done right, Pride movements will expand past LGB to TQI2, etc. etc. etc. Done even better, they will one day eliminate those letters and categories altogether, and in so doing expend energy on acquiring a more critical edge about gender, race, class, and society.

THE PRICE OF GAY MARRIAGE

'It is unfortunate that the movement's two great victories of the last decade – the right to serve openly in the military and the right to be married – have come as progress has stalled or reversed in so many other areas of civil rights: equal pay and reproductive choice for women; housing and school segregation; police violence against minorities; and the prospects of a decent wage and a modicum of job and retirement security for all.'

Stewart-Winter, T. The price of gay marriage New York Times June 26, 2015. www.tinyurl.com/hccp67o

How Must We all Matter?

Once we have thoroughly rejected the gender binary, then what? First, it's a question of opening up our minds and giving up the secure containers in which we fit and in which we place others. But then the key challenge is addressing how we engage each other in gender transformative thinking that reduces, not increases inequity.

The tired phrase 'win-win' comes to mind. Or 'win-win-win...' Perhaps that's what we really need to think about, if we hope to see revolutionary change in the world on gender inequities. The only truly gender transformative programs and moments and shifts will occur when men and boys are asked to, guess what, think about themselves more. It's counter-intuitive for sure. But it focuses on the costs and benefits of gender (and sex) for them as people, and then maybe in relation to others, such as girls, women, gays, lesbians, transgender people, other men, etc. etc.

Men, specifically white men, have had expectations placed upon them of late to fix some or all of this problem, but historically women of all kinds have often led the charge and borne the brunt of such burdens. Across the globe, women and girls remain vulnerable to a complete absence of human rights in some settings, and widespread violence, disfigurement, objectification, victimisation, overwork, underpayment, and oppression in most.

People of colour and Indigenous people, male and female, are disproportionately poor, ill, incarcerated, or uneducated and shut out of mainstream power structures. Again, this is true in particular settings and in every country. And gay, lesbian, transgender, ambiguous, or extra-spirited people as we have seen, are emerging from invisibility and pain into a place of visibility, in some cases, re-emerging and experiencing considerable danger in the process in many countries.

But counter-intuitively, men need to spend more time thinking about themselves. Why? Part of this is about embracing their own internalised privilege, as you might expect, but the other part is about understanding their lack of privilege. This is better understood as seeing, feeling, and sharing the constraints of being male, in addition to the benefits. This type of thinking leads to acknowledging the gender container in which men are also locked, as well as addressing their own vulnerabilities, victimisation histories, trauma, lost hopes, hurts, injustices, fears, pressures, and missed aspirations.

This approach is late in coming. How do men, collectively generalised as oppressors, break out into more nuanced roles and identities? How do men, within and among themselves, address gender inequity in an honest way? Part of this requires good, old-fashioned consciousness-raising but more often it also requires some structure and support. And even permission. That might sound like an odd word, but it does apply to men in general. The container of gender and the elements of heteronormative masculinity form a rigid box. In some settings, there are very few options for any deviation.

Hence, men may be offered no options for rethinking masculinity, themselves, their own sexuality, gender identity, attitudes, and values about women and girls, or indeed about other men. They may have no platform for addressing their own abuse histories,

REDEFINING MASCULINITIES

'The programmes generally seem to view the behaviour and attitudes of individual men and boys as emerging from socially and historically constructed gender inequality and accordingly design programme activities to target both the individual and the broader social setting.'

Barker, G.; C. Ricardo, and M. Nascimento. "Engaging Men and Boys in Changing Gender-Based Inequity in Health: Evidence from Programme Interventions." Geneva: WHO, 2007: 27. www.tinyurl.com/5ok5qq

GENDER FOR ALL

'Gender matters everywhere in the world. And I would like today to ask that we should begin to dream about and plan for a different world. A fairer world. A world of happier men and happier women who are truer to themselves. And this is how to start: we must raise our daughters differently. We must also raise our sons differently.'

Ngozi Adichie, C. We Should All be Feminists. New York: Vintage Books, 2014

trauma, victimisation, or bullying. They may have no place to discuss sexism, racism, classism, or ableism no matter what role they play in all of those issues and processes.

WOMEN'S AND MEN'S WORK

'91% of fathers took time off after the birth but only 29% of fathers took more than two weeks.'

"Women and Work: The Facts." UK Business in the Community, The Prince's Responsible Business Network. www.tinyurl.com/zvu6wtl

Gender transformative programs for men attempt to do all or part of this. Such initiatives address negative gender stereotypes that, if rejected or avoided, could free men as well as women from their clutches. In particular, women and children and gender nonconforming men can benefit from addressing the elements of masculine hegemony among men. People of colour and Indigenous people can benefit from shifts in power and redressing and reconciling historical harms, but Indigenous women and women of colour will benefit the most in a new order by shifts in attitudes and behaviours and laws and opportunities redressing both sexism and racism.

Gender transformative work with men can be as simple as teaching and valuing nurturing and caring among fathers and rendering it masculine and strong. Or it can be as difficult as sharing domestic work in the home, by redefining it as men's *and* women's work, or rebalancing power in sexual relationships by generating a value to women's autonomy, different modes of sexual communication, and the rewards of consent.

Usually, such initiatives exist to address an issue such as a health crisis, domestic violence, or sexual assault. But along with addressing the issue, there is an equal commitment to investigating the gendered patterns, assumptions, stereotypes, behaviours, laws, regulations, or expectations that go along with the problem or crisis. This forms the basis for genuine change; addressing root causes and finding root solutions.

This enlightened approach had its beginning in low-resource countries. It is to the benefit of the entire globe that this way of thinking about gender transformation and equity is beginning to be diffused to middle- and high-income countries. It may be a harder sell in countries where women's lot and inequity, in general, may seem or feel less dramatically unequal. Or it may be a harder sell in high-income countries where men may have more to lose in the way of power, money, or prestige. But there is no doubt that it is just as necessary.

Typically, these programs often emerged after linear, shallow programs failed, such as those attempting to stop the transmission of HIV/AIDS or those attempting to quell domestic violence or sexual assault. Linear thinking leads to campaigns, programs, or messages that exhort and maybe shame, use typical 'hooks' such as gender stereotypes about femininity and masculinity and often rely on authoritative voices. But many such approaches failed to get results. Why? Because they didn't actually get to root causes, and hence, avoided root solutions. And root causes are critically important.

How Women Matter

So how do women fit in to this? At first blush, it might look like women have lots to gain and nothing much to lose from gender transformative thinking. And while they will have lots to gain, especially if they are experiencing several interlocking oppressions at once, there will still be lots for women to do. Centuries of patriarchal systems have institutionalised women's inequality and generated race-based inequities and in so doing have blunted the aspirations and cultural expressions of girls and women in general. Numerous waves of feminism over the past century have dealt with almost every aspect of women's lot from suffrage, to working conditions, to sexual harassment, to violence, to pay equity, to body image, to sexual freedom to reproductive rights, to property to...well the list goes on and on.

FEMALE APPLAUSE

'The father of the modern Olympic movement, Pierre de Coubertin argued in 1912 that "the Olympic Games must be reserved for men." The Games, he wrote, were for the "solemn and periodic exaltation of male athleticism," and they had "female applause as reward."...Shot put has been part of the modern Olympics since the beginning in 1896, but women did not compete in it until the 1948 Games in London.

Michelle Carter [gold medalist at the 2016 Olympics] believes that there's a stigma in the United States for women who compete in events like the shot put that require enormous amounts of brute strength and the bodies that go with it.'

Pilon, M. "You Throw, Girl: An Olympic Shotputter's Feminist Mission." The New Yorker, August 11, 2016. www.tinyurl.com/hs6nhxg

BOYS AGAINST FGM

In some countries, men oppose female genital mutilation at a higher rate than women... In Guinea – the country with the second highest prevalence of female genital mutilation (FGM) in the world –38 percent of men are against the practice, compared to just 21 percent of women, per new data from UNICEF. The same is true in Sierra Leone... Some of the biggest support for ending FGM is actually coming from young boys. In Sierra Leone, for instance, 40 percent of the boys between the ages of 15 and 19 are against the practice. 'Women feel obliged to uphold the tradition and aren't aware of how many men are actually against it', according to Francesca Moneti, UNICEF's senior child protection specialist

Ruiz-Grossman, S. "More Men Than Women Oppose Female Genital Mutilation in These Countries." The Huffington Post, July 19, 2016. www.tinyurl.com/joekghp

But centuries or decades or even sometimes just years of patriarchal culture and law promote lowered expectations among girls and women, that is until consciousness-raising takes hold. These lowered expectations can cut to the core of our aspirations and render them sterile or minuscule. It can slash any hope we may have had as girls and change that into resignation and silence as women. Without control over our own bodies, we can end up exploited, assaulted, raped, mutilated, sold, bought, or repeatedly pregnant. Without access to money or property, we are stalled, stuck, liabilities, appendages, or just plain poor. Without respect for our words, products, skills, or abilities, we are rendered secondary, worthless, invisible, and without meaning.

But worse, we can come to believe these things about ourselves and other women, and internalise sexism, objectification, body image definitions, sexual roles, brutal 'humour', and cutting language. We can become the agents of damage to girls and women, through role modelling, categorising them, cutting them, or delivering them to beauty rituals. We can and do enter into bride-price negotiations, persecution of daughters-in-law, attacks, and worse when 'family honour' is threatened when girls or women express will, agency, plans, or ideas. Stories abound where all of this is currently happening. And yes, women are not immune to internalising the rules and being gender-unequal operatives. Women have long been soldiers in the patriarchal army.

Choice comes into this. There are some complex definitions of 'choice' bandied about by women, designed to rationalise their paths in life. Much of this is attributed with thanks to feminism, even though the choices might not be feminist. For example, undergoing voluntary labia shaping surgery has been framed as a choice, as has selling one's body to strangers for money night after night after night. These 'choices' are often framed as offshoots of feminism: the result of freeing up space for self-expression, improving one's body image, or taking particular career paths.

A gender transformative approach to any of this is to understand root causes and root solutions. Why would someone want labia shaping surgery, or why do the majority of young women in contemporary society shave their pubic hair? Well, because a pervasive multi-billion-dollar pornography industry leads us there, slowly but surely, by framing sexual desire and preferences for women and men, even to the point of violence and torture, and by promoting heterosexual and male-centric versions of sexualized beauty. Or why do many girls and women find themselves stuck selling their bodies to strangers for a job? Because women's poverty is extreme, and women's trauma and violence and addiction histories can get in the way of climbing out of traps set by pimps, fathers, husbands, or boyfriends, or because there seems to be nothing else available.

Some women use 'choice' to justify their traditional roles in life, to stay out of the public sphere or the workforce, or to rationalise a lack of ambition to achieve or make decisions. Some women ignore or even exploit gender inequities in others in order to progress their own lives or reach their own successes. But many successful women still reject the label of feminism, distancing themselves from simplistic stereotypes of feminists or to 'pass' among men. Women whose lives and sometimes their fame or wealth or political power have been made possible by feminism often use these latter arguments, but they want no part of the feminist movement, or in giving back.

So when feminism is said to be about opening up choice for women, without a critique it can really be a can of worms. This is why gender transformative thinking is so important for women. But it is also why adopting gender transformative thinking is as hard for women as it might be for men. It will question the limits and habits of women as well as their aspirations

WHOSE VERSION OF A VULVA?

'...should [women] go under the knife to make their vulvas more closely resemble the airbrushed versions on display in mainstream porn, such as the "clamshell," in which the labia minora, or smaller, inner lips of the vulva, are barely discernible. The artificial aesthetic proliferated by porn is having an effect... a British medical group saw a threefold increase in the number of labiaplasties being performed in 2007–08, while inquiries rose sevenfold over the course of three years.'

Johnson, G. "Reality Check: This Is a Vulva." The Georgia Straight, February 23, 2011. www.tinyurl.com/zebddhh (review of Wrenna Robertson's 2011 book I'll Show You Mine. Vancouver: Show Off Books.)

TOMBOYS AND BOYS

'*Tomboy Survival Guide* is not just for women who keep their hair short, a pocketknife in their boot-cut jeans, and a set of socket wrenches close to hand...

"I have no desire to create some kind of a box that people can feel alienated by," explains storyteller and saxophonist Ivan Coyote... "My intention is to celebrate people who push the gender norms a little bit. For me, it [being a tomboy] was a space that existed, as a trans person, before I came to terms with that word [trans] in my own life," ... "It's not necessarily a safe space, but it's a safer space, where you're sort of allowed to want to do so-called boy things, or wear so-called boy's clothes... To me, it's a loose category, and it's an identity that I'm happy to share with anyone who feels like it resonates for them... I wish there was a space that allowed biologically assigned male children a similar exploration... In North American culture, anyway, I don't see that."'

Varty, A. "Tomboy Survival Guide pushes gender norms." Georgia Straight, April 22, 2015. www.tinyurl.com/jc57a6c

review of Coyote, I. (2016). *Tomboy Survival Guide*. Vancouver: Arsenal Pulp Press.

and comforts, and will loudly rattle the walls of the gender container called women.

How Transgender People Could Matter More

We have already seen how transgenderism has helped to smash the concept of the gender binary and how some transgender people have led the way, in the past and present, in atomizing gender expectations, presentation, aspirations, language, and human rights. You might think this is enough of a contribution. And it is significant. But in fact, there is a lot more that can be done to achieve gender transformative thinking.

It's one thing to smash the binary. And it's a good thing. It's a contradiction, though, to then define others in a binaried category or to call oneself 'non-binary' if one understands gender as a continuum. We are well past the 'third sex' as a concept, and into a fluid and potentially fairly limitless continuum of sex, gender, sexual orientation, and everything else that goes into gender identity, the body, gender relations, or sexual life. If transgender rights movements are interested in helping to push the issues of gender, equity, inequity, and transformation to their logical conclusions, then concepts of fluidity and movement need to replace categories. And that means some serious thinking on all of our parts about language and labels. Absolutely all of us.

As a corollary, it's not especially useful to name others as 'cisgender' – a term that is meant to indicate that one's gender identity parallels one's sex assigned at birth. It may be true for a lot of people, or even most people, but it really doesn't matter much. It is at best an observation and situation that reflects only a point in time, either then, or now, and certainly doesn't resemble the freedom of the fluidity that many trans people enjoy, desire, ask for, and explore. Over the years, trans people have developed different terminology to self-describe and others need to develop the same options.

What about the transformative thinking part? Some transgender people have been forefront in the LGBTQI2S[7] movement, and have been credited with standing up to police, taking risks, formulating demands for human rights, and much more. One of the issues about becoming women, however, is to confront the issues of gender inequity and incorporate them into activism and thinking. It can be theoretically confusing to explore gender fluidity and acquire a new identity, with all of its gendered trappings. But transgender people are in unique positions to understand those experiences. And often in the front row of experiencing gender-related inequities.

For example, transgender men experience the privilege and perquisites of being men, layered on a previous lifetime of being women in a sexist, misogynist world. Handling that dissonance is part of transitioning, and can be done with reticence or gusto, with silence or noise. It's arguably easier, and perhaps safer, to become a male bystander to sexism, but it creates a very uncomfortable spot for thoughtful, progressive people. In many ways, transgender men and women are very well placed to confront the impact of the gender hierarchy and the essence of gender inequity and injustice.

—

7 LGBTQI2S This refers to an ever-changing list of sexual orientations and gender identities – for example Lesbian Gay Bisexual Transgender Queer Intersex Two Spirited. The list may also include Questioning and Asexual.

As gender theorist Raewyn Connell (formerly Robert Connell) writes:

> Much of what transsexual women need is already contained in feminist agendas: equity in education, adequate child care, equal employment conditions and wage justice, prevention of gender-based violence, resistance to sexist culture... Given the depth and inter-woven character of gender inequalities, the best guarantor of justice for transsexual women is a gender-equal society. However hard it is to acknowledge... transsexual women have a broad interest in supporting feminist causes.[8]

But in reality, there has been a fairly long history of clashes between feminists and transgender women. Much of this has centred on requests from transgender women to enter often hard won women-only spaces. It may be time for finding paths forward and requests for rights that don't increase inequities for others. Asking to be in women-only spaces where women gather who feel vulnerable as women because of their bodies and share lifetimes of accumulated experiences, can be construed as invasive.

It's not a surprise that many of these arguments are about spaces and projects that women-born-female, and avowedly feminist, have painstakingly built as sites of safety; cocoons of communication and identity formation. It should be easy to see why, given rampant gender inequity in the world and the vulnerability of female bodies to violence from men. It's less often the case that men-born-male go out of their way

GARNERING EVIDENCE

'The University of Victoria today announced the establishment of the Chair in Transgender Studies—the first of its kind—to tackle essential issues that matter and to inspire research and discussion to help make a difference in the lives of some of our most vulnerable people in society... Dr. Aaron Devor will work with some of the world's top researchers and scholars, thought leaders, transgender community activists and students to further research into a broad range of topics concerned with the lives of trans and gender nonconforming people and to explore crucial issues such as healthcare, poverty, discrimination and suicide.'

Dr. Aaron Devor - World's Only Chair in Transgender Studies." University of Victoria, Sociology. www.tinyurl.com/j968x2r

—

8 Connell, R. "Transsexual Women and Feminist Thought: Toward New Understanding and New Politics." *Signs* 37, no. 4 (Summer 2012): 872

to create such spaces, or that transgender men want to join in with them and offer a challenge to masculinity.

None of this undermines the veracity of the problem of violence against transgender persons or trans women in particular or the need for safety. Or of the identity formation derived from trans communities. But gender transformative thinking requires an objective assessment of what gender inequities exist, who is most vulnerable, and how committed an individual or community is to reducing those inequities. The gender order exists out there, and all communities are rendered 'something' in that order, sometimes favourable and sometimes not. This has consequences for all of us in different ways. Raewyn Connell, again on transitions and the gender order:

> It is structured by the inequalities of the gender order; the process is not the same for transsexual women and transsexual men. Transsexual women are shedding the patriarchal dividend that accrues to men as a group in labour markets, finance markets (e.g., housing), family status, professional authority, and so on.

The struggle for recognition of the rights of transgender persons is finally and rapidly gaining ground legally, morally, and strategically. It is to be supported by all of us. It carries with it the burden and the responsibility of confronting the gender order in ways that feminist or gay rights movements have not been able to. It has embodied direct experiences of gender changes and offered stories of pain and hope, seeking and belonging, and it has demonstrated beyond a doubt how far we have come and how far we have yet to go in conceptualising a gender transformative order that includes everyone, without diminishing anyone. This is truly a very tall order.

Gender Transformative Revolutions

So what's to be done? How do we include everyone, so that there truly is a 'win-win-win...' and without losses encountered along the way? Addressing inequities of gender necessitates all of us to look at all possible genders and expressions of gender, and to build on history and theory from all sectors. This includes scholars, communities, activists and lawyers, feminist and men's movements, trans, gay, lesbian, and queer movements. It means we are all in this together, and we cannot ignore gender inequities that persist even if we personally are not feeling that particular pain. This is not a call for blinders as we traverse an idealistic sweet path forward, but rather it's a call for eyes wide open and doing good as well as doing no harm to anyone.

CHAPTER 5

Loss and Profit

Equity involves thinking about money. In fact, from its sub-title some might have thought this book was about money and capital. And in many ways it is. Our world operates on a language of money, economics, capital, and capitalism that affects all of us. Our lives are increasingly globalised and interconnected not just by money and its drivers, but also the attitudes and processes that drive investment, reward, profit, and loss.

Normally we say 'profit and loss,' but here we will start with loss. For very frequently in our world we see unused assets, assets that are not nurtured or sustained, the foregoing of returns on investments, and the eroding, ignoring, and denigrating of human, social, and moral capital. These sound like bad ways to run a company. But that's how we're running things right now. The only assets most companies have are people and resources, and sometimes real estate, equipment, and intellectual property. If we view ourselves as a company, there are some immediate tweaks we need to our business model. At the moment, we are experiencing a lot of losses. These need rectifying. They all involve how we treat our collective assets. They all reflect inequity and often gender inequity.

OLD ADVICE

'That the principle which regulates the existing social relations between the two sexes – the legal *subordination* of one sex to the other – is wrong itself, and now one of the chief hindrances to *human improvement; and that it ought to be replaced by a principle of perfect equality, admitting no power or privilege on the one side, nor disability on the other.* '

Mill, John Stuart. The Subjection of Women. 1869.

Losses

It seems highly counterproductive to undervalue those who do the most work in the world, reproduce the next generation of workers, and run domestic households for no pay. UNICEF estimates[9] that compared to boys, girls as young as five to fourteen spend forty percent more time, or 160 million more hours *a day*, on unpaid household chores and collecting water and firewood. Think about that for a minute. This is probably what your mother and grandmother did. It might be what you do or what your partner does. Without this unpaid work – gendered unpaid work – there would be no one to work with. The world's business model would come to a halt, and we would all die off.

PRESIDENTIAL TREATMENT

And no woman seems to be immune. At the Republican National Convention in the USA in 2016, the following buttons were on display as commentary on Hillary Clinton's unsuccessful candidacy for president: *'Life's a bitch, don't vote for one'*, and *'KFC Hillary Special: 2 fat thighs, 2 small breasts, left wing'*.

This is rather an important asset. Women and girls perform the vast majority of this unpaid, caring, reproducing work. McKinsey Global Institute estimates that the unpaid work in the world is thirteen percent of the global GDP, and women do seventy-five percent of it. In the current setup, this is free labour and household equity is grown by this invisible amount. While this might be an asset for your home and possibly the factory down the way, it's a loss for those women and girls who spend their capital in this limited way.

Then there are the natural resources in our world, ranging from water, to air, to minerals, rocks, and trees. It is clear that we have abused these resources and are now in a planetary crisis. The temperature of the earth has increased rapidly in the last few years, and melting ice will drown several countries

---

9 "Girls Spend 160 Million More Hours Than Boys Doing Household Chores Everyday." UNICEF Press Centre, www.unicef.org/media/media_92884.html

and shift coastal life around the world to a very different rhythm.

Some species will be threatened, and climate change will generate all manner of costs to the current bottom line. Many of these costs will accrue to those who have the least. Equity is a critical part of the story of climate change. Many coastal communities and many low-income groups will be victims of rising sea levels, and many women will shoulder the burden of climate change in uniquely gendered ways.

Transforming gender is also becoming key to conservation and keeping species alive, whether threatened by climate change or other reasons. In Melanesia, men have historically been rangers protecting the sea turtles and women historically excluded from even visiting the habitats. The extent of women's roles in conservation was cooking food for the men. Now,

> Research demonstrates that involving more women in community conservation projects is key to their success, but without conscious effort they aren't always included. So Nature Conservancy scientist Robyn James is changing the way conservation projects in Melanesia incorporate women — and using her experience to develop gender-inclusive conservation strategy and policy recommendations for the entire organization. [10]

And what about intellectual property, talent, invention, and innovation? It seems, if you look back in history, that this was all the domain of men, usually white men. In many countries, our museums,

CLIMATE CONTROLS

'For the past three decades, since the Intergovernmental Panel on Climate Change was created and climate negotiations began, the refusal of our governments to lower emissions has been accompanied with full awareness of the dangers. And this kind of recklessness would have been functionally impossible... without all the potent tools on offer that allow the powerful to discount the lives of the less powerful. These tools - of ranking the relative value of humans - are what allow the writing off of entire nations and ancient cultures. And they are what allowed for the digging up of all that carbon to begin with.'

"Naomi Klein on the Racism That Underlies Climate Change Inaction." The Saturday Paper, June 25, 2016. www.tinyurl.com/jnchrhk

—

10 Hausheer, J. E. "Why Conservation Needs Women: Supporting Women's Networks for Community Conservation." Cool Green Science, July 22, 2016. www.tinyurl.com/j6lpogo

libraries, and art galleries are full of men's products. Our monument collections, lists of famous leaders, scientists, writers and composers... well, they are populated by men. And those in charge of major institutions, revolutions, war, peace? Prime ministers, presidents, bishops, imams, popes, colonels, CEOs...etc. Review the history we are all fed, and we must conclude that this is gendered too. Or is it sexed? Do you just need a penis to make a decision and a difference? Even when women made important discoveries or literary contributions, they were hidden. In many cases, males took the credit for innovations and discoveries, or women published these achievements under male names.

It seems a highly shoddy business decision to ignore the intellectual capital, talent, and innovation of much of the world's population. That's like leaving money on the table, food in the ground, inventions unmade, compositions unplayed, crops in the field, books unread or...well, it's an endless list of ignored and unused capital. It's a business model based on waste or misrepresentation. And it remains a fairly common approach to running families, schools, communities, universities, governments, international agencies, etc.

SEEING, NOT BELIEVING

'Quantifying the gender gap is an inexact science. By some estimates, over 50% of visual artists are women, but less than 5% of the artists featured in the world's most popular art museum galleries are female... Even though new female artists have a much better opportunity to make it into museums than their predecessors...if art keeps being added to the National Gallery [US] at the current rate...we estimate that it will be a little after the year 2600 before half the painting you see in the museum's collection are by women.'

Priceonomics. "Just How Big is the Gender Gap in Fine Art?" www.tinyurl.com/jmyauz3

PRIZE DISCOVERY

Rosalind Elsie Franklin (1920–1958) was an English chemist who discovered the molecular structures of DNA. However, two American male scientists who had been exposed to her work took credit for the discovery and went on to win the Nobel Prize for the discovery.

Lee, J. J. "6 Women Scientists Who Were Snubbed Due to Sexism." National Geographic, May 19, 2013. www.tinyurl.com/bzgor2t

What Return on Investment?

The World Economic Forum publishes a stark reminder of this on a regular basis. They calculate the 'economic gender gap' across all levels of development, from high- to low-income countries. Over the past ten years, they dismally report that the global economic gender gap has closed by only three percent. The good news is that many, many, countries are increasingly investing in the education of girls and women, and in some countries, women's educational achievement is equal to or surpassing men's. But in every country, the bad news is that this does not translate into higher incomes for women, or even higher rates of economic participation.

Talk about ignoring your investments! And failing to reap the returns! The barriers, as they say, are complex. But essentially it's about process not content. It's not about women not being educated or skilled or willing or ambitious, it's about assumptions, stereotypes, or negative attitudes. This results in discrimination. These manifest as barriers ranging from benign presumptions to outright aggression; from subtle condescension to outright harassment; from lack of professional networks to different pay rates, labour codes, or job roles for men and women. Sometimes, the lack of female bathrooms is offered as the reason. So the good news is that more investment in girls and women's education is being made. The bad news is the world is not getting the rewards. Sometimes, just for the sake of a few toilets.

And this doesn't begin to get at how human assets are abused. Not only is a rather large proportion of our human assets often left undeveloped, but it is also badly treated. It seems highly unwise to abuse and threaten the health, bodies, and very lives of those who serve, give care, are indentured, or are slaves. This is like collective self-harm. Without these services, things could get uncomfortable; sexual services not transacted, children not born, families not fed, factories not supplied with workers, houses not cleaned, and crops unpicked. But this is the story for many girls and women who are in situations with little or no agency, protection, or prospects. These women are the most overlooked, in ways that threaten their very existence.

In a business model, it also seems unwise to harass, limit, ignore, denigrate, or pass over those who begin to make inroads by breaking out of their confines and starting to take a place in the system

KIDNAPPED AND RAPED

On April 14, 2014, close to 300 school girls were kidnapped from Chibok, Nigeria, by the militant group Boko Haram. Boko Haram is a militant terrorist group, whose name roughly translates to 'Western education is forbidden.' Following the abduction, Evon Idahosa, a Nigerian-born lawyer, activist and a leader of America's #BringBackOurGirls advocacy group, told MTV News 'I think one thing I want the West to understand is there's a much deeper issue here that extends beyond education, I think it really has to do more with how women are viewed and valued in society. It could be education today, but tomorrow it will be unequal pay. It will be doors slammed in the face of women when they try to enter the doors of politics. It's this issue that women are chattel and they can be carted off in the middle of the night.'

Davidson, D. "One Year after #Bringbackourgirls, Why Are They Still Missing?": MTV News, April 10, 2015. www.tinyurl.com/jnkrchh

and the world. Think of all those women and girls who may get to school or university for the first time. Or all the firsts: the women who blaze the trail in a company, industry, or field as a minority of one. Think of the stereotypical (yes, unfortunately) female firefighter, harassed and sexualised, or bullied into submission. Or the harassed woman soldier, or police officer. Think of the gently excluded and ignored woman in the boardroom, whose opinion is taken up and claimed by some guy before it gets heard. Think of the female leaders and politicians who are forced to ignore barrages of haters, reputation-rapists, on-line bullies, cyber attackers, sexist pranksters, fashion critics, body police, and more.

GAPS AND SPACES

People and their talents are among the core drivers of sustainable, long-term economic growth. If half of these talents are underdeveloped or underutilised, growth and sustainability will be compromised. Moreover, there is a compelling and fundamental values case for empowering women: women represent one half of the global population—they deserve equal access to health, education, earning power, and political representation. The current inequalities risk being exacerbated in the future...

World Economic Forum. "The Global Gender Gap Report 2015." 2015: Preface V www.tinyurl.com/zmako27

In the world of business, some of the most important principles are: recognise your resources, grow your assets, get return on investments, and protect your assets. If we agree that people who are inequitably treated in this world are really assets, then we are making some very bad business decisions. But perhaps they are not seen that way. Perhaps there is such a sensation of distanced privilege washing over those who run things that the assets are just taken for granted, invisible, assumed, and not counted. So could counting be the key?

Money, Money, Money

Economic costs of things do matter. So perhaps the calculation of costs is critically important to developing understanding, and generating better economic decisions? Not sure. In the mid-1990s, we were engaged in assigning economic costs to violence against women. In fact, such costs were calculated in several jurisdictions around the world. These were painstakingly and carefully compiled and then broken down by type of costs such as; policing, emergency room care, missed work, insurance, etc. etc.

The purpose of doing these exercises is to shine a different light on the problem of violence against women and to make the point that everyone, including victims and survivors, pays. Actually pays hard cash. It also re-frames the problem for governments as a financial issue, not 'just' a social issue. And we all do pay. Those paying include insurers – and therefore individuals paying raised insurance premiums; governments – and therefore taxpayers; employers – and therefore consumers, and on it goes.

These efforts do get some brief front-page attention, or a shout-out in legislatures, and violence against women enjoys a different kind of analysis. People are shocked, briefly, to see an annual monetary figure attached to what they had considered a private, personal problem. In 2004, the UK Home Office reported that domestic violence, only one discrete form of violence against women, was costing the state 23 billion pounds per year.

> There are an increasing number of studies that show that violence against women places significant burdens on individuals, governments and economies, including a 2003 report from the US Center for Disease Control and Prevention that estimates that the costs of intimate partner violence in the United States alone exceeded USD 5.8 billion per year while a more recent study conducted in Australia in 2009 by the National Council to Reduce Violence, in collaboration with KPMG, estimated that violence against women and their children cost the Australian economy an estimated $13.6 billion in that year alone. A number of developing and middle-income countries have also conducted costing exercises of violence, including Fiji, Macedonia,

MONEY DOESN'T ALWAYS TALK

Research prepared for a World Bank Group report on challenges to gender equality, shows domestic violence has a significant impact on a country's GDP: 'This underscores that the loss due to domestic violence is a significant drain on an economy's resources. Violence against women and girls is a global epidemic, with devastating consequence for individuals, communities, societies, and economies. Addressing this challenge head-on promises to significantly advance our efforts to end extreme poverty and increase prosperity for all...'

Jeni Klugman, World Bank Gender and Development Director in press release Nov. 25, 2013. www.tinyurl.com/j6ftjaj

Uganda, Nicaragua and Chile, and Vietnam using various methodologies. [II]

These forms of analysis have also been applied to child abuse, incest, and specific calculations made for the health care system, the criminal justice system, educational systems, insurers, etc. But have these exercises ended violence against women? Not at all. In fact, twenty years later not only are we still dealing with the same issues but also surfacing additional and more complex versions of violence against women. But we do have more players paying attention and playing a role, including employers, unions, insurance companies, and governments. So perhaps naming the 'costs' has to be done, and done in many different ways?

IGNORED AND UNCOUNTED

'Much of the world's economic activity takes place in the form of unpaid work by women, from fetching water, carrying firewood and tending animals in subsistence agricultural countries, to caring for children, the sick and elderly in both developing and developed nations... a large portion of this activity still left out of GDP calculations and policy decisions...

"When you don't have all of that in front of you, you just make really bad policy...You make very bad policy about the next generation, about the environment." Marilyn Waring, author of *If Women Counted: A New Feminist Economics* said'.

Langeland, T. "Women Unaccounted for in Global Economy Proves Waring Influence." Bloomberg June 18, 2013. www.tinyurl.com/j8lq2gb

Exploit

But how does the world of capitalism fit into this counting exercise? In general, it's all about making profit. It likes to think it's building equity, in that its assets outweigh its liabilities. But many capitalist processes, such as competition for markets and the cost cutting that goes on to achieve this seem to be working against the grain in the world of equity. When the aim is to produce the cheapest product, then contracting out labour or undermining union organising is the way to go.

In addition, in the name of creating markets, products, and demand, businesses actively and consciously generate and exploit gender inequity. First,

II "What Works: Economic and Social Costs of Violence Programme." What Works to Prevent Violence www.whatworks.co.za/about/costs-of-violence

there are gender-specific services, such as charging higher costs for cleaning women's shirts compared to men's shirts, or for cutting women's hair compared to men's hair. Then there are gender-specific products that mean charging more for a deodorant or soap marketed to women, when it's the same product.

The effect of these differences is sometimes called the 'pink tax', and has been calculated by sources in several countries as a substantial figure, totalling thousands of dollars a year. Women pay more for cars than men, and black women pay more than white women, according to the state of California. Women also pay more for insurance. But don't forget, women make substantially less money than men, and black women even less than white women.

As gender lines blur and a few innovators strive to create products such as genderless clothing lines, mainstream companies apparently want to keep the lines in place. This is another way in which gender matters to manufacturers. Gender creates a wider market. Instead of producing just shirts, they produce and market women's, men's, girls', and boys' shirts. Now there are four products, not one. And four manufacturing and design initiatives.

This is music to the big ears of capitalism. Not only is there an opportunity to charge different prices, but, more sinister and long lasting, there's a chance to continue to communicate gender via products. And this then generates wants and needs in girls and boys, and women and men that are markers of a supposed identity. And this starts early. Marketing to girls regenerates gender categories, giving them perpetual life. If capitalism gains from gender categories, then smashing the binary is going to take a lot longer, or require different tactics and evidence.

And this is the obvious stuff. In the structures of capitalism, there are different pay scales, different jobs, different interview questions, different promotional paths, different starting salaries, different

STEMMING THE TIDE OF GIRLS

'The perception of somebody who works in technology is a pizza guzzling-nerd who cannot get a girlfriend. This perception is pushing women away from studying "STEM" subjects – science, technology, engineering and maths', says Lady Geek's Belinda Parmar.

Those brands brave enough to break the stereotypes see instant benefits. Respondents in the [Little Miss Understood] research reacted very positively to an advert from GoldieBlox, a brand that makes toys and entertainment for girls to encourage them to become engineers.

Chahal, Mindi. "Why Brands Are Losing Relevance with Girls. Research Shows Brands Need to Go Beyond Pink and Princesses." Marketing Week, Feb. 18, 2015. www.tinyurl.com/h3vdsvc

hiring hurdles and promotional benchmarks, different workplace hazards and bullying techniques, and different sorts of marginalisation, depending on your gender and race, your ethnicity and accent, your immigration status and...well, all the components of inequity show up right here.

MISSING

In a 2016 *Lancet* journal series on transgender health, researchers and advocates for transgender health note that we don't know how many transgender people there are nor what their health needs are. Knowing is complicated by how some people live with their gender incongruence; some make a social transition only, while others seek out clinical care for transitioning. It is further complicated by the choice of non-binary gender identities. And health surveillance in most countries does not assess gender identity as an equity stratifier.

"Transgender Health." The Lancet (June 17, 2016). www.tinyurl.com/h7c533o

Whose Expense?

When tallied, inequity costs money. Lots of money. Not only to those enduring the inequity but also to the world that supports us all. Many global debts could be paid with this money. Various smart people have calculated these costs. McKinsey Global Institute is the research arm of McKinsey and Company, a global consulting firm that has recognised the costs of women's inequality and monetised them.

They offer the startling estimate that *$28 trillion per year could be added to the global GDP by 2025* – the size of the economies of China and the USA in 2016 – if gender inequity were erased, and women and men participated in the economy equally. This would mean that women could be in the workforce, unpaid work was measured in the GDP, laws and regulations were changed to promote gender equity, and health and security issues were addressed. This astonishing estimate illustrates what is lost by ignoring women's value, and by not addressing access to equity.

Growing the Assets

What business or economy doesn't want to grow its assets? But investing in developing human capital means that those who are typically disenfranchised need more attention than others, at least for a while.

This is the heart of equity. It's why some people matter more than others at some points in time.

It's why Black Lives Matter in the chaos of repeated police shootings of black men. It's why British girls of African descent matter when they are being railroaded through airports on their way to school holiday clitoridectomies. It's why Indigenous girls and women in Canada matter when they continue to be murdered and go missing and are ignored by the powers-that-be. It's why gay men mattered in the 1980s when an unchecked and unknown virus was killing them. It's why poor, pregnant women in Brazil matter as Zika-laden mosquitos generate birth defects and governments block anything remotely approaching socially just solutions.

These injustices emerge and recede and manifest differently, but ignoring them creates ongoing loss of human capital and generates less growth. Gender inequity, global economic inequities, and race and ethnic inequities persist and more emerge every day, piling on to these historical understandings and experiences. But even with this cascade, there is little interest in growing assets. Even when it comes to the ultimate challenge – replenishing the workforce:

> Gender equality has been relegated to a superfluous concern in the grand march towards economic 'reform.' Even the falling birth rate has hardly registered as a danger signal of this neglect. [12]

If states were interested in replenishing the population, there would be free day care, universal care

MATTERING TOGETHER

'When we say Black Lives Matter, we are broadening the conversation around state violence to include all of the ways in which Black people are intentionally left powerless at the hands of the state. We are talking about the ways in which Black lives are deprived of our basic human rights and dignity.
Black Lives Matter affirms the lives of Black queer and trans folks, disabled folks, black-undocumented folks, folks with records, women and all Black lives along the gender spectrum.'

www.blacklivesmatter.com/about/

—

12 Pollert, A. "Gender, Transformation and Employment in Central Eastern Europe." *European Journal of Industrial Relations* 11, no. 2 (2005): 228)

for elders, home care for people with disabilities, and parental leave for all concerned.

Indicators

MORE OF THE SAME

'For years I worked at the BBC, making and presenting business programmes for TV and radio, and I was always asking, "Where are all the women?" The majority of interviewees are of the suit and tie variety: male, pale, stale (hair optional). In 20 years, my question went unanswered, and so it goes on. Recent research shows a consistent male to female ratio of 4:1 for contributors invited onto news programmes as experts.'

Haslam, Penny. "The Power of Visibility: Why We Need to Keep Asking 'Where Are All the Women?'." The Guardian, May 8, 2015. www.tinyurl.com/jayg7b7

So how do we transform assets using gender transformative thinking? This leads us to what we need to measure to support gender transformative thinking. As you can see, we are fairly good now at measuring the gender gap, globally and locally, and at pinpointing the issues where assets and labour could be better utilised, grown, or invested. But how do we measure transformation? How do we comment on what would allow us all to know if equity, not just equality, is reached? This is a far more complex question and requires some innovative thinking about indicators.

Typically, we measure things like educational levels, income levels, access to property and health care, or morbidity, mortality, and rates of disease. For many years, we just measured a few of these, and we didn't even differentiate among women and men. This told us absolutely nothing about women's lot; it rather just indicated some averages. After a lot of agitation, disaggregation of statistics and information became more common. So as we are getting better at measuring these by the binary of gender, male and female, we could now think about how to get even more precise once we start measuring the status of transgender people.

But taken at face value these kinds of data will only help us with assessing equality. These measures will tell us who gets more cancer, or who dies in childbirth, or who has less education than the other. While critically important, the processes of gender stratification are more subtle and complex, and they operate at numerous levels. Cultural, sect-based, tribal, social, media-inspired, cyber-controlled, community-based...

these are some of the parameters that might really matter to increasing gender equity and seeing transformative thinking take hold.

So what might these be? In searching for fundamentals, we think about autonomy, including freedom of movement, visibility, bodily autonomy, household decision-making power, control over resources and land, access to information, reproductive choice and freedom from reproductive coercion, freedom from threats and fear, etc. etc. If you are experiencing none of these or just a few of these, you are imprisoned in your own skin, and maybe your home, physically and emotionally. All of these components, you would agree, are very real components of quality of life for any gender, but especially pronounced for women and girls.

Let's take visibility. In Melanesia, the women were formerly in the kitchen, not helping to conserve sea turtles. In various Middle Eastern countries, women are not seen much in public, or if they are, are invisible behind layers of cloth covering hands, faces, and bodies. In many countries, even where women roam the streets at will, and wear whatever they want, they may still be invisible in politics or business or law. In other situations, women and girls try to become invisible through deliberately shrinking their bodies, or just staying quiet.

Reproductive coercion, another unmeasured indicator, takes many forms but involves removing from women and girls the decision-making about whether to have children or not. This can include men refusing to use contraception or sabotaging contraceptive efforts. It can involve pressure to have numerous pregnancies to produce male children, or to give up female children. It can involve pressure to keep unwanted pregnancies, or in some cases, the opposite. It is common in the context of intimate partner violence, but its range is much broader. In short, it's about women not having bodily autonomy over their reproduction, and being unable to exercise agency.

The more you think about this, the more real it seems. It likely goes on in some form in every corner of the world. But it is not often counted, researched, measured, or asked about in health and social care or surveys. It is certainly not discussed much in public. This is an indicator whose time has come.

Autonomy is often multi-faceted, and can be complicated to measure. It's not just about what a woman can do on her own, but it's also about what influence she might have on her family and community. It includes the respect she might gain for her opinions, and this combines with her level of education, class, occupation, and age. Digital access, freedom of movement, and household decision-making powers are additional indicators that reflect on lived experiences of men and women. At base, however, autonomy is critical to anyone's welfare; whether a prisoner, a slave, a child or an elderly person. Without it, wings are clipped or never grown and certainly consent is hard to come by.

Freedom of movement is often seen as the heart of agency and scope. This is critical for many women and girls around the world who cannot go out on their own or without male company, for reasons ranging from male patriarchal controls, to danger from sexual harassment or sexual assault, to laws forbidding women to drive. Such freedoms are limited by custom, clothing, rules, laws, dangers, or social pressure and serve to domesticate, limit, curtail, and cut into the influence women and girls might have on the world. Freedom of movement is linked to other controls, in that it might be limited for reasons of modesty, sexual control, enslavement, confinement, or blocking access to education or paid work.

Household decision-making is a bit easier to measure as researchers pinpoint the elements of decision-making: whether on food choices, expenditures, education, politics, health, or fertility. These can be broken out and measured in women, men, and

VISIBLE EQUITY

Frances Morris (Head of Collections, International Art at Tate Modern) is optimistic about improvement in gender representation in art as she describes how 'the western paradigm is now shifting, so it's not all about European and North American art. If you start chipping away at the core, in geographical terms, then I think gender has a better chance of getting in as well. That master system and narrative is collapsing.'

Elderton, Louisa. "Redressing the Balance: Women in the Art World." The White Review, July 1013. www.tinyurl.com/gny89fv

extended family members of different classes or castes in any society.

Men often dominate in public spaces, occupy the plazas and parks from New York in Athens, jog at night in any neighbourhood, sprawl in ungainly postures taking up three seats instead of one on public transit, take up prime TV time when playing sports, and get prime time in recreational hockey rink rentals. Visibility and gender take many forms. And the ability to be visible needs measuring.

Women become invisible if their names are lost at marriage and when their children are given only their father's names, leading to family histories and genealogies that are only about men and impossible to fully reconstruct. This gives historians great female vacuums to work through. When women's own voices don't make it to the history books or art galleries, this too results in invisibility. Women also become invisible in societies where their energies – sexual, economic, and intellectual – are circumscribed by culture, tradition, fashion, religion, decree, laws, or worse, self-containment.

Rebecca Solnit calls this 'obliteration,' and talks of this and the legal ways in which women are merged into men's property and lives by being denied agency. She also talks about the obliteration rendered by the veil and, in particular, the burka. On reflecting on a photograph of an Afghan family in the *New York Times:*

> ...I saw only a man and children, until I realized with astonishment that what I had taken for drapery or furniture was a fully veiled woman. She had disappeared from view, and whatever arguments people make about veils and burkas, they make people disappear. [13]

—

13 Solnit, Rebecca. *Men Explain Things to Me.* Chicago: Haymarket Books, 2014: 68

What to Do?

Generating social change is complex when it comes to gender. The entrenched relations between men and women, and the entrenched and culturally specific resistance to understanding a range of gender expressions set up some difficult terrain. Clearly, measuring such common indicators as legal and human rights, or access to education or property are very important in understanding gender equity.

But there are all manner of other indicators of gender inequities that need examination and measuring, many of which don't get discussed, despite their numerous manifestations and lived realities. And these lived realities are not limited to the categories of men or women. Race, sexual orientation, gender identity, and age also determine and sometimes limit the ability to roam, leave a neighbourhood, experience a safe walk at night, or drive a car without recrimination or fear.

The evidence seems to be in. Inequality is a loser economically as well as morally, socially, and legally. Shouldn't the 'captains of industry' be moved by these arguments? Change might depend on not just the counting, but also on consciousness-raising and effective leadership among both the counters and the counted.

> Making the economic case for equality requires persuasion, effective leadership, and awareness-raising activities to convince a wider number of decision-makers, but once the longer-run benefits of gender equality policies are accepted then viewing equality as an investment in our economic future becomes inevitable.[14]

---

14 "The Economic Case for Gender Equality": European Commission, Directorate-General for Employment, Social Affaires and Equal Opportunities, August 2008.

CHAPTER 6

Leading

We've talked about equity, gender, principled action, how we all matter (differently) and what inequity costs us. It's all challenging to think about. But how do we move forward? Now it's time to figure out how to galvanise things in order to make changes. This means strengthening what works, accelerating in the right direction, fortifying ourselves, and fighting against corrosion. Change requires clarity, courage, and ongoing engagement. It doesn't happen on its own.

Risks of Not Doing Anything

The risks of doing nothing about equity are obvious and significant. It leads to the overlooking of great resources, especially, but not only, girls and women, or even the retreat of women from the workforce. It can lead to the continued relegation and invisibility of women and girls of colour and all that unused potential, creativity, writing and art, industry, invention, production and innovation, leadership, activism, and achievement. It inevitably affects trans women, gays and lesbians, and all others who live outside any assumed heteronormative binary. It leads to harm.

It also leads to the ongoing marginalisation of men and boys. There will be little progress without an equity-informed approach to defining masculinities, boy socialisation, male feminism, responding to perpetrators and prisoners, and challenging pornography and prostitution. Without male leadership tuning in to equity and gender and addressing violence, conflict, and bystanderism there will be no significant changes for men either.

OUTSIDE THE LINES

Three groups of adolescents are consistently targeted for victimisation in middle school:

1. Boys who are perceived as not masculine enough;
2. Girls who are perceived as not feminine enough; and,
3. Girls whose bodies mature before their peers.

In each case, policing gender norms or punishing some sort of perceived gender non-conformity is clearly integral to the attack.

TrueChild. "Gender Norms: A Key to Combating School- and Cyber-Bullying and Homophobic Harassment among at-Risk Youth." 2009. www.truechild.org

As more and more people in personal and political terms challenge the still-dominant gender binary, it also means that ignoring gender inequity becomes even more complex, and involves issues, settings, and personal and political costs yet to be measured. In all cases, though, there are people with real lives and potential whose future and present circumstances are threatened, economically, socially, legally, and physically. This can and does range from inconvenience to death. So there's a lot at stake in understanding how gender equity is critical to moving forward and how transforming ourselves is an utter necessity.

Take pay equity, for example. Some of the most advanced countries in the world have significant gender gaps in pay. In other words, women get paid less than men for work of equal value, even in large public universities, as well as in companies and factories. In Canada, universities, one by one, are painfully rectifying the wage gap between their female and male faculty by giving women professors, as a group, raises across the board. These inequities have been noted and measured for over two decades and are only now, slowly being rectified. The goals are extremely modest and the progress extremely slow. The expressed goal of the Australian effort to reduce gendered pay inequity, for example, is to erase gender pay inequity in a generation. Not tomorrow, or in five years. A generation!

Intelligence from South to North

As a solution, gender transformative thinking represents an interesting diffusion from the so-called 'developing' or low-income countries to 'developed' or higher-income countries. Other than importing 'exotic' items through colonised trading and exploring centuries ago, diffusion generally has happened in the other direction as inventions, customs, products, and attitudes tend to flow one way.

But critical equity issues in low-income countries have been so dramatic and seemingly intractable and so difficult to shift on the ground that gender transformative thinking has accelerated and been tested in some of the most difficult and dire circumstances. Responding to the HIV/AIDS crisis or to the issues of reproductive mortality in many countries with high fertility, low literacy, insufficient health care systems, and little money has compelled the development of gender transformative approaches. These issues have not only formed urgent national crises, but also thrown gender into stark relief and galvanised serious action on gender inequities in many so-called 'developing' countries.

These crises have rendered gender transformative thinking essential based on seeing, in life or death terms, the impact of negative gender stereotypes and norms that render HIV an epidemic. These are norms such as: masculinities that encourage multiple partners and femininities that encourage silence and create powerlessness. Powerful heterosexual gender norms that do not let equal decision-making surface, control over condom use be shared or allow meaningful consent to sexual relations. These kinds of issues make it necessary to act on root causes and take immediate action.

Consequently, the generation of many gender transformative ideas and much testing of theory and practice is taking place in communities and countries facing some of the most dire and dramatic hardships and some of the most overt gender inequities. It's no surprise that conditions in these settings are also bad for men and utterly life threatening for transgender persons or gay and lesbian people. Sticking to the rigidities of the gender binary, whether in Somalia or Kentucky, renders life difficult for all people wherever they sit on the gender spectrum. But so far, only a few communities facing extreme inequality and life or death problems have had the courage to address them in a gender transformative manner.

OBSERVING INEQUITY

Three women who lead a United Nations working group on discrimination against women, visited Alabama, Texas, and Oregon to evaluate a wide range of US policies and attitudes, as well as school, health, and prison systems. 'The delegates were appalled by the lack of gender equality in America. They found the US to be lagging far behind international human rights standards in a number of areas, including its 23 percent gender pay gap, maternity leave, affordable child care, and the treatment of female migrants in detention centers. The most telling moment of the trip, the women told reporters on Friday, was when they visited an abortion clinic in Alabama and experienced the hostile political climate around women's reproductive rights.'

Bassett, L. "The U.N. Sent 3 Foreign Women to the U.S. To Assess Gender Equality. They Were Horrified." The Huffington Post, December 16, 2015. tinyurl.com/z869p56

Leadership

It has taken true leadership to listen to these pragmatists and respect the incredible insights of gender transformative thinking, programming, policy-making, and legislation that have already taken place, and then transport them and adapt them to new environments, particularly in the developed world.

But leadership involves more than learning with an open mind and then adapting. It also involves cultivating courage, clarity, and taking action at a range of levels. It means constant questioning and trying new approaches. It means never letting up on consciousness-raising.

Theories are great, as they make us think about the deep dive. But the danger is getting stuck underwater or letting theoretical debates deter us from addressing the real life, urgent, obvious issues confronting us. In the last few decades alone, we have struggled with essentialism, determinism, post modernism, post-structuralism, feminist theories, intersectionality, queer theory, etc., and whether to take radical, liberal, or conservative approaches, etc.... These debates, although theoretical, are likely to divide us rather than merge our energies.

When it comes to gender equity, there have been many turns in the road. We have moved from noting and reacting to the limiting and crude frame of 'sex differences' to more complex approaches, including gender(s), sex- and gender-related factors and interactions, gender-based analyses, diversities, and intersecting factors affecting equity.

We have moved to debating the finer points of sex, gender, gender identity, gender relations, and the intricacies of measurement, the false confidence of categories, and the challenges of fluidity and comprehensiveness. We have labelled approaches to change as gender specific, gender sensitive, gender exploitive, gender accommodating, and gender transformative and debated the place and utility of each. We have even seen some claim that a progressive and fair approach demands a gender-neutral stance, while others see that as a gender-blind copout. Some or all of these debates and tactics can be seen as pieces of progress, but none of them have yet resulted in winning the equity sweepstakes or ending the gender inequity travesties of our time.

Creativity

Seeking true gender transformation requires that we get more creative. It also means that we must multitask on purpose and deliberately generate programs and actions that accomplish more than one thing at once. This means that while addressing a health crisis, an environmental issue, migration, a labour force problem, a legal vacuum, or a conflict, there is a parallel and integrated aim to generate improved gender equity.

This ensures that we are forward looking and consciously addressing root causes. Gender transformative thinking often means that we work with all genders and gender identities and create gender synchronous approaches. Such approaches ensure that we build content and goals tailored to different experiences of gender inequity. Programs such as building relationship skills in young people to prevent bullying, violence against girls and women, dating violence, or sexual assault are gender synchronous, working with both men and women, boys and girls, or heterosexual adolescents and queer adolescents in simultaneous but different ways, in order to generate new attitudes, behaviours, or results. Such approaches blend the universal and structural fixes with some tailoring to specific groups, who might matter more or differently at certain points in time.

While these binary-based initiatives are easier and easier to imagine, there is still a dearth of gender transformative approaches that embrace the full range of gender categories and identities. Programmes need to keep up with a wider range of lived realities for people in any country but especially where interventions, policies, legislation, or rules for transgender and other 'non-binary' people appear to be under constant query and contention.

The content of these initiatives needs creative and incisive analysis. Some of the atomization of gender categories expresses itself in claiming the opportunities or territory of a binary-defined group. An example would be transgender women claiming spots on women's sport teams. While some scientists, human rights officials, and transgender women might view it as progress that they are allowed to compete in women's sport, it is ironic that blasting open gender categories results in a desire to firmly plant oneself in one of those. It causes more than ruffled feathers. It makes it urgent to immediately generate analyses and measures of the impact on inequity and equity on all gender categories at the same time.

Will 'women-born-female' be at a disadvantage when competing with transgender women who may have sex-linked characteristics that give them more strength, speed, or endurance? Will women's sport lose anything, from tangibles like medals and records, to intangibles like hard-won places of safety, success, and respect for women's bodies and abilities? Girls and women have had to depend on anti-discrimination legislation and persistent campaigns to generate social changes in attitudes to women's sport. It has taken decades to acquire respect for women's and girls' abilities in the context of over attention and over investment in male sport and the idealisation of male bodies' athletic abilities. These are the sorts of issues at stake, not easily boiled down to using testosterone levels as a criterion for decisions about admissibility.

These questions have to be asked in the context of the past as well as the future in order to understand the equity sweepstakes. How do you weigh the intense desire and rights of transgender women to not only play sport, but to have safe toilets and safe prisons, let alone appropriate and respectful health and social services and opportunities to thrive without barriers, threats, and recrimination? And then set that beside the deep-seated attachment that 'women-born-female' have to hard-won spaces and places such as rape crisis centres, women's music festivals, and women's sport teams that come from years of lived experiences including vulnerability, assault, and centuries of obliteration?

The defining features of these battles need to be viewed through a lens of gender inequity and power. For transgender persons to acquire power through being perceived as removing options, spaces, and opportunities from other powerless groups will probably make everyone unhappy. These will be sour victories. Even when the gender binary is being smashed in a social and legal sense, biological characteristics and years of experiences don't necessarily dissolve. This is particularly relevant in competitive sport. Indeed, the International Olympic Commission (IOC)

TENTATIVE WINS

The 2016 Olympic Team from Great Britain included two formerly male transgender athletes who reported that, if selected, they may hold back from winning medals to avoid bad press and ridicule.

Manning, S., and I. Gallagher. "Transgender British Athletes Born Male Set to Make Olympic History by Competing in the Games as Women." MailOnline, July 3, 2016 www.tinyurl.com/j2lxf3b

is in ongoing chaos about gender categories. They have had to confront policy issues regarding intersex, transgender, and other athletes who may have unfair advantages due to biology. The policy on transgender athletes for the 2016 Olympics took a wide view, when the IOC issued a statement saying:

> To require surgical anatomical changes as a precondition to participation is not necessary to preserve fair competition and may be inconsistent with developing legislation and notions of human rights.
> www.tinyurl.com/heo46vj

It is not surprising that men and males are less worried about transgender men joining their ranks, in business, clubs, or sport. It may be far less threatening to men who have always had power and retain power, and in general, have fewer struggles for positioning among gender categories. It is less likely that male athletes worry about transgender men integrating into competitive male sport, at least from the medal or record-setting point of view.

Some transgender athlete activists want to dispense with all gender categories in sport and devise a more ability- or characteristic-based system of ordering classes of competition. But at the moment, this solution is way ahead of science. Such a solution will depend on scientists stepping up their relatively nascent efforts on gender and sex research and measurement, a field that is still groping for funding, ideas, standards, support, and insight. But even with some future science in the mix, smashing the gender binary on the backs of girls and women enjoying hard-fought spaces, funding, recognition, and attention in sport would be bittersweet if it does not reflect and respect overarching historical and present power and equity issues.

There is no doubt that we need to expand and extend gender synchronicity to encompass all forms of gender identities and sexual orientations. This requires some innovation and creative engagement with communities and leaders. Gender binaries may be passé in reality, but institutions and laws are slow to reflect this.

But this work cannot advance without sensitivity and critical thinking. In order to respond to contemporary understandings of life and gender, we need to integrate the past, the present, and the future, and not kill historical accomplishments in the name of liberation or human rights.

In the context of rapid change around sex and gender science and policy, as well as lived realities, it is essential to base our future on some principles. A careful inventory of tangible and intangible gains and losses and direct and indirect consequences is required, fully contextualised in a power analysis that incorporates accurate measures of gender inequity. Not to mention some ethical principles about how rights are understood and granted. We are still a long way from this.

Courage

The true tests of leadership in reducing gender inequities come with drawing lines between events and issues that may have become obscured. This often means embracing root principles as well as root causes and rejecting neutrality or relativism as an acceptable stance. The ability to do this is sometimes complicated by adherence to other values, such as tolerance and freedom.

Take dress for example. The contemporary liberal position is that dressing how one wants is a freedom, and freedoms are sacrosanct in secular, multicultural societies. In progressive societies, it is deemed to be especially important where women's dress is involved, making sure that sexism isn't controlling the positioning or surveillance of dress. So wearing a burka or a veil, especially in some Western societies, is often considered a freedom not to be interfered with by legislation or regulation as is wearing thigh-high shorts or cleavage-revealing tops. Attempts to regulate dress in progressive societies, whether on a beach in France or in a school in Leeds or Berlin, are seen as dangerous.

But none of this can be cause for avoiding mentioning the implications of women's dress. Patriarchal authorities, religious and secular, have defined the boundaries of women's attire for centuries, artfully and effectively channelling the male gaze. Centuries of tradition have involved men in creating standards – often having women enforce them. Colonisers spent enormous energy on curtailing the dress habits of the people they encountered. Particularly the women.

While women in burkas and women in mini shorts may say they choose to wear these items, and even if a liberal society doesn't interfere with that choice through regulation, it can still be seen as an opportunity to critically analyse these practices.

Yes, it does matter that a multi-billion-dollar fashion industry creates sexualised clothing for three-year-old girls, who become teenagers going to schools in micro garments with visible midriffs. And it does matter that hijab-like onesies are for sale for infants. Yes, it does matter that centuries-old customs across many cultures and religions indicate that veils protect women from the male gaze and symbolise purity and that if they falter at maintaining modesty, there are ramifications, whether in tribal settings, synagogues, or the Vatican. That these examples occupy opposite ends of the modesty scale is no contradiction as forces are at play that are greater than individual women or cohorts of girls.

MARKETING TO GIRLS

'When I recently stepped into a Toys R Us store in Cairo, it was quite shocking to see a Fulla doll clad in a headscarf and a full length abaya, the box proudly proclaiming "Fulla in her outdoor clothes," in effect telling little girls that there is only one proper way to dress outside the house. Many defenders of the hijab point to the influence of "decadent Western culture," endlessly criticising how Western TV sexualises and objectifies women, though they fail to understand that they are doing the exact same thing to little girls when they constantly promote the hijab. If it is so important to cover up, there must be something worth covering up and hiding from men. Inevitably, little girls are taught to view themselves as sexual objects that must be covered up from an early age – and it is this culture permeating the minds of our younger generations.'

Ibrahim, B. "This Trend of Young Muslim Girls Wearing the Hijab Is Disturbing." The Guardian, Nov. 23, 2010 www.tinyurl.com/gsk2hx2

All of this requires a critical eye. It is essential to go back to indicators, especially the ones rarely measured, and to address each person's freedom of movement or personal autonomy as building blocks in our analyses. Women are often confined by their dress in various ways, or their health is threatened by their dress, whether through vitamin D deficiencies from covering too much skin, or through deformed feet from 'stylish' shoes. There are many practices that undermine health and reduce freedom of movement, such as breast augmentation, the proliferation of diet pills, or the imposition of high heels as a job or fashion requirement. All of the examples expose the argument that women are safer or protected from the male gaze when covered up in burkas, or alternatively, enjoying 'freely chosen' fashion expression in stilettos. We can avoid naming the root problem; the male gaze, patriarchal customs, marketing, and related industries and edicts, by relying on choice, claiming tolerance and freedom, and leaving it at that. But should we?

Clarity

So why *do* girls and women have to pay for the exigencies of the male gaze by coverings that impede vision and hearing, cause overheating and Vitamin D deficiency, lead to a range of chronic health conditions such as obesity, diabetes, and osteopenia, and impede movement and physical activity? The same may be asked about life-threatening breast implants, labia shaping surgeries, or fallen arches. It is not courageous to avoid this discussion in order to appear tolerant, to look as if you are not trying to regulate a 'freedom', or interfere in another's concerns. To remove oneself from the talk because it's not your group, your culture, or your place to comment is a cop-out. The root solution is in engaging women, men, and transgender people in fixing the male gaze, knowing history, analysing power and custom, and either regulating it or containing it or exposing it for what it is.

REALITY CHECKED

'The problem is—the problem has always been—that feminism is not fun', Zeisler [*Bitch* magazine cofounder] declares. 'It's not supposed to be fun. It's complex and hard and it pisses people off. It's serious because it is about people demanding that their humanity be recognized as valuable. The root issues that feminism confronts—wage inequality, gendered divisions of labor, institutional racism and sexism, structural violence and, of course, bodily autonomy—are deeply unsexy.'

Bianco, M. "We Sold Feminism to the Masses, and Now It Means Nothing." Quartz, May 26, 2016. www.tinyurl.com/jqws6q2

Bodies and sexualities are often the site of control, whether through cosmetic surgery, labia-changing surgery, full body depilation, or female genital mutilation. While some would still refer to FGM as a 'cultural practice' and opt for gentler language and gentle changes, if any, it is now seen internationally as a health-compromising, sexuality-snuffing, occasionally deadly crime against women that is illegal or opposed in many countries.

Similarly, some refer to labia-changing surgery as a 'cultural practice' reflecting a prevailing view of women's sexual organs spread by pornography that has reshaped the views and desires of both men and women. It is useful to equate these examples as they all reflect the desire to control a woman's behaviour by literally reshaping her to be a male-defined sexual object without her bodily characteristics and desires interfering with patriarchy-defined men's sexual goals. That these practices exist in the name of 'modesty' and in the name of 'sexual liberation' at the same time is a testament to the cunning and adaptable methods of patriarchy.

Adopting non-heterosexual orientations and gay and lesbian activity is still against the law in many countries, under a large umbrella of laws, religious rules and regulations, stigma and discrimination. Again, these laws function to control sexualities and protect ideas of masculine sexualities, even in situations where many men may cross the boundaries on a regular basis. The punishments can be severe, up to and including death. The quest to impose a male-female heteronormative, two-gender, heterosexual paradigm is strong and compulsory even in countries that allow same-sex relating. These gender identity expressions need transformation as much as any and smashing the gender binary will allow for more transformative movement. But considering that lives are at stake and being lost as we ponder this situation, there is comparatively little meaningful global intervention into regimes where such practices and stigmas continue to exist, whether it's FGM or murdering gays in the name of compulsory heterosexuality.

Incisive Leadership

So leadership matters a lot. And with leadership comes the responsibility to take action, and to act with courage and clarity. And this can be difficult. Lots of theorising can sometimes stall us and prevent us from acting, as we worry about all of the repercussions of taking a stand. We may also worry about all of the factors affecting a practice or situation and locating ourselves appropriately, so much so that we are paralysed in intersectional gridlock. Or we may censor ourselves from noticing or noting gender inequities, for example, by committing ourselves to relativist thinking. We might all too often take moral or cultural relativism so seriously that we fail to see the forest for the trees. Or worse, we might fail to act when we do.

For example, we may ignore, rationalise, or resist naming issues such as female genital mutilation, violence against women, bride dowry customs, cosmetic surgery, diet industries, exploitative sex, the lack of male birth control, or... We may ignore the gendered commerce at the root of child marriage, prostitution, pornography, or sex trafficking. We may just be too afraid to say the roots of these things are inherently gendered and unequal and usually not in the interests of women and children.

But saying these things takes courage. It's much easier to say 'choice' or 'freedom' or 'tolerance' and avoid the subject all together. It's much easier to

GOOD DEEDS

'One gender-transformative project we support is an effort by the international non-profit organization Landesa to improve food security and income for 200,000 households in rural India by increasing women's land ownership. Landesa facilitates state government programs that grant small plots of land—enough for a home and a kitchen garden—to low-caste people. It works with the state governments to put land titles in women's names, either jointly with their husbands or individually. The project includes community meetings to explain the practical benefits of land ownership for women and to encourage men to support this social change. Landesa knows the relative position of low-caste women in India and understands their limited access to assets. It has designed the project to change systems that can undermine women's empowerment and productivity.'

"What We Do, Gender-Responsive Agricultural Development Programs." Bill & Melinda Gates Foundation. www.tinyurl.com/nbpdqm9

question these trends and practices in private, not public. It's much easier to say, 'to each their own' and to avoid comment on anyone outside your own community. It's a persistent liberal ideal to say the group in question must come to its own understanding of these practices in its own due course. This is dangerous.

It does not require a request for regulation, ostracism, or shunning and it does not mean that we fuel the fires of discrimination or stigmatisation or any kind of phobia. It means that if we are truly interested in gender transformative change, we need to have conversations that confront root causes and therefore seek root solutions. And to make sure that no one is left behind.

ETHICAL INVESTMENT

Gates Foundation - $80 million for eliminating gender inequalities

Maclean's - 'How is this new focus on gender equality transforming the foundation? What have you needed to do differently?'

Melinda Gates - '... We're putting the question out to the whole foundation: within your strategy, if you invested in women and girls, how would you get different outcomes? Would you even know where to invest? Do you even have the right data?'

Mercier, Noemi. "Melinda Gates on Ending Inequalities between Sexes." Maclean's, September 10, 2016. www.tinyurl.com/glyuooj

Rerouting the Money

So along with clarity, courage, and leadership, money also talks. Governments and international agencies fund a lot of projects. Most of these are golden opportunities to advance more than one objective at once. In particular, gender equity goals can ride on the back of any project, from curtailing tobacco use to mining natural resources, to creating building codes, to environmental protection, to improving health, preventing disease, ensuring safe maternity, and any other kind of social change. While many current gender transformative projects are concentrated in low-income countries, their experiences apply to any society.

Philanthropists and other funders have a key role to play in gender transformative thinking and practice. For example, the Gates Foundation funds only projects that recognise gender and engage women. They explicitly reject proposals that are gender neutral, and explicitly favour projects that are gender transformative, such as agricultural programs that recognise gender inequalities, and emphasise the transformation of relationships between women and men.

These are grand and important gestures by a very important global philanthropy fund. However, they do draw a line. Gates clearly states:

> Changing culture and society is not our role. We acknowledge that all development projects will affect individuals, households, and communities—we hope for the better. When we ask grantees to address women's needs, we are simply asking that they apply smart design principles that support women—not undermine social norms or effect changes that are unsustainable or unwanted by the community itself.[15]

This limitation raises interesting questions about the quality of social norms and the range of social changes that could be effected. Surely there are some, indeed many social norms that undermine equity for women and others and changes to those would presumably be resisted? Otherwise, they would have changed for the better on their own. And what levers, if any, can be used or should be used? The expressed wish to not make changes that meet with resistance reflects a classic problem of liberal tolerance.

On a 2016 radio interview, Melinda Gates discussed these limits where she suggested that contraception could be used 'covertly' instead of overtly in situations where women encounter resistance (May 10, 2016, *Melinda Gates on the "ingenuity" of women in the developing world.* The Current, Canadian Broadcasting Corporation). While this is potentially empowering

—

15 "What We Do, Gender-Responsive Agricultural Development Programs." Bill & Melinda Gates Foundation. www.tinyurl.com/jynuyys

and conducive to autonomous decision-making, it can also be risky and unsafe, unless root causes and attitudes are addressed and changed. Hoping that the community comes to this on its own, or that the women funded by the projects ultimately rise up and demand change is a strong strategy, but not necessarily gender transformative.

CARE is another development organisation that reduces poverty, and does it by concentrating on women and girls. They know from experience that when women and girls are enhanced and developed, the whole community prospers. However, their key intent is to transform gender relations in the context of their projects, whether they are promoting microfinancing, cottage industries, sanitation projects, or better post-disaster planning. They also engage men and boys in specific ways, by reshaping gendered power structures, not by simply shifting existing power around.

CARE knows that engaging men and boys in social change is complicated. They start from the premise that gender relations are complex and multifaceted and need to be understood in the local context, and that staff and leaders need to be reflexive before they start the work. Shifting gender relations is a long and sometimes rocky process, but it's impossible without men's engagement as well as women's ability to change. In short, CARE is starting social movements in communities via projects on a range of issues that generate economic improvements for women.

So money can make change. Funding, philanthropy, or simple donations can be done with gender transformative thinking in mind. We can't blithely support the status quo, but must ask for other goals to be met along with the project or charity we are supporting. We must demand that our governments fund only projects that explicitly reduce gender inequities.

FUNDER'S LESSONS

The meta-analysis of 22 Fund for Gender Equality programme evaluations found that successful strategies have aimed at:

- Increasing women's incomes while supporting greater control over earnings
- Increasing women's understanding and ability to exercise their rights
- Strengthening women's trade unions to advocate for political reforms
- Increasing awareness and promoting legislative changes for marginalised groups
- Connecting/creating networks for economically marginalised groups
- Engendering existing government employment schemes
- Closing gender gaps in technology

UN Women Fund for Gender Equality. "Fund for Gender Equality Annual Report 2015." New York: UN Women, 2015: 16 www.tinyurl.com/j5wlcex

Change Your Story

Wicked problems require wickedly inventive solutions. And gender inequity is one of the world's most wicked problems. Gender inequity affects all of us: men, women, boys, girls, and transgender people, whatever our sexual orientation, age, ability, race, or location. It is also true that we are collectively used to thinking about our own lives and in our own ways. This translates into silos of thought, disciplines in education, and departments in governments. It renders religion important to some, science to others, politics to others. It makes guiding lights hard to find when considering how to unravel the universal wickedness of gender inequity.

It may be true that our systems of evidence and education, our ethical frames and our indicators of success are, at the moment, inadequate to the task of resolving gender inequity. But fixing these deficiencies then becomes our collective agenda. A thorough and deliberate adoption of transdisciplinarity and transectoralism could help. This means rising above some age-old categories, shifting our thoughts, and exercising our leadership to reach across divides to create melded and more inspired and shared approaches to how we think about things and organise ourselves. It means we must be Renaissance people, reaching into all other areas to inform ourselves, and deliberately developing shared languages and methods for making change.

The costs of doing nothing are incredibly high. They include pain, illness, and death. The cost of being ineffective in our efforts is punitive. It includes lost resources, wasted potential, and thwarted progress. The promise of being successful is in reviving hope, joy, optimism, and liberation. The allure of gender transformative thinking, especially in a gender-atomized world, is that it has the potential to improve life for *absolutely everybody*.

In our own lives, roles, jobs, communities, or families, there is a lot of scope for galvanising equity. Along with courage, clarity, and leadership, we can be unceasingly and unflinchingly critical about root causes and root solutions. We can all reduce our own ignorance and take issue with those who want to dwell in theirs. We can all smash the binary, get out of our theoretical caves, and embrace the unknown as more and more people are free to express themselves and shape their lives and bodies.

Everyone has gender in a rapidly changing world. Sensitive and multi-faceted gender synchronicity in our programs and policies is essential to enact gender transformation, but always in the context of measuring ongoing inequities. Gender transformative approaches are the goal where inequities are deliberately and systematically reduced by courageous and clear thinking people who are unafraid of criticism and leadership. Gender transformative approaches unabashedly address power dynamics, traditions, gendered relations, and culture. Everyone is affected by the unchaining of gender. There are no holds barred. Indeed, everyone has a stake in, and a responsibility for, shifting a bit for the better.

INFLUENCES ON OUR THINKING

Barker, G., Ricardo, C., & Nascimento, M. "Engaging men and boys in changing gender-based inequity in health: Evidence from programme interventions." WHO. 2007

CARE International SII on Women's Empowerment Series. www.care.org/our-work/womens-empowerment/gender-integration/strategic-impact-inquiry-womens-empowerment 2009

Commission on Social Determinants of Health. "Closing the gap in a generation: Health equity through action on the social determinants of health." WHO. 2013

Connell, R. *Gender in World Perspective*. Cambridge: Polity Press. 2009

Coyote, I. *Tomboy Survival Guide*. Vancouver: Arsenal Pulp Press. 2016

Daly, Mary. Gyn/Ecology *The Metaethics of Radical Feminism*. Boston: Beacon Press. 1978

Dea, S. *Beyond the Binary: Thinking about Sex and Gender*. Peterborough: Broadview Press. 2016

Feinberg, L. *Transgender Warriors*. Boston: Beacon Press. 1996

Freire, Paulo. P*edagogy of the Oppressed.* New York: Continuum. 1996

Greaves, L., Pederson, A., & Poole, N. (Eds.) *Making it Better: Gender -Transformative Health Promotion*. Toronto, ON: Canadian Scholars Press. 2014

Greene, M. E., & Levack, A. (2010). *Synchronizing Gender Strategies: A Cooperative Model for Improving Reproductive Health and Transforming Gender Relations*. www.igwg.org Accessed 2010.

Hausmann, R., Tyson, L. D., & Zahidi, S. *The Global Gender Gap Report 2009 and 2010*.

Hooks, b. *Teaching Community: A Pedagogy of Hope*. New York: Routledge. 2003

Interagency Gender Working Group. *"The 'so what?' report. A look at whether integrating a gender focus into programs makes a difference in outcomes."* www.prb.org/igwg_media/thesowhatreport.pdf Accessed 2004

International Planned Parenthood Federation. "The Men and Boys Collection: Stories of gender justice and sexual and reproductive health and rights" www.ippf.org Accessed 2009

Kaufman, M., & Kimmel, M. *The Guy's Guide to Feminism*. Berkeley: Seal Press. 2011

Krieger, N. *Epidemiology and the People's Health*. New York: Oxford University Press. 2011

MenCare+. "An advocacy brief: Policy recommendations for Gender-transformative approaches." www.rutgers.international/sites/rutgersorg/files/PDF/2016_Mencare_positionpaper.pdf Accessed 2016

Mohanty, C. T. *Feminism without Borders: Decolonizing Theory, Practicing Solidarity*. Durham, NC: Duke University Press. 2003

Ngozi Adichie, C. *We Should All be Feminists* New York: Vintage Books. 2014

Nussbaum, M. C. *Women and Human Development: The Capabilities Approach*: Cambridge University Press. 2000

Ricardo, C., & Verani, F. "Engaging men and boys in gender equality and health: A global toolkit for action." www.menengage.org/resources/engaging-men-boys-gender-equality-health-equity/ Accessed 2010

Ridgeway, C. L. *Framed by Gender: How Gender Inequality Persists in the Modern World*. New York: Oxford University Press. 2011

Solnit R. *Men Explain Things to Me*. Chicago: Haymarket Books. 2014.

Spoon, R., & Coyote, I. E. *Gender Failure*. Vancouver, BC: Arsenal Pulp Press. 2014

TrueChild. "Gender Norms: A Key to Combating School- and Cyber-Bullying and Homophobic Harassment Among At-Risk Youth." "Gender Norms: A Key to Improving Health & Wellness Among Black Women & Girls." "Addressing Masculine Norms to Improve Life Outcomes for Young Black Men: Why We Still Can't Wait." www.TrueChild.org Accessed 2009, 2013, 2015

Tuana, N. The speculum of ignorance: The women's health movement and epistemologies of ignorance. *Hypatia, 21*(3), 1-19. 2006

UNFPA. "Gender Transformative Programming Engaging Men in Gender Equality and Health: A Global Toolkit for Action"

McKinsey Global Institute. "The Power of Parity: How advancing women's equality can add $12 trillion to global growth." 2015

World Economic Forum. "The Global Gender Gap Report 2015: 10th Anniversary Edition." www.reports.weforum.org/global-gender-gap-report-2015/

The Joker

UNAUTHORIZED

JACK NAPIER

ISBN-13: 978-1503006713

"These eyes will deceive you, they will destroy you, they will take from you, your innocents, your pride, and eventually your soul. These eyes do not see what you and I see. Behind these eyes, one only finds darkness. These are the eyes of a psychopath."

JACK

PROLOGUE

I walk into an empty house, the sound of my footsteps uneven. One is clear and hard, the other slightly muffled. My heart is broken into a million pieces. A rusty gas can dangles from my hand.

In the living room an old brass lamp spills a dim light across a pile of toys that have taken over the room. I move from room to room, slowly pouring gas over everything I see, each drop bringing back the painful memories of my life. I drench the couch, its faded roses running together in a puddle. I pour my hatred over the armchair and its ottoman. I nod in satisfaction as I move to the television resting on a stand in the corner. Gas splashes from the worn wood to the floor as a white colored ring forms on the plastic casing surrounding the TV. My distorted reflection appears on the dusty screen. Not giving it a second look, I continue.

Lurching down the hallway, I enter a room on my right. My eyes automatically fall on the bunk beds that line the back wall. I am overtaken with humiliation and grief. The pain I have suppressed for so long starts to make its way up my spine, determined to corrupt my brain. I slowly walk to the other side of the room and run my hand over the trophies that sit on the tall dresser adjacent to the bunk beds.

I think about my family while the fractured pieces of my heart beat rapidly. I soak the mattresses with gas, then stumble across the carpet to the door and look back. Anger and loathing crowd out reason as my mind takes one last snapshot of my old life.

Moving slowly down the hallway, I see a black lab with gray hair around her eyes. She cautiously steps

toward me, her movements hesitant and unsettled. She looks up and whimpers, then walks down the tiny corridor as if she is looking for help.

I continue to a narrow door. I enter a long, shotgun-style bathroom lined in dingy-white subway tiles. Like a shadow, the black lab is at my side. Wild-eyed, she senses what is about to happen.

A huge window is ajar on the back wall. A breeze whispers through its opening. Crickets chirp as though this is like any other night. The hoots of night owls join the chorus from their nests in the trees outside.

The lab waits as I walk towards the window. Confused, she follows me, her tags jingling from her collar. Oh how that sound once brought me great pleasure. I stop to remember the beautiful family I once had. I then move on.

Exhausted, I slump on the toilet seat and admire the handgun I have removed from the back of my jeans. I cannot get the memory of what happened out of my head. The familiar jingle starts again. My friend comes to my aid. She walks up and gently licks my hand. She cries, begging for attention.

I slowly reach into my pocket and pull out a lighter. Hands as steady as a heart surgeon, I flick the cheap Bic lighter. I watch its delicious flame, hungry for something to touch. I make it wait. I can see the fire dancing in the reflection of the dog's eyes. She howls more loudly, pleading me to stop.

The flame is starving, begging me to set the house on fire. I do. With a quick move, I let it begin to eat.

Fire slowly devours the wall. Out of the bathroom it works its depraved hunger towards the rest of the house. It ingests drywall and wood floors in its need to be full. I watch and smile as the flame follows the path of gasoline like a hungry demon taking its prey.

I get up and step in front of the mirror. I look at the reflection in front of me. I hate what I see. My skin is

pale, my wiry hair long and unkempt. My sad eyes stare back at me. They are both empty and confident at the same time.

Suddenly, in a mad rage, I punch the mirror. Looking at myself through its broken pieces, I scream, "I HATE YOU!"

I punch the mirror again and again like a madman. My hands are dripping with blood. Abruptly, I stop and sit back down on the toilet. I pick up the pistol. I put its shaft into my mouth. I can feel its cold metal on my lips as I place my forefinger on the trigger. I sit frozen in this position, tears running down my face then onto the barrel of gun. I watch them roll slowly down to my trigger finger.

I remember my last conversation with Brooke as my stomach becoming an angry sea of remorse.

TEXT MESSAGES

Jack says:
May 31, 2015 at 10:47 am

I got the final divorce decree today.

Jack says:
May 31, 2015 at 11:47 am

Really, you won't even respond to my text!

Jack says:
May 31, 2015 at 11:48 am

How many guys are you fucking now! I hear you have become quite the slut!

Jack says:
May 31, 2015 at 11:50 am

What a good example you have become for our boys! I just hope you don't fuck them up like my mother did me.

Jack says:
May 31, 2015 at 11:51 am

I will never let that happen!

Reply

Brooke says:
May 31, 2015 at 11:55 am

Jack you're being extremely rude and immature right now. I've never had anyone talk to me like this before. Its disrespectful!

Reply

Jack says:
May 31, 2015 at 11:57 am

I will not allow my boys to have a whore for a mother!

Reply

Brooke says:
May 31, 2015 at 10:47 am

Jack, I'm not going to let you talk to me like this. My attorney has recommended that I file a restraining order on you. In fact, from here on out if you want to communicate with me you will need to contact him.

Reply

Jack says:
May 31, 2015 at 10:47 am

You're probably fucking him too! You used me Brooke. You hurt me!

You have no idea how much pain you have caused me! I won't allow you to hurt my boys! I swear if they see the shit you're doing I will burn your fucking world down!!!!

Reply

Brooke says:
May 31, 2015 at 10:47 am

Do u not realize how emotionally crazy u sound right now? I'll pray for u Jack.

Reply

Jack says:
May 31, 2015 at 10:47 am

You need to pray for yourself!

Jack says:
May 31, 2015 at 10:50 am

Be very careful how far you push me Brooke!

JACK

CHAPTER ONE

"All that we see or seem is but a dream within a dream."
~Edgar Allan Poe

Jack – Day 1

Let me explain how I have come to my current state of mind. This morning I woke abruptly, my hands balled into fists as I screamed at the gray ceiling tiles. I tried to move the rest of my body but couldn't. Confused, I slowly rolled my head, examining what looked to be a hospital room. Next to the monitor that was taking my vitals, I caught sight of someone sitting in a chair. She was reading from a notebook.

"Who are you?" I asked.

"My name is Harleen. I was called in to help you. Can you tell me your name?"

I had to think for a minute before I could remember. Then it came to me.

"My name is... Jack."

"Jack, do you know where you are right now?"

"No, I don't."

"You're in the hospital," Harleen replied.

My mind became a tsunami of clashing memories, one

thrown against another. Brooke crying, then the words "I'm no longer in love with you." Inside my head, the pain was trying to break its way out. I started to retch. Harleen rang for a nurse, who quickly elevated my bed, which made me feel like I was being launched into space. She held a plastic pan under my mouth. I vomited, heaving until there was nothing but bile and blood.

Picking up the phone, the nurse spoke quietly to someone on the other end. She then injected a medicine into my IV before lowering my bed. Wetting a washcloth, Harleen wiped my face in an effort to soothe me. I was so anxious, jittery, in the midst of a full-blown panic attack.

That was, until the valium kicked in.

"What's happening to me?" I asked.

Harleen pulled her chair around so I could see her face.

"Jack, do you remember what happened to you?"

"What are you talking about?" I replied.

The flashes of memories began again. This time more slowly. I am tied to a chair. A strange face appears then vanishes in into darkness. I hear Brooke scream!

Looking at Harleen, I began to cry like a desperate man trying to swim to shore, knowing he will never make it.

"Where is my family? Where is Brooke? Why isn't anyone but you here?"

"Jack, I am sorry to have to tell you this, but you had a mental breakdown. When you got to the hospital and came back to consciousness you were in shock, unable to communicate, choking on your own vomit. You became extremely violent. They had to sedate you."

"What do you mean? I don't remember any of that!"

"Jack, something happened to you the night we found you that triggered this. Some things are so disturbing to us that our brain shuts off our ability to remember. In clinical terms, it is called Trauma Induced Dissociative Amnesia," Harleen explained.

I felt like I'd been sucked into the universe. The pounding in my head was like asteroids colliding. While gazing at Harleen, the memories flew at me at the speed of light, one image of Brooke after another. I couldn't make it stop. At that moment my world had been consumed by a monster's gaping maw, a black hole that chewed on me until I groaned. I was speechless, staring at the ceiling, not moving. I wanted to make the world spin back to the day before. The day I could remember.

"This doesn't make any sense to me!" I shouted.

"Jack, when you got to the hospital you tried to commit suicide."

"What! Why would I do that?"

"I don't know, that's what we're trying to figure out."

I could feel the blood rush from my face. Harleen gently put her hand on my shoulder.

"Jack, it's going to be alright, I'm here to help you work through this."

I broke like a dam collapsing. Torrents of emotion poured through me. Grief began to wrack my body, growing inside of me until I could barely breathe. Harleen reached out and took my hand. I let her; the touch of human flesh was comforting.

With a warm smile, Harleen removed a notebook and pen from her briefcase. She handed them to me.

"Jack, I encourage you to write down any thoughts, feelings, or images you might have. Maybe start with what you remember about your family. Journaling is a powerful tool that connects us to people, places, and events in our life. The brain has a way of opening our minds through our hands, of letting our thoughts pour out onto the paper. Often we find out things about ourselves that we have repressed, demanded to be silent."

Turning my head, I stared at the empty table near my bed.

"Jack, you need to rest. You were brought here without any personal belongings. Are there some things

you would like?"

"Yes, I would like my family to be here with me."

"I'm sorry Jack, but, they can't be here."

"What do you mean they can't be here!?"

"Jack, you're sick. We need to focus on getting you better. We need to understand what triggered your breakdown."

"But I need to see my family! I need them to be here with me!"

"Jack, you need to work with me. We need to understand what happened first. Then we can talk about your family."

The valium was preventing me from protesting.

"Will you at least bring me a picture of them?" I asked.

"Sure, Jack, where can I find one?"

"There's one on the dresser in my bedroom."

Harleen's comforting eyes landed on mine, which made me feel a little better.

"Of course Jack, I will get the picture. Now, get some sleep. We will talk in the morning."

Harleen touched my arm endearingly. She gathered her things, tapped on the door, and left.

DREAM

I am sitting next to my mother, who is signing a pile of consent forms in a doctor's office. A nurse walks out of the back room and calls for my mother.

"Cindy, we are ready for you sweetheart."

My mother gets up and grabs my hand.

"Sugar, you might want to leave him in the lobby."

"He's fine!" My mother demands.

"I am not sure that's a good idea," the Nurse challenges.

"Don't tell me what's good for my son!"

Conceding defeat, the nurse escorts us into an

examining room.

"You have been here before, Cindy. You know the routine," the nurse explains.

My mother sits me down in a chair in the corner of the room, then hands me my favorite Dr. Seuss book.

"Sit here and read while I talk to the doctor," she tells me.

My mother removes her clothes and puts on a medical gown. sShe walks over to the examining table and puts her feet into a set of metal stirrups.

I start to laugh. I tell her she looks funny.

"Be quiet, goddam it!" she barks at me.

"Sorry," I say as I go back to reading my book.

The door opens and the doctor walks into the room, flanked by two nurses in traditional white uniforms. The doctor says good morning and my mother returns the greeting. Then the nurses began to prepare her for the procedure.

"I don't want this baby! Get this thing out of me! I don't want to make the same mistake twice!" my mother yells.

Looking at a picture of Sam-I-Am, who was holding a plate of green eggs and ham, I hear the hate in her voice.

I see the doctor holding what looks like a vacuum hose that is literally sucking the life out of her.

"Ahhhhhhh! Get this thing out of me! I hate you. I hate you! Get out of me!" my mother screams.

Startled, I get out of my chair. I get closer. I see a head coming out of her womb. Horrified, I step back when I see the baby's face. It was mine!

When I woke my mind wouldn't stop racing. I was completely alone, just myself and my thoughts. Bound to my room, I couldn't escape them. I don't know why my dream made me think about Brooke. Maybe it's because she and my mother are the two people who have hurt me the most in life. Yet I couldn't stop loving them. I kept

thinking about how messed up things with Brooke had become as I stared at the discolored cracks in the concrete floor.

Each memory of her was a rift that was part of an even bigger fracture of time. Before I knew it, I was lost in a labyrinth of painful experiences, trying desperately to escape.

Suddenly, the thought of her with another man invaded my mind. I could envision them in our bed, the place where my children once slept with us. Sadness crowded out my anger.

How did we get to this place? I thought.

Our relationship wasn't always bad. Some of my best memories in life were with Brooke. Like the secret hand signal we would give each other when we wanted to say *I love you.* We would curl our index finger between our nose and upper lip, then gently swipe it downward towards our chin until it met our thumb. There could be a thousand people around us and not one person would know that we were secretly telling each other *I love you.*

BROOKE

CHAPTER TWO

" "So heavy is the chain of wedlock that it needs two to carry it, and sometimes three."
~Alexandre Dumas

Facebook Message from Tyler Ward 5/28/2014 at 9:02 am:

Hey Brooke,

It was awesome seeing you at the Alpha Kappa Psi reunion last night! What a blast! I'm feeling it today big time :-(how are you feeling?

Facebook Message from Brooklyn Page Napier 5/28/2014 at 9:05 am:

I'm feeling it today too! Do you remember Matt talking about starting a sexual revolution?! WTF! I guess some things never change :-)

Facebook Message from Tyler Ward 5/28/2014 at 9:08 am:

OMG! Matt was so drunk! What are u doing today?

Facebook Message from Brooklyn Page Napier 5/28/2014 at 1:57 pm:

I need to meet my dad for dinner, but I'm so sick I can't get out of bed. Ugh!!!

Facebook Message from Tyler Ward 5/28/2014

at 2:01 pm:

I know, it’s 2 in the afternoon and I haven’t gotten out of bed yet!

Facebook Message from Tyler Ward 5/28/2014 at 8:18 pm:

How was dinner with your dad?

Facebook Message from Brooklyn Page Napier 5/28/2014 at 8:22 pm:

I didn’t make it :-(I’m too hungover.

Facebook Message from Tyler Ward 5/28/2014 at 8:30 pm:

That sucks!   I just took a sleeping pill and I’m about to go night night LOL I’ll talk to you in the morning :-)

Facebook Message from Brooklyn Page Napier 5/28/2014 at 8:32 pm:

Goodnight :-)

Facebook Message from Tyler Ward 5/29/2014 at 7:45 am:

Good morning! Have you ever heard the song "Do You Wish It Was Me" by Jason Aldean? I can't get it out of my head.

Facebook Message from Brooklyn Page Napier 5/29/2014 at 7:49 am:

Yes, I love that song!

Facebook Message from Tyler Ward 5/29/2014 at 7:52 am:

Does it remind you of me?

Facebook Message from Brooklyn Page Napier 5/29/2014 at 8:01 am:

Maybe :-)

Facebook Message from Tyler Ward 5/29/2014 at 8:04 am:

Not pursuing you in college was one of my biggest mistakes.

Facebook Message from Brooklyn Page Napier 5/29/2014 at 8:07 am:

Well, that was a long time ago and I was a much different person then.

Facebook Message from Tyler Ward 5/29/2014 at 8:11 am:

Sometimes I feel like I was totally invisible in College. I was so shy back then :-(

Facebook Message from Brooklyn Page Napier 5/29/2014 at 8:14 am:

I know! I always thought you were cute, but you never seemed interested in me.

Facebook Message from Tyler Ward 5/29/2014 at 8:16 am:

Really? I had no idea.

Facebook Message from Brooklyn Page Napier 5/29/2014 at 8:18 am:

Yes, ding dong!

Facebook Message from Tyler Ward 5/29/2014 at 8:19 am:

Now, I'm starting to blush lol

Facebook Message from Brooklyn Page Napier 5/30/2014 at 8:03 am:

I was thinking about you last night.

Facebook Message from Tyler Ward 5/30/2014 at 8:04 am:

I was thinking about you too. Guess what?

Facebook Message from Brooklyn Page Napier 5/30/2014 at 8:06 am:

What?

Facebook Message from Tyler Ward 5/30/2014 at 8:08 am:

I wrote a book.

Facebook Message from Brooklyn Page Napier 5/30/2014 at 8:10 am:

Seriously! I didn't know u were a writer... I want to read it! Is it published?

Facebook Message from Tyler Ward 5/30/2014 at 8:11 am:

Not, yet. It needs a lot of editing still.

Facebook Message from Brooklyn Page Napier 5/30/2014 at 8:12 am:

How long did it take you to write it?

Facebook Message from Tyler Ward 5/30/2014 at 8:14 am:

I have been working on it for years, but it's finally done. I just need someone to edit it now.

I will email you a PDF copy tonight. Thanks for reading it :-)

Facebook Message from Brooklyn Page Napier 5/30/2014 at 8:16 am:

Absolutely... I'm a reader... Love to edit too... I'll edit it for you. I will be having a beer and reading it tonight. Can't wait!!!

I have wanted to write about my dysfunctional childhood... but never seem to have the time!!!

Facebook Message from Tyler Ward 5/30/2014 at 8:18 am:

Lol the story you are reading is my f'ed up childhood wrapped up in a crazy fictional twist. It gets real crazy and a lot of its true!

Facebook Message from Brooklyn Page Napier 5/30/2014 at 8:20 am:

Can't wait... Are your parents still living? Mine continues to be absolutely crazy. Esp the last three years...I want to get it down but don't know where to begin. Maybe reading yours will help me get started!!!

Facebook Message from Tyler Ward 5/30/2014 at 8:23 am:

My mom overdosed on pills 2 yrs ago and died. That's when I started the book. I think I needed to get stuff out :-). My dad is still alive but he is a mess lol

You should record your thoughts and stories. That's what I did. Then I wrote from that.

Facebook Message from Brooklyn Page Napier 5/30/2014 at 8:25 am:

I'm sorry about your mom :(

Both my parents are a mess, my brother too... I thought I came to terms with a lot of the crap... But I'm not soooo sure. Sometimes it all still feels so crazy. And trying to protect my kids from all of it... Btw your girls are precious!!!

Facebook Message from Tyler Ward 5/30/2014 at 8:28 am:

I know the feeling. I do everything to protect my kids from the crap I went through at the expense of my own happiness. I thought I was dealing with things well until my mom died. It brought a lot of stuff back.

Facebook Message from Brooklyn Page Napier 6/1/2014 at 9:30 am:

Wow... Just read... At lunch now... Okay give me chapter 3 I'm hooked...

Was Joe the guy in chapter one...the one in the dream? Well, I think it was a dream ...

Facebook Message from Tyler Ward 6/1/2014 at 9:35 am:

Thanks! I will send you the first 6 chapters

Facebook Message from Brooklyn Page Napier 6/1/2014 at 9:37 am:

Oh... Okay... I will read it tonight and give feedback...

What I have read so far makes me want to know more....

I want a take of your first million... Ha!!

Facebook Message from Tyler Ward 6/1/2014 at 9:39 am:

I will send you ch 7 this weekend it's about Joe meeting the love of his life. Do you want me to send you the word doc version so you can just put your notes there?

Facebook Message from Brooklyn Page Napier 6/1/2014 at 9:40 am:

Sure

Facebook Message from Brooklyn Page Napier 6/5/2014 at 5:27 pm:

I just finished chapter 7. You are on to something... It's good... I really like it...

I love the story

We need to meet in person and talk about the book... Send me the rest... Btw who was the love of your life? Kim? Sorry, I meant Joe's love :-)

Facebook Message from Tyler Ward 6/5/2014 at 5:29 pm:

LOL you will have to keep reading to find out :-)

Facebook Message from Brooklyn Page Napier 6/7/2014 at 6:07 pm:

OMG Chapter 8 was the best... Very well written. Wouldn't change a thing!!!! Do Joe and Kim get married?

Facebook Message from Tyler Ward 6/7/2014 at 6:08 pm:

You need to keep reading! I don't want to spoil it for you.

Facebook Message from Brooklyn Page Napier 6/8/2014 at 3:02 pm:

I'm about halfway done with the book now. It's really good, Tyler. It makes me "feel" and that is what good writers do... I feel for Joe and want to know more about what happens to him...it makes me think of all the "boundaries" that were not upheld or respected in my upbringing. I think when kids do not see adults respecting boundaries it affects them deeply and the choices they make as teens and adults. Okay I'm rambling...

Facebook Message from Brooklyn Page Napier 6/9/2014 at 9:00 am:

I just wanted to say hi .., I'm sure ur busy with your girls... Reading your book has brought back some memories of my own!!! Keep writing.. Lmk if you need anything!

Facebook Message from Tyler Ward 6/9/2014 at 9:02 am:

I really want to thank you again for reading my book and sending me feedback. You have no idea how much this is helping me. Have you read chapter 10 yet? It's very intense.

Facebook Message from Brooklyn Page Napier 6/9/2014 at 9:05 am:

Yes... Remember the Noble Romans? I spent a lot of time there. So did my parents (in the bar)... We lived in the "poor" Williams Creek, where my parents drank almost every night and on weekends the house turned into "swingerville" or where fights broke out! If you need any good stories lmk...ironically I spent most of my time at the creek or in the woods..... Or at my Grandmas!!! I have a lot in common with Joe!!!

Facebook Message from Tyler Ward 6/9/2014 at 9:08 am:

Awwww. It's crazy how these things affect us. You will like the rest of the book, but not sure about the end.

I am sorry you had to experience that as a

kid.

Facebook Message from Brooklyn Page Napier 6/9/2014 at 9:11 am:

What doesn't kill us makes us stronger! Did you have a first love in high school like your character Joe?

Facebook Message from Tyler Ward 6/9/2014 at 9:12 am:

Kim was the first girl I ever dated. We met my senior year in college.

Facebook Message from Brooklyn Page Napier 6/9/2014 at 9:13 am:

What! You weren't a virgin were you?

Facebook Message from Tyler Ward 6/9/2014 at 9:15 am:

LOL, no! I had my share of high school and college hook-ups. They were just never serious enough to turn into a steady thing.

Facebook Message from Brooklyn Page Napier 6/9/2014 at 9:17 am:

The first time I ever met you I thought u were cute and nice... How gay is that? I think we were at a party... Maybe at one of the fraternity parties?

Facebook Message from Tyler Ward 6/9/2014 at 9:18 am:

:-)

Facebook Message from Brooklyn Page Napier

6/9/2014 at 9:20 am:

Kind of wish I had known some of this stuff about you in college. I always thought I was the only one going through crap.

Life is funny. Glad we reconnected...

Facebook Message from Tyler Ward 6/9/2014 at 9:22 am:

Yes me too.

I think a lot of us were going through stuff, but didn't tell anyone.

Facebook Message from Brooklyn Page Napier 6/9/2014 at 11:11 am:

True!!!

I don't know whether to laugh or cry. My dad just called drunk and screaming and crying. He shot all his turkeys and goats to put them out of their misery!!!! When does the drama end????? Did it finally end for you... Joe?

Facebook Message from Tyler Ward 6/9/2014 at 11:15 am:

When our dysfunctional parents start to die off it gets less crazy, but you actually miss them.

I think you have to embrace them for who they are :-)

There was something in their past that made them that way just like things in our past made us the way we are.

Facebook Message from Brooklyn Page Napier 6/9/2014 at 11:17 am:

Yes I know... Didn't mean to dump ... Just funny how as much as things change... they stay the same!!!

Btw did u end up in a foster home like Joe?? You don't have to share that info with me if you don't want to tho…

Facebook Message from Tyler Ward 6/9/2014 at 11:20 am:

It's complicated.

Facebook Message from Brooklyn Page Napier 6/9/2014 at 11:23 am:

I'm sorry, I don't know about the rest of your life, but you have a great story just about you... What you went through... I think you need to consider a memoir for your next book!

Facebook Message from Tyler Ward 6/9/2014 at 11:24 am:

Thanks for saying that :-)

Facebook Message from Brooklyn Page Napier 6/10/2014 at 10:05 pm:

It's been a rough day. I've had a few glasses of wine, actually make that a few bottles of wine LOL

By the way, thanks for buying lunch yesterday :-)

Facebook Message from Tyler Ward 6/10/2014

at 10:06 pm:

What's wrong?

Facebook Message from Brooklyn Page Napier 6/10/2014 at 10:08 pm:

Like I said yesterday, Jack and I are having problems. Today things have gotten really bad.

Facebook Message from Tyler Ward 6/10/2014 at 10:09 pm:

What happened?

Facebook Message from Brooklyn Page Napier 6/10/2014 at 10:14 pm:

Jack and I are sleeping in separate rooms. We hardly ever see each other anymore. It's like we are roommates. When we are together he makes me feel like I'm not good enough for him. He wants me to dress and act a certain way. It's like he wants me to be someone else. I want him to love me for who I am.

Facebook Message from Tyler Ward 6/10/2014 at 10:19 pm:

I'm sorry to hear that. Marriage is hard. Kim and I have been married almost 15 years and the last few have been really challenging. We hardly ever have sex anymore and when we do it feels like it's out of obligation. All I want is to feel like she wants me.

Facebook Message from Brooklyn Page Napier

6/10/2014 at 10:21 pm:

OMG, I can totally relate. Jack and I haven't had sex in over a year.

Facebook Message from Tyler Ward 6/10/2014 at 10:22 pm:

What!!!!

Facebook Message from Brooklyn Page Napier 6/10/2014 at 10:23 pm:

I know :-(

Facebook Message from Tyler Ward 6/10/2014 at 10:25 pm:

My situation isn't that bad, but I know what it's like to not feel wanted.

Facebook Message from Brooklyn Page Napier 6/10/2014 at 10:28 pm:

I don't know if I'm "in love" with Jack anymore. I mean I love him, but I just don't feel it anymore. He is so distant and when we're together he makes me feel like I'm not good enough for him.

Facebook Message from Tyler Ward 6/10/2014 at 10:30 pm:

Was there something that triggered this or has it always been like that?

Facebook Message from Brooklyn Page Napier 6/10/2014 at 10:40 pm:

It all started when we were trying to have kids. Jack wanted children and I wasn't

sure I was ready yet. When I told him this he got upset, then he became cold.

As time went on he was more and more distant. It wasn't until I agreed to try and have children that things got better. Instantly, he became more attentive. I craved the affection. In a few months I got pregnant and Jack was over the moon with excitement. He brought me fresh daffodils, my favorite flower, almost every day. I was again the center of his attention.

Then I had a miscarriage. When I told Jack, I could see how disappointed he was. He made a weak attempt to try and mask his feelings, but it was so obvious that he was disheartened. Shortly after that he took a position that required him to travel. We would go weeks without seeing each other.

When Jack would come home he was distant. I desperately wanted our marriage to work, so I tried hard to get pregnant. I knew that's what he wanted. I read fertility books, took all the right vitamins, and made sure we had sex when I was ovulating. I was determined to make this happen for our marriage.

After months of trying I got sick as a dog one morning. I was nauseous and I couldn't keep my breakfast down. As I suspected and the pregnancy test proved, I was pregnant again.

Excited to tell Jack the news, I called him. He was in Tampa for work. He answered his phone but didn't say hello, which I thought was odd.

I kept calling his name but he wouldn't say anything.

He didn't answer. I heard voices in the background, and then I heard Jack talking to someone.

"Things are not good between Brooklyn and me," he said.

"We are so different. I want kids and she could care less. And sex, we hardly ever have it, when we do its out of obligation. It's gotten so bad I have trouble even getting aroused."

Jacks words hit me like a car accident, totally unexpected then painful as hell. My heart broke into a million little pieces. I then heard a fuzzy voice say what sounded like "That's so sad". It was so distorted by the background noise that I couldn't tell if the voice was that of a man or a woman.

Then the line went dead. I was devastated. I wondered if Jack was having an affair. I couldn't believe what I was hearing.

Facebook Message from Tyler Ward 6/10/2014 at 10:42 pm:

So, was he having an affair?

Facebook Message from Brooklyn Page Napier 6/10/2014 at 10:47 pm:

Honestly, to this day I don't know if he had an affair or not. But I decided to not tell him about the baby until I knew what

was going on.

When he came home from his trip I didn't confront him about it. I made an effort to be warm and affectionate to him. I even made him a nice dinner and offered to rub his back. But he told me that he had to go to a work dinner, which meant he was going out with his friends. I begged him to stay. When he looked at me I could see the disgust he had for me in his eyes. When I went to kiss him, what once felt electric was now like kissing a dead fish. Hugging me he just patted me on the back like he was placating a child.

When he got home late that night he slept in the guest room using "I didn't want to wake you up" as an excuse. The next day he was off to Tampa for work. While he was gone I struggled with the thought of having his child. I now secretly hoped for a miscarriage.

Facebook Message from Tyler Ward 6/10/2014 at 10:49 pm:

OMG, Brooke that's not good.

Facebook Message from Brooklyn Page Napier 6/10/2014 at 10:50 pm:

:-(I know!

Facebook Message from Tyler Ward 6/10/2014 at 10:51 pm:

I need to go to bed because I have a meeting in the morning, but I want to hear more. How about we meet for a drink

tomorrow night?

Facebook Message from Brooklyn Page Napier 6/10/2014 at 10:53 pm:

That's would be nice. Let me see if I can get my friend to watch my boys. I'll get back with you in the morning. Goodnight!

Facebook Message from Tyler Ward 6/10/2014 at 10:54 pm:

Night :-)

Facebook Message from Brooklyn Page Napier 6/11/2014 at 8:23 am:

Good morning! I'm so sorry but my friend can't watch my boys tonight :-(Raincheck?

Facebook Message from Tyler Ward 6/11/2014 at 8:25 am:

No problem! Maybe we can meet for a drink this weekend. So, finish your story. You said you were hoping for a miscarriage when you suspected that Jack was having an affair.

Facebook Message from Brooklyn Page Napier 6/11/2014 at 8:27 am:

Yes, over two months went by and no miscarriage. This time it stuck. I should have been so happy, instead I was depressed. I wasn't sure I was "in love" with him anymore. I wasn't sure I wanted to have his child in me.

When Jack opted to stay the weekends in Tampa instead of coming home to me, I no longer wanted to be pregnant.

Facebook Message from Tyler Ward 6/11/2014 at 8:30 am:

What did you do?

Facebook Message from Brooklyn Page Napier 6/11/2014 at 8:31 am:

I had an abortion.

Facebook Message from Tyler Ward 6/11/2014 at 8:32 am:

OMG, I'm speechless.

Facebook Message from Brooklyn Page Napier 6/11/2014 at 8:36 am:

I haven't told anyone about this, not even Jack, especially Jack! So, please keep this confidential.

Facebook Message from Tyler Ward 6/11/2014 at 8:37 am:

Of course, I would never tell a soul.

Facebook Message from Brooklyn Page Napier 6/11/2014 at 8:45 am:

I know this is a sin and I wish I had never gone through with it. I felt that I had no other choice.

I was so ashamed at what I did that I thought about killing myself. I begged my doctor to put me on anti-depressants, which

helped mask my pain for a while.

It was around that time that I started to lose my faith in God. How could God love me after destroying the life of an unborn child? Every time I saw a pro-life bumper sticker I felt swallowed by guilt. My self-loathing was at an all-time high. I couldn't stomach the thought of going to church. It would only remind me of what I had done.

Here it is 10 years later and I still can't escape the guilt. If Jack ever found out I don't know what he would do. I'm afraid he might hurt me.

Facebook Message from Tyler Ward 6/11/2014 at 8:47 am:

What? Why would he hurt you?

Facebook Message from Brooklyn Page Napier 6/11/2014 at 8:53 am:

Well, first of all, Jack has a horrible temper. I have seen him snap several times. I'm afraid if I tell him he will go crazy. When I was in college I had a roommate who thought she was pregnant. When I mentioned to Jack that she was considering having an abortion he went off on a tirade. Ranting and raving about how he would never allow anyone he was with to have an abortion. How his mother wanted to abort him and how his grandmother stopped her. How lucky he was to be alive.

There was something about the way he said this that was so intense. I could see the

seriousness in his eyes. It was bit unsettling. So, you can see I could never tell him about this.

JACK

CHAPTER THREE

"Art enables us to find ourselves and lose ourselves at the same time."
~ Thomas Merton

Jack Napier- Day 6

I have been in the hospital six days now. I'm not sure exactly why I'm here. Every time I ask about my family, Harleen avoids the question.

I fear something has happened to them and Harleen is afraid to tell me. Today, she asked me to journal about the day before I blacked out.

I remember sitting on the couch watching TV. Brooke and I had gotten into an argument earlier about one of her old "guy friends" who always liked all her pictures on Facebook. I'm not the jealous type, but this guy had a lot of balls. I told her I wanted to confront him. She insisted that I leave it alone.

"Why do you care?" I questioned.

"He's just a friend, now leave it alone!"

"It's disrespectful, Brooke!"

"You don't control me, Jack! And why are you going

through my Facebook page? It's none of your business!"

"When you post pictures of our kids on Facebook it's my business. Do you understand?!"

Brooke glared at me with clenched teeth. Without saying a word she gathered up the kids and left the house.

Something didn't feel right about this guy. I pulled up his Facebook page. His profile picture was a photo of him and his three girls. He was a nice looking guy with sandy blond hair, chocolate brown eyes, with a lumberjack's scruff. He was in good shape, unlike me. After Brooke and I got married I put on a few pounds, but I held it well and she never complained.

In his profile it said that he graduated from Indiana University, but I didn't remember him. There was no information about his age or what year he graduated. I just assumed that Brooke knew him from college before she and I reconnected in Finland. However, something about him looked familiar. It was driving me crazy.

I read through his profile a little more. Tyler was the youth minister for a local non-denominational Christian church. His relationship status was "Married to Kimberly Richardson Ward". I don't know why, but it was comforting to know that he was married.

Looking through his pictures, he appeared to be a very happily married man. His daughters were beautiful like their mother, and he had photos from all over the world from his mission trips. It was hard not to secretly like the guy, so I let it go for the time being.

My birthday was that weekend. I had planned on spending it with my boys, until I got a call from Brooke's mother informing me that my wife and kids were going to be staying with them for a few weeks. She explained that Brooke needed time to "figure things out".

Figure things out? What the hell did that mean? So, I spent my 37th birthday alone, drunk, and I guess blacked out. That's the last thing I remember before waking up in the hospital.

The only thing that's keeping me calm right now is my journaling. Remembering my childhood is both arduous and nostalgic at the same time. My memories are often blurred. I find myself filling in the gaps with versions that are appealing to me. It's like I have been given a chance to relive my life.

When I was a kid, art was my outlet. Along with my comic books and writing, it was my escape, my safe place. When life got hard I would immerse myself in my creative world, drawing pictures of my favorite comic book characters. I got so good my friends would beg me to draw different superheroes for them.

I can recall one day in elementary school my teacher telling the class there would be a Thanksgiving art contest. Everyone was going to draw a turkey and color it in. The student who received the most votes from the panel of teachers judging the contest would win a prize. Of course, they didn't announce what the prize would be, but we were all excited anyway.

My turkey was very unique compared to the others that hung next to it on the wall. After all, in my short yet dysfunctional life, I had lots of time to discover my creative side.

The turkey itself was well done. I had developed a special technique for coloring it in. I drew very heavy with each crayon I used. The wax built up thick, creating a 3D effect. It even broke off in chunks, adding to the realism of the feathers. I loved it!

After we handed in our drawings the panel of teachers studied the collection of art that covered the hallway. Keeping up the suspense, they sent us home before choosing the winner. It was killing me! I barely slept that night.

The next morning, the boring announcements scratched across the classroom speaker. All of my classmates were excited, making predictions about who they thought the winner might be. We even had to sit

through the lunch menu before they would announce the winner. After the word of the day, they finally got to the art contest.

"Now, for the announcement you all have been waiting for, we have the name of the winner of the Thanksgiving art contest. I would first like to say that all of you did a great job on your drawings. They were all so wonderful. It was a hard choice to make. But the judges finally did choose a winner. And that winner is..." The kids started banging their hands against their desks to mimic the sound of a drumroll, "... Jack O'Malley!"

Me! I won the contest for the best drawing! All of my friends patted me on the back as I was instructed to pick up my prize at the office after school. I was a celebrity for exactly one whole day. Kids were congratulating me as I walked down the hall and at recess.

What could the prize possibly be, a pair of skates, a baseball glove, what? When I got to the principal's office I was handed a giant cage with a live turkey inside.

"GOBBLE! GOBBLE! GOBBLE!"

The principal walked up to me with a huge smile on his face and said, "Jack! This is your prize. Take it home with you! It's yours!"

"GOBBLE! GOBBLE! GOBBLE!"

I could barely hear him over the turkey. The cage looked like a space ship that was piloted by a fat, feathery alien with a bright red gobbler dangling from his chin. I am sure my jaw hung open. Why couldn't I have won something normal, like movie tickets or a gift certificate?

Trying to walk with the cage was impossible. Principal Hilgenberg tried to jump in and help when he realized I was falling. Turkey, cage, and disappointment all fell on top of me.

Struggling and with no help from my friends I managed to carry the turkey, clucking and gobbling, all the way home. The cage hit my ankles every step of the way. By the time I got to our townhome, my arms hurt

like I'd been doing push-ups all day.

Wrestling the kitchen door open, I brought the turkey inside. I set the cage down in the middle of the kitchen. I took a few breaths, then I studied the beast in front of me. His brown and white feathers were majestic like body armor. On his neck were a trail red moles that led to two large red ones that resembled a ..... set of very unhealthy testicals.

Figuring there was only one place for such a pet, I opened the basement door and dragged the cage down the stairs. Every step brought another scrape to my ankles, while the gyrating motion made my new friend more anxious. Once I reached the bottom step, I rested. Taking a moment to catch my breath, I admired my new buddy. When I noticed the turkey looking at me, I didn't move a muscle in an effort to not scare him. His head cocked to the side as his raven-like eyes connected with mine. This only lasted a second. That's when I decided that feeding my new friend might be the nice thing to do.

Not knowing what turkeys eat, I went upstairs and rummaged through the cupboards. Cornmeal should work, I guessed. Taking it down stairs along with a bowl of water I made the peace offering.

My plan was to watch my friend all afternoon, just to figure out what a turkey does. What I quickly discovered is that turkeys don't do that much. Really, what can you do with a turkey in a cage? Bored, I headed upstairs to my room.

Hours later, my grandfather came home. Who knows when my mom finally dragged her ass in? I fell asleep thinking everything was okay. That is, until six o'clock in the morning, when it sounded like a fire alarm went off. A loud cackle rang throughout the house. GOBBB-GBOB-GOBBLE! Then that noise was followed by another loud cackle, GOBBB-GBOB-GOBBLE!

Popping out of bed, I ran down the stairs, meeting my grandfather in the kitchen. Grandpa Bob glared at me

with bloodshot eyes that were half-open. Standing in white boxers and a dull gray tank top, he flailed his arms and yelled cuss words. In came my mother. She was not happy either. Then we heard the sound again.

"GOBBB-GBOB-GOBBLE!!"

"GOBBB-GBOB-GOBBLE!!"

"I know it's close and when I find it I going to wring its neck!" Grandpa shouted.

When I saw him looking toward the basement door I panicked, feeling my eyes pop right out of my head. I did the only thing I could think of... I stepped in front of the door, but my grandfather pushed me aside. Flinging it open, he started down the steps.

That's when the loudest cackling sound nearly ruptured my eardrums GOBB – GOBB-GOBBLE! Grandpa Bob's cussing could be heard in the next county.

"What in the hell? Where in the...what in God's name...?"

My mother joined in his tirade as they tried to figure out why there was a turkey in their basement. Suddenly, my new friend was quiet. It was like someone hit the snooze button on the turkey alarm clock.

I ran down the steps to protect my prize, asking them what they thought they were doing with my turkey.

"This is your turkey?" my mother yelled. "How in the world did you get a turkey?" She stood in front of the cage, blocking my view of Grandpa Bob. I tried to see around her, but I knew to pay attention when she was mad.

I started to answer, telling her about the contest. She quickly interrupted, telling me she had no interest in some bullshit made-up story about my artistry. I kept telling her it was true.

"I don't want to hear it, Jack!"

"But Mom, he's my friend!"

"Goddam it, Jack! I don't need this shit right now. You are nothing but a pain in my ass!"

She glared at me with her all-too-familiar look of

resentment. A look that said "I wish you had never been born."

I waited for her to tell me how I was holding her back. How she should have aborted me. How she should be a model in New York City. She said nothing - the expression on her face said it all.

I started to protest. Before I could continue, my mother announced that the turkey was going to her cousin's farm. I knew what that meant. My friend was on his way to becoming someone's turkey dinner.

I begged for his life, but no one was listening. At that point I lost it.

"It's not fair! He is my friend! He needs me!"

"Quit whining. You know I hate when you do that," my mother barked at me like an angry dog.

Knowing I was powerless to stop what was about to happen, I marched upstairs. I didn't even saying goodbye to my Turkey. When I got to my room, I felt like a coward. That turkey liked me. I didn't fight to try and save him. I was sure he would feel like I abandoned him.

Taking out a piece of paper I began to draw. It didn't matter what is was. I just wanted to get far away. I didn't want to think about day I just had or the friend I just lost.

CINDY

CHAPTER FOUR

"There are wounds that never show on the body that are deeper and more hurtful than anything that bleeds."
~ Laurell K. Hamilton

Cindy Napier's Diary

January 12, 1978

Oh my god, I am two weeks late! My period is always on time. Like clockwork. Debbie agreed to come over and take me to the drugstore to get a pregnancy test. Thank God she went in to buy it for me. I honestly can't imagine having to do it myself. We went straight back to Debbie's house, only to confirm what I had initially thought. I am pregnant! I am only seventeen! Why? Why me? So many of my friends had sex with their boyfriends. This didn't happen to them! I can't believe I'm pregnant. I have no idea what I'm going to do. I am too young to have this baby. I guess I will either put it up for adoption or have an abortion. I want a future. I want to move to New York City and become a model. That has been my dream ever since I was old enough to remember. This cannot be happening to me!

January 13, 1978

I would be lost without Debbie. After making some phone calls and staying up all night we have come up with a solution to the problem that's growing inside me. The answer is in Kentucky. It's the closest state to Indiana that will allow me to have an abortion without my mother's consent. We called the clinic and made the

appointment for January 15th. Debbie has agreed to take me. We are going to tell both our parents that we will be spending the day shopping at Glendale Mall.

When I made the appointment, the nurse said that there might be some protesters outside the clinic. She said I should just ignore them and walk straight in as fast as I can. I was told under no circumstance should I talk to anyone outside of the clinic.

January 14, 1978

I don't know why I decided to write a letter to my mother explaining what I was about to do, but I did. When I was done I put it in the drawer in my bedside table. I had no intention of giving it to her right away, if ever. I just needed to write out my feelings. This way if something happened to me during the procedure she would know how I felt. How I got myself in this mess. The letter gave details about my plan, my love for her, and how sorry I was to disappoint her.

Later that night Debbie and I were watching The Sound of Music at her house when the phone rang. It was my mother. She was crying hysterically, telling me that she had found the note. She said she was on her way to pick me up. Did I subconsciously want her to find out about my plan so she could stop me? No, no way in hell! She was probably just being nosy going through my room and found it. While I waited for her to come get me I wondered how she was going to react. Was she going to be furious that I did this behind her back or would she understand and be supportive of me and my decision? Am I feeling a sense of relief that she knows? God I don't know. I guess deep down I want my mother to know and approve of my plan to have this procedure. She is all I have now that my father is nowhere to be found. She is the only person in my life who is here for me. I desperately need her.

Surely she wants me to have a life, to make something of myself, and to finish high school and go to college. She will agree that having the procedure is the best choice for me and my future.

When my mother got to Debbie's house she didn't bother to come in, she just honked her horn. She didn't say anything the whole way home. When we pulled into the driveway she broke her silence telling me how late it was. How I needed my rest. Walking me to my room she said goodnight. To my surprise she hugged me and began to sob. I thought, oh my God, she does understand? I'm sure she will go with me to Kentucky. This whole thing will be over with soon. I will have my mother's acceptance, which is the most important thing to me. Her next words changed everything.

My Mother: "Cindy, you will not be going to Kentucky tomorrow with Debbie or anyone else. I will not allow you to kill your unborn baby."

Me: "What? You are crazy if you think you can stop me. I am going to have this done whether you like it or not. It's my body, my choice!!!"

My mother told me that my only options would be to have the baby or put it up for adoption. She didn't even bother to ask who the father was. She just assumed it was my boyfriend Sam. She told me she would be calling Sam's mother to discuss the matter. Then I lost it. I told her that Sam didn't know about the baby. How I wasn't sure it was his (Oh God, how I wish I hadn't told her that). Besides, there wasn't going to be a baby anyway, so he didn't need to know. I screamed at her, telling her she couldn't control me, that she had absolutely no right do this to me. My last words to her were, "I hate you! Get out!"

January 15, 1978

I snuck out of the house this morning before my mother woke up. Debbie picked me up in her mom's car and we left for Kentucky. I was quiet most of the ride, knowing my mother was going to be furious with me. When we got to the clinic all we could hear were protesters yelling and shouting as we walked towards the entrance. I was so nervous I couldn't make out what they were saying. It was all a bunch of white noise to me. When we reached the front of the clinic it was lined with angry faces. I could hear them shouting, "Murderer!" They begged me to save the life that was growing inside of me. I just ignored them and went inside.

In the reception area were mostly young women like me. Most of them looked like they were in their 20s, but a few looked older. After about 20 minutes, a nurse came out and read off four last names. One of which was mine. The nurse led the four of us back to a small room at one end of the hall. It looked just like the reception area only much smaller. She handed each of us a paper cup containing two pills. She gave us water and instructed us to take the pills. She said they would help relax us before the procedure.

After the nurse made sure we took our medicine, she left. Shortly after, I started to feel dizzy. I was tipsy like I had drunk a few glasses of wine. I thought about asking some of the other girls how they came to their decision to have the procedure. Then I realized that was not a good idea. None of the girls were making eye contact or talking. So I decided it was best for me to just leave it alone. After what seemed like a long time the nurse came back and called my name. She escorted me down a long hallway to a restroom where I changed into a gown. She then took me to the place where they were going to do the procedure.

I felt present, but not really, like I was in a dream, or rather the start of a nightmare. I saw three nurses with blank stares on their faces. I was expecting the doctor to

come in and introduce himself. He just entered the room and directed me to get on the table, put my legs in the stirrups, and scoot down. He told me that I would hear a loud noise that would sound like a vacuum. He continued to explain that I would feel some cramping, but the procedure would only take a few minutes.

I started thinking about my baby never having the memory of life, never filling its lungs with the Earth's air, and never experiencing love or fear. Who am I to deny this baby growing inside of me these things? Like my mother said, it's not the baby's fault I got pregnant. But how can I love something that is the product of something so awful?

All of these thoughts were starting to make me feel sick. I couldn't take it. I had to get out of there. I could feel my mother's presence hovering over me like a ghost. I stopped the doctor, telling him I didn't want to go through with the abortion.

"This is a common reaction, you just need to relax. It will all be over in less than 15 minutes," he explained.

All I could picture was my mother looking at me with disappointment in her eyes. I told the doctor my mind was made up, that I no longer wanted to have the procedure. He immediately became irritated.

"You have wasted my time! I hope you understand that you will still have to pay for the procedure," he shouted.

I didn't care. I just wanted to get the hell out of there. When I got back to the car, I told Debbie I couldn't go through with the abortion. She held my hand. I cried all the way home. I was not ready to be a mother. Regret was now filling my stomach with fear and doubt. I felt like I just made the biggest mistake of my life.

January 25, 1978

I got home from the clinic an hour ago. I can't stop

crying. While I am not ready to have a baby, I just couldn't go through with the abortion. My mother has gotten her way. She has forced her will on me once again. Now, she keeps asking whether or not I am 100 percent sure Sam is the father. Sam's mom must have questioned it when my mother called her. Sadly, I have no idea who the father is. I am pretty sure it's either Sam or Mike. But Mike was a one-time thing and I just don't think it was him. Odds are its Sam. Plus, Sam is easy to explain to everyone because we have been seeing each other for almost seven months now. No one will question it, not even Sam.

I met Sam at the Riviera Club, my second home in the summer. I first noticed him at the snack bar. I recognized him from high school. He was a senior, very good looking, and very popular. He has shaggy brown hair and light blue eyes that accentuate his dark tan. Asking around, I found out that he had broken up with Barbara, the girl he had been dating off and on in that spring. I decided that I was going to be his "girl" that summer. After I finally got his attention he introduced himself to me. We instantly clicked and started dating. He is smart, kind, and most of all fun! But I got bored. Summer was not a time to get tied down. Besides, what Sam didn't know wouldn't hurt him.

Yes, Sam has to be the father! He would certainly be a good one. He is a hard worker in school, gets good grades, and works at the Nora bowling alley on the weekends. He has told me about his dreams of going to the police academy like his father and grandfather. Most guys our age have no plan for their life. Sam is motivated. He will be a good provider for me and our baby.

The thought of making a life with Sam brings some comfort to me even though I truly feel like my life is basically over. Now, I just have to figure out when and where to tell him. Maybe his mother already has? He has been avoiding me. I bet that's why.

March 1, 1978

I told him! Sam was surprised to see me at his front door today. I told him there was something important we needed to talk about. I informed him that I was pregnant. That he was the father. At first he stared at me with a blank look on his face. Like I was joking. Then strangely he smiled. I told him that I needed his help to raise this child. That's when the seriousness of the situation hit him. His facial expression dropped. Then his body sort of closed in on itself as he glared back at me. Shaking his head Sam had the nerve to question how this could have possibly happened. He asked if I lied about being on the pill. That really pissed me off! I laid into him good, telling him not to even think this baby wasn't his! He then told me the reason he had backed off a bit in our relationship was because someone told him that I had cheated on him with Mike Salinger.

"That's crap! You are the only person I have slept with in the past seven months." I yelled stormed off the porch.

Following me he grabbed my arm. I pulled away, telling him to get his hands off of me. He let go, begging me to forgive him.

"Look, I wasn't expecting this! I'm sorry! I will be there for you and the baby," he pleaded.

I trumped up some tears as Sam pulled me in closer to him. He assured me that we would figure this out together. I was still angry, but Sam hugging me, along with his words, brought relief to me.

April 12, 1978

Sam asked me to marry him today!!! He took me to El Matador, my favorite restaurant. It's a dive, but they serve the best Mexican food in town. Flacco, the bartender, is always willing to serve me a strong margarita without asking for ID. God knows I wanted one

today. Considering my condition I decided not to, a coke for this mommy-to-be...

Its spring now, and after the hard winter we had I think everyone in the city was out walking the Broad Ripple strip. Hoosiers always get overexcited about spring. They prematurely breakout their shorts and flip-flops. It can be 50 degrees out and in their minds it's 70.

Sam reached in his pocket and pulled out a little red box. He then began his "speech."

"Cindy, I know this is not what either of us expected or planned. But I have loved you from the first moment I laid eyes on you. While we have had our ups and downs the past few months, there have been way more good times than bad. Yes, we are young, but I know we are meant for each other. Let's be a family. Will you marry me?"

I couldn't believe what I was hearing. Weren't these the words I was waiting to hear? My mother would be so happy... but will I? Is this what I really want, to be a wife and mother?

I can't raise this baby alone. A part of me does love Sam. We can make this work.

When I finally said yes, Sam walked around the table. In front of everyone he placed the diamond ring on my finger. Two couples sitting next to us raised their margarita glasses and yelled , "Congrats! Cheers!"

Sam continued to assure me that all would be fine, that we would make it work, especially since we had his parents' blessing.

My ring is nice, not something I would have chosen, but simple and pretty.

While we were eating, Sam was talking a mile a minute about his plans for our future.

I knew marrying Sam was the best option for me and my baby. It will keep my mother off my back and the local gossip to a minimum.

JACK

CHAPTER FIVE

"Many men go fishing all of their lives without knowing that it is not fish they are after."
~ Henry David Thoreau

Jack Napier- Day 11

I asked Harleen again today about my family. She blew it off like she did the last time. I told her I couldn't wait any longer, demanding I see them immediately. Harleen was expressionless, like one of those mannequins you see in a Macy's display window.

"I have done everything you have asked. Please let me see my family," I pleaded again.

"Jack, I am so sorry to have to tell you this, but your wife and children were found dead in your home the night you were brought here."

"What!" I shouted.

"The police received a call from one of your neighbors that Friday evening reporting that they heard what sounded like gunshots. When the officers arrived they found your wife and children unresponsive. You were unconscious. Tied to a chair."

The shock that paralyzed my body quickly morphed into anger.

"Why didn't you tell me this when we first met?!" I shouted.

"We wanted to see if you remembered anything. Several hours had gone by and you still had not been able to recall or shed a light on what happened that night."

My body started to shake.

"I want to help you remember," Harleen said, "so we can find out what really happened. I needed to make sure you were stable from a medical and mental standpoint. The last thing I wanted to do was blindside you with this news. I am so sorry this happened to you. I am here to help you, Jack."

I felt the blood rush to my face. My head was tingling. Sweat trickled down my neck.

"Is there anything you can remember from that evening?" Harleen prodded. "If not, what about the day?"

"You lied to me!" I screeched. "You let me believe my family was alive, that I would get to see them!"

"Jack, I never lied. My job was to make sure you were mentally prepared before I could share the news. Our focus now needs to be on finding out what happened that night. Please try and remember. Did you go to work that morning?"

I leaned into Harleen, so my face was within inches of hers.

I screamed, "YOU LIED TO ME!!!!"

"Jack, I never—"

"I DON'T BELIEVE YOU! YOU ARE LYING TO ME NOW!"

I could see that Harleen was scared as she rang for the nurse. When the nurse and the guard entered the room, all hell broke loose. Security was called and it took several officers to hold me down so they could sedate me. Then it was lights out.....

When I eventually woke, I realized my family was in

danger, or even worse, they were gone. Something felt very suspicious about this whole situation, like I was being set up. I knew I had to keep my cool if I wanted to find the truth.

I needed to take my mind off the current situation. I had to regroup and figure out what was really happening.

When I was a kid, I would go to the Broad Ripple Canal when I wanted to clear my head. That's where I met Jim, my fishing buddy and one of my best friends.

Jim and I would cast our lines in the canal, then we would sit and talk for hours about the mysteries of life. Like whether or not Goofy was a dog or a human with a dog-like face. Jim would joke around telling me that one of his ex-girlfriends had a face like Goofy.

What I liked most about Jim was that he always had time for me and all of my silly questions. Being that I was a kid with no father in sight, Jim was a godsend at that time in my life. He taught me about life and most of all, how to put the right bait on my line to catch the big catfish, the one worth telling a story about.

By the time I was seven I knew all the Broad Ripple Village shortcuts, which dogs to avoid, and which old ladies to stay clear of. I was a scrappy little guy with long, curly-blond hair. I was bony and malnourished with a ruddy complexion from spending every possible minute outside. I was adventurous, wandering along the train tracks and around the canal. What the Mississippi River was to Huckleberry Finn, the train tracks were to me. It was my escape from reality.

The train that ran along the Monon Railroad passed right by our three-bedroom townhouse, slicing Broad Ripple into two equal halves. Walking along the tracks, hopping from one tie to the next, took me through parts of town where I met the most interesting people, many of whom became my dear friends. Best of all, the train tracks led right to my favorite place, the Broad Ripple canal.

The canal had carved its way through the once-tiny village decades ago. Now it's lined with restaurants, bars, and the after-wash of late night riffraff.

Back when it was a child's paradise, I would tiptoe as soon as my feet hit the bank, so as not to stir up any dirt. Then I'd flip a rock, catching a crawdad before it had a chance to scurry away. I was really good at catching crawdads.

"They make mighty-fine bait," Jim would tell me.

When it got cold, Jim would go to the local homeless shelter to live for the winter. I wouldn't see him for months. That was one of the many reasons I hated that season. I could barely wait until spring, so Jim and I could get back to fishing. We would spend hours casting our lines, hoping for a bite, and me asking a lot of questions.

The thing about Jim was he genuinely wanted to be my friend, which made me feel loved. I asked him once why he lived under the bridge. He told me he couldn't be tied down to just one fishing hole. Then he called me Ponyboy. He liked to call me that and he always said it with a giant smile.

Ponyboy was the main character in Jim's favorite book, The Outsiders. Jim kept a worn paperback copy in his back pocket. He liked to read it to me, and I loved to listen. While we were fishing, I would ask him to read my favorite parts over and over again.

I never really knew why Jim loved to call me Ponyboy until I was old enough to read the book on my own. I was Ponyboy to him, and he wanted me to stay golden. It wasn't until much later in life that I realized what a gift it was to have him as a friend.

Looking back, I suppose it was kind of weird that my best friend was a forty-five year old black man who barely survived the jungle hell of Vietnam, only to take up temporary residence under a bridge in Broad Ripple. Jim's face was worn and callused like his hands. He was

built like a soldier, lean but muscular. His hair was long (afro style) with a chin curtain beard that was speckled with grey. Jim would tell me all about his adventures in Vietnam, the good ones, that is. When I would push to hear about the bad ones, he would simply say, "Leave it alone, Ponyboy," and I would stop.

As soon as I woke up in the mornings on summer break, I would run to the canal to see my old fishing buddy. Jim was easy to spot because he was always in his Army fatigues with all kinds of different patches on them from his service in Vietnam. My heart would glow when I saw him sitting on the bank of the canal with his bamboo pole in hand. He didn't have a reel, but he managed to catch fish just fine.

One particular morning on my way to go fishing, I saw Jim at the canal, right at the dam where it meets White River, where the railroad tracks cross. Jim was excited because he just got a huge bite on his line. He yelled at me to come help him. This was no regular fish nipping at the bait. We both knew "who" it was. It had to be the legendary catfish that had teased many a fisherman for years. Jim and I called him "Old Man." He'd lived longer and avoided more fishing hooks than seemed possible.

The bobber didn't just sink, it popped below the surface, back up, and then down deep. Each time the fish made a run for it, Jim and I grew more excited.

Just as Jim was pulling it to shore, the line broke. The biggest fish in the canal still held the title of "The One That Got Away."

Jim already had six catfish and a smallmouth bass sitting in his bucket on the bank. But this was the one he wanted. It was the fish everyone coveted, the one we all talked about. This guy was a catfish worth one hundred fishing stories.

Jim balled up a piece of crawdad into a piece of bread and went at it again. After putting the bait on his hook,

he cast his line. The bobber floated peacefully on the top of the water like a swan. Jim and I never looked away, never relaxed, didn't talk, just waited and waited.

Suddenly the sinker was pulled under the surface with such force Jim had to hang onto the pole with all his strength. Up and down the bank he followed the giant catfish. He wanted to tire the Old Man out.

At one point Jim got pulled so near the bank he lost his footing, his pole slipping out of his hand. He managed to grab it and kept fighting. He yelled for me to get the net. The battle raged for nearly half an hour. My palms were sweaty. I felt like I was going to jump out of my skin.

Jim pulled and pulled on the line until the Old Man was close to the shore, then he yelled for me to throwing the net over the Old Man.

As we pulled the net out of the water, the giant catfish fought like a prizefighter, thrashing to get out of the net, refusing to accept his fate. Jim and I shared a grin of victory. Jim figured the catfish to be about eight pounds. I was pretty sure it was more like sixty.

Jim carefully cut the line. Then he grabbed his pliers to get the hook out of the fish's mouth. That monster was still fighting. Catfish can cut you like a knife, you know. Jim put his gloves on and fought to get it to hold still. Removing the hook, he threw the Old Man in the bucket with the rest of his fish. It was odd, because a catfish like that deserved to be in his own bucket, not one filled with inferior fish. I would have thrown the other fish back in the canal, freeing up the bucket for my prize.

Jim had quite a load in that old plastic paint bucket he found in the dumpster behind the drugstore. It was enough food to feed him for a week. He looked at me with a huge smile on his face while we watched our captive flop around in an effort to escape the crowded bucket of water.

The satisfied look on Jim's face was what you would imagine seeing from someone who just climbed Mount Everest. Breathing heavily, he looked out over the water.

He was the most content man I ever saw.

Jim then told me to take the bucket of fish home. He said I could have the tackle box as well. It didn't make any sense; he used that tackle box every day.

"Jack, you're a good friend," he said. "One of the best I ever had. I am glad I met you."

"Me too," I told him.

I felt like I had ants in my pants because I wanted to show the fish to my friends so bad. I asked Jim again if he was sure he didn't want the Old Man for himself.

"Nah, you take him", he said, "take 'em all." Then Jim said, "Stay golden, Ponyboy," like he was saying goodbye for a long time.

I told him thanks, that I'd see him in the morning. I didn't think much about what Jim said at the time, but I would later regret not staying longer with him that day.

Not thinking about the consequences, I put the giant catfish in the sink when I got home. I ran through the neighborhood, yelling to my friends, who all came running in to catch a glimpse of the legendary catfish. They looked at the monster in the sink in disbelief. They couldn't believe their eyes!

I did just what Jim had instructed. I told everyone I caught the Old Man singlehandedly. My friends had no choice but to believe me. The indisputable proof was right there in the sink.

One of my buddy's grabbed his mother's Polaroid camera and took a picture of me holding the legendary catfish. Everyone made a big deal out of it, which made me feel really special.

This had been one great day.

The next morning was not so great. I woke to my Grandpa Bob yelling.

"What the hell is that smell?" he screamed.

I ran down the stairs into the kitchen that reeked of dead fish. In fact, the stench was so bad I could smell it upstairs.

When I told my story, Grandpa Bob Bob settled down. He told me that in all his days, he had never seen a catfish that big. I could tell by the way he looked at me with his crooked smile that said despite being annoyed by the nasty fish smell, he was actually very impressed. He spent the morning skinning my prize. Wrapping it in tinfoil to put in the freezer. I wanted to have it mounted and hung on my wall, but I knew better than to push my luck with Grandpa Bob.

As usual, my mother, who had stumbled home late, was hungover and sleeping upstairs. She didn't smell a thing. I was so anxious to tell Jim all about how much fuss everyone made over the catfish that I lit out of the house like I was on fire. I raced to the canal.

My adrenaline started pumping when I heard the sound of a train coming. I pulled out a penny from my pocket and placed it on the rail. Then I jumped into the ditch just below the tracks as the train passed.

Woooh! Wooooh! The train whistle blew, the ground vibrating like a 6.0 earthquake.

When the ground stopped shaking I made sure the train was gone, climbed out of the ditch, then went to find my penny. It took me a while, but I located the smashed penny with Abraham Lincoln's head smeared like an alien. It was perfect! It would make a great addition to my collection of other smashed coins. Collecting these coins was something all the kids in the village did. Every Saturday we would all meet to show them off and make trades. I am proud to say I had one of the finest collections in town.

Running to the canal, I was surprised to see an ambulance, a fire truck, and several police cars parked in the area. I slowed down when I saw a big crowd of people gathered by the bridge.

As I was walking toward the scene to find out what was going on, someone grabbed me by the arm. I spun around to see Mr. Swindle from the drugstore. There was

a look of concern on his face that he quickly masked with a smile.

"Hey, Jack! I want to show you something."

Naturally, I asked what was going on down at the canal.

"Oh that. There was a car crash or something. Don't worry! They have to send all these people out here as an extra precaution," Mr. Swindle explained. "Come with me, I've got a new candy I want you to try!"

I looked back at the canal, but candy was candy. I followed him into the drugstore to get his treat. Mr. Swindle was a very thin man of average height who wore circle-rimmed spectacles that defined his narrow face, which made him look very sophisticated. Behind his glasses were a set of blue eyes, the kind that were comforting to look at.

I met him one day when I was looking for odd jobs to support my growing addiction to candy. Mr. Swindle was so impressed he gave me a part-time job. Our friendship blossomed from there.

Pointing at the new candy he said, "You can have as many as you want, however, you have to eat them here."

I supposed it was some kind of test to find out which version of the candy would be the best seller. There was a huge array of sugary treats surrounding the counter which were enough to get my mind off of the ruckus at the canal. I saw Mr. Swindle keeping one eye on my candy testing, and the other on the commotion outside. Something was going on that he didn't want me to know about.

When the last police car finally cleared out Mr. Swindle said, "Hey, you know what? I've got some cleaning to do. Why don't you grab yourself a handful of candy and go play?"

"Okay, Mr. Swindle! Thanks!" I replied stuffing my pockets with candy.

I ran out of the store looking for Jim. I didn't find

him that day, or the next. More than a week had gone by since we landed the world's biggest catfish, and I was really concerned. I visited the canal every day looking for Jim, but he was nowhere to be found. I started asking around town to see if anyone had seen him.

I even asked my mom if she would help me look for Jim. She told me in no uncertain terms to stay away from the men who lived under the bridge. I found this ironic because she never cared where I went or when I came home. I think she just said it to make herself feel like she wasn't a horrible mother.

Finally, I found someone who did answer, a miserable old man named Rudd who was homeless like Jim. Jim didn't like Rudd at all. When he would fish at one of our spots, we would move to the other side of the canal to avoid him. Rudd was a big guy with a chubby round face that looked like he was always blushing.

When I asked him about Jim, he removed a pint of whiskey from his back pocket and took a giant pull.

"Jim killed hisself. He jumped off the dam and drowned right here where I cast my line. They have been searching for his body for weeks. With all the rain we've been having and the current being so strong, who knows if they will ever find him," Rudd explained.

"You're lying!" I screamed. "Jim would never do that!"

"Believe what you want! Now get away from me!" Rudd shouted.

I hate to admit it all these years later, but tears ran down my face that day. I yelled, calling him things I had heard my mother say, not even knowing what they meant.

About that same time, I heard someone behind me. It was Mr. Swindle. I ran up to him, pointing back at Rudd.

"He said Jim drowned! That Jim killed himself! Is that true?" I yelled.

Mr. Swindle looked at me with broken eyes. "I'm sorry, Jack. I am sorry you found out this way. Jim was sick. He just couldn't take Vietnam sneaking up on him in

the night anymore."

I knew Mr. Swindle wouldn't lie. He liked Jim, and he knew how much I liked Jim as well. Mr. Swindle used to give Jim food and money when he needed it. I knew his puffy red eyes held the truth. I didn't even thank him for telling me what really happened; I just tore off for home. When I was halfway there I got such a stitch in my side that I had to stop running. I couldn't catch my breath. I kicked rocks, throwing them at the tall maple trees that lined the railroad tracks.

Why would Jim kill himself? To a 7 year old kid it made no sense. I was angry with God for taking Jim away from me. Angry that I had a mother that didn't want me, angry that I didn't know who my father was. I felt like an old toy that was no longer desirable, left in the toy box and forgotten about.

Losing Jim made me feeling a deep loneliness I had never experienced before. I swore never to go back to the canal, ever. There was no reason to return, Jim wouldn't be there. I went to my tree house. I started drawing a picture to capture the scene of Jim and I on the canal. I thought maybe if I put us together on paper, then he wouldn't really be gone.

CINDY

CHAPTER SIX

"Many a man in love with a dimple makes the mistake of marrying the whole girl."
~Brooken Leacock

Cindy Napier's Diary

July 26, 1978

Two weeks ago, Sam and I tied the knot. It wasn't the fairytale wedding I've always dreamed of, but it was nice. Everyone seemed to have a great time. Over three hundred people attended the wedding, which was held at Christ the King Catholic Church. It was a quaint little church where Sam and his family were parishioners. They attended service every Sunday.

All seven of Sam's brothers and sisters had been baptized there. So, Sam's parents were adamant about us getting married there. To them, this was non-negotiable. They were becoming a little too controlling for my taste.

Sam's family filled the pews on the right side of the church. The left side was for mine, which numbered far less than his. The church was a sea of blue. Police blue ran in the veins of the O'Malley family. Sam will be the fourth generation O'Malley to serve on the Indianapolis Police Department.

When I was walking down the aisle of lopsided wedding attendees, I felt a little annoyed that more of my family didn't attend. It was embarrassing to see the inequity of people representing my side of the aisle. Focusing on the moment I noticed all eyes were on me. I felt like I was floating in my gorgeous wedding dress as my father walked me to the altar.

One of the few things my mother helped out with was finding and paying for my dress. She surprised me by suggested that we stop at Abigail's and look for a wedding dress one Saturday morning. I was shocked! Up until this point she had not seemed to show much interest in me or my wedding. I think she was still angry about my pregnancy. The dress I chose was ivory and satin with an empire waist and A-line skirt. The scalloped neckline brought all eyes to my face. There was lace around the hem. It was an elegant dress with delicate frills all around that covered my body quite well.

Approaching the altar I looked at Sam. I was thinking how I was grateful that my father was able to walk me down the aisle—sober. After we exchanged our vows, we had our first kiss as Mr. and Mrs. Samuel O'Malley. The audience clapped and cheered. When we walked out of the church and down the steps to Sam's car, our family and friends threw the ceremonial rice. I found this to be quite annoying. I was not pleased when I got to the car and realized that my hair was covered in wedding rice. Sam laughed it off, which annoyed me even more.

When we arrived at the Scottish Rite Cathedral we entered the ballroom located on the second floor. The DJ introduced as Mr. and Mrs. O'Malley, and the party began. Well, it began for everyone but me. While it was wonderful being the center of attention and receiving so many compliments, what I really wanted was a drink. Many were well on their way to getting drunk and I wanted to join them. I snuck a glass of wine. It instantly calmed my nerves, so I had another. When Sam's mother saw what I was doing she went over to him to say something. Mary Alice was acting like a total bitch. She was ruining my special day!

Like her puppet, Sam came over and told me to slow down with the drinking. I asked him if he had any idea what it was like to be pregnant. He just gave me a blank stare. I told him to back off, that if he ruined my wedding

day I would never forgive him. Like a good boy he left me alone, but his mother was another story.

Later that night Mary Alice found me smoking with some friends in the parking lot. She pulled me aside and said she couldn't believe how careless I was being with the child growing inside of me. I had been holding back for way too long, so I unleashed on her. Seeing this Sam grabbed me by the arm. He dragged me to his car kicking and screaming.

"It's my body, I can do whatever I want." I shouted.

Then I slipped, telling Sam how my mother was forcing me to have this baby. How I wanted an abortion, how it was my body, my decision. How my mother guilted me into having the baby. Sam was in shock.

While it had been a nice evening up to that point it wasn't what I had dreamed about. Maybe that's why I drank so much. I didn't feel like a princess. Was it because deep down in my heart I knew Sam wasn't really my prince? I'm not sure why, but I am grateful of one thing... No one questioned our marriage. They seemed to believe Sam and I were two young kids in love who wanted to spend the rest of our lives together. I know this made my mother happy.

August 22, 1978

It's been about a month since the wedding. Thank God my morning sickness has subsided! I spend most days in our little apartment sleeping. My visits to the Riviera Club are much less frequent due to the fact that my belly is showing. The only people that know I am pregnant are a few close friends and our families. I'm sure when I can no longer hide my baby bump the gossip start and the calculations will begin.

"When did they get married?"

"She looks much farther along than just a couple of months. Sam must have knocked her up. That's why he

married her."

"I wonder when she is due?"

"I wonder if she is going back to school in September to finish her senior year?"

I can just hear all the rumors now. I don't care that much, but my mother will. She is always thinking about how this has affected her... and oh, the poor baby. I know she is worried about what kind of mother I will be. She continually reminds me that my partying ways will be over. That life will no longer be about me, but rather my baby and my family life with Sam. Oh how I resent these comments. I want her, Sam, and everyone else to know that I will get my life back! I will be a good mother to this baby. I it will not stop me from doing things for me, like getting my body back and looking for a modeling agent.

I desperately want a modeling career. I will not let this baby will not stop me!

November 14, 1978

I gave birth to John Michael O'Malley at 1:30 pm yesterday. He is 8 pounds 1 ounce and 20 ½ inches long with no hair! Sam and I named him Jack after his paternal grandfather. Labor was far worse than I expected. The last several weeks have been miserable since sleeping was so difficult. It started with cramping in my back, which crept around to my stomach. I woke Sam at 2 in the morning and we headed down to Methodist Hospital. After almost 10 hours of labor and two whole hours of pushing, Jack finally arrived.

When he was placed in my arms I didn't know what to feel. It was almost like the nurse handed me a doll. I didn't FEEL anything but tired and sore. All I could think about was having Sam get me a milkshake from Steak-n-Shake. Is this bad? Should I be feeling like I am madly in love with this little being? He is awfully cute, but he looks just like him, "him" not being Sam.

I thought about how I might be deceiving Sam when I filled out the birth certificate. I know deep down that Jack is not his baby. I have started to believe my own lie. The last time we slept together before our break up was Valentine's Day. He had taken me to Hollyhock Hill. After dinner we decided to head to Holliday Park for a hike. Having sex in the car was not ideal, but both of our parents were home for the night and there were no other options. After we finished, Sam asked about my plans for the upcoming weekend. I told him I was going to a movie with Julie, Scott, and Greg. He said it sounded like a double date. I assured him that we were all just friends. (Sometimes Greg and I were friends with benefits. Greg wasn't boyfriend material, but he was so cute.)

This led to a huge argument that ended with Sam dropping me off at the Peaches Record Store on the Broad Ripple strip. That was the end. Until the day I arrived on his porch step to tell him I was pregnant.

A part of me feels guilty for harboring this secret. I know exactly who the father is. The thought of it makes me sick!

My plan has worked. So, I have to move past these guilty thoughts. I need to focus on my life with Sam and Jack.

The birth certificate reads......

Mother: Cynthia Ann Napier
Father: Samuel Paul O'Malley
Child: John Michael O'Malley
Birthdate: November 14, 1978

December 1978

It's Christmas time! The Broad Ripple villagers are out and about getting ready for all the festivities, while I'm stuck in this little house on Crestview with a baby who won't stop crying. I'm alone almost all the time. Sam

works nights then picks up extra shifts on his days off. My only outlet is to take Jack to my mother's or to Mary Alice's so I can go out with my friends. I have been doing this more often and I think Sam is starting to resent the fact that I am spending so much money. He gives me an allowance which I seem to go through faster and faster each week.

I tell my mom I am going to the grocery or a movie then I meetup with my old drinking buddies at the Monkey's Tail. Part of me feels bad about this, but I am just so bored. I feel so cooped up at home. I find myself constantly thinking about the life I had planned before I got pregnant.

My dream of modeling is now a broken reality. My plan was to move to New York City after high school and get signed with the Ford Modeling Agency. I am only ten pounds away from my pre-baby weight. I know in my heart this will never happen. I am stuck in this little house, with this little baby, and with little love for the man I am married to.

March 16, 1978

I can't believe I haven't written in so long. So much is still the same, yet so much has changed. My double life has doubled back on me. It all started when I was pulled over for drinking and driving. Of course, my father-in-law tried to help as best he could, getting the charges dropped. But a few weeks later I was busted with marijuana. Greg and I had decided to get high before a 4 pm movie at Glendale. We stopped by Broad Ripple Park for a quick smoke down by the river. On our way back to the car a police officer stopped us. He started asking questions, like why we weren't in school. We were so stoned we couldn't stop laughing. Then the officer noticed a pipe sticking out of Greg's blue jeans. Now he had probable cause to search my handbag, where he found an

ounce of pot. I was arrested for possession of an illegal substance.

I was numb. I just didn't care anymore. This time my father-in-law was furious. He couldn't even look at me, let alone speak to me. He did his best to keep the arrest from Sam, but eventually he told him. As usual, Sam was silently angry. I begged him to talk to me. I thought he would yell, but his silence was far worse. I grew up in a home where we argued and got our feelings out. The silent treatment was a new experience for me. I didn't like it at all. When Sam did speak, all he could say was that he was extremely hurt and disappointed with me. That was it!

My next "offense was the final straw for Sam. Drunk and high one evening with my friends I left the bar with this cute guy who had been buying me drinks all night. Though he was a stranger, there was a confidence about him that turned me on. Sam was a cop, but he wasn't very manly at all. I felt like the man in our relationship, which made sex with Sam a very undesirable thing. The guy from the bar was all man. There was something about a bad boy that got me hot. Plus, they know how to fuck the way I like it, hard and rough. We had nowhere to go so we ended up fooling around in his car.

While I was going down on him we got busted by a cop. The next thing I knew we were charged with public indecency, performing a lewd act in public. Looking back now, I think I wanted to get caught so I could get out of the miserable existence I was living.

The charges swept through the entire police station like lightning. Sam heard it before his father had a chance to tell him. Humiliated and upset, he left early from his shift. He went back to our house, and began packing. I tried to talk to him, to explain I was just acting out because I was bored. I would have never done any of those things if I had not been drunk and high. I begged

and pleaded, telling him I would get counseling. When he finished packing his suitcase and duffel bag he left. He didn't even say goodbye. He shut me out of his life completely. He wanted nothing to do with me. The next day Sam filed for divorce. Oh my god how am I going to support myself and my baby. I'm still in high school and Sam will not be able to support us financially. Why did I push him away. I'm am so screwed! I shouted inside my head. I guess the only option for me now is to head back to Mommy Dearest or Drunken Daddy.

JACK

CHAPTER SEVEN

"True love is finding your soulmate in your best friend"
~ Faye Hall

Jack Napier - Day 18

As a child I was shuffled between a feuding mother and daughter like a chess piece that my mom held hostage, but my Grandma Daisy cherished.

Living with my mother never lasted for long. That's because we lived with Grandpa Bob. Together they were a full-fledged codependent couple. Their relationship was not one of a father and daughter. It was more like Sid Vicious and Nancy Spungen.

After my mother's wedding, Grandma Daisy filed for divorce and Grandpa Bob disappeared for several years. I think when he returned and came back into my mother's life he tried to make up for not being there after she got married.

There was uncomfortable undertone to the way they interacted with each other. Nevertheless, they were

inseparable, always there to support each other's addiction. When Grandpa Bob got really drunk he would start pimping my mother out to his friends like she was a prostitute. When this happened I'd sneak out to my treehouse and draw. I don't even want to know what went down when I was gone. Like Grandma Daisy once told me, "Some things are better unknown; revealed they can leave a permanent scar." Grandma was right, I didn't have much room for another scar and scars on top of scars start to disfigure one's soul.

Grandpa Bob would go on drinking binges, disappearing for weeks at a time. When this happened, my mother would be stuck with me. This was never a good situation. She would try to behave because she knew Grandma Daisy would find out, which would give her grounds to get custody of me. My mother wasn't about to give up her shiny chess piece. So when she couldn't cruise the bars, the party was brought to the house. It was pretty horrible. There was an endless parade of men in and out of the house. Having a ten year old kid around was definitely a buzzkill. During these times my mother would break down and send me to Grandma Daisy's.

At one point it got so bad Grandma Daisy forced my mom to enroll me in the elementary school in her district. This way she didn't have to keep driving me back and forth. School 45 was just a few blocks from her house, so I could walk to school in the morning and back in the afternoon. Each public school in Indianapolis had an individual number. There were about forty-eight in the city. I swear I had already attended about half of them.

That year, I was starting fourth grade for the second time. My mother's instability was affecting my grades. Even though I was held back I was still way behind the other kids in my class. I felt stupid, but school hopping made keeping up more than difficult. Especially for a kid who lived with a mother who didn't give a shit about him. Like many things in life if it hadn't happened this way I

would have missed out on something great.

I will never forget the day I met my soul mate. Although she wasn't my soul mate at the time, I knew the minute we met I could love her forever. I think people often misunderstand the meaning of soul mate. It's so much more than love itself. It's what love eventually evolves into. It's what we feel when we are old, when vanity and lust have withered away, when the only thing that matters is true friendship.

Like the beginning to all good love stories, I noticed her from across the room. She was the most beautiful girl I had ever laid eyes on. My body was consumed by a feeling I had never felt before. It was a mixture of fear with a jolt of pure adrenaline.

I was the new kid in the class getting the "who's that" stare. Brooke's earthy green eyes focused on me, only me. Her glance made my heart pound. It felt like a thousand butterflies had invaded my stomach.

She was so beautiful. She had thick, black, curly hair, and emerald green eyes. Her skin was smooth, with round cheekbones that accentuated her soft, warm, smile. She was absolutely breathtaking. All these years later the image of her at ten is seared into my brain. I even remember what she was wearing. Brooke made her simple dress with pink flowers look stunning. As she walked up to the teacher in her white, open-toed flats, she glided like a figure skater on ice. I was so fixated on her that I saw no one else in the room.

I was abruptly brought back to Earth when the teacher introduced me to the class. Color rushed up my neck and into my face like a thermometer. I suddenly noticed all the kids in the room staring at me from their wood topped desks with shiny chrome legs. The chalkboard in front of the room had the alphabet displayed across the top in bold colors.

Not being a shy kid, after I was introduced to the class, during our bathroom break, I splashed some cold

water on my face. I walked over to the beautiful girl and introduced myself.

"Hi, my name's Jack. What is your name?"

"I know your name," Brooke giggled. "The teacher just introduced you, silly." I was so nervous that my legs were shaking.

"I'm Brooke." Her smile and soft eyes pierced straight into my soul. I was in love. Yep, ten and in love, or so I thought. Numb with excitement, I couldn't stop thinking about her. I had never wanted something so badly in my life.

"We need to know everything about this girl. Like, what was her favorite color? Does she like boys? Has she ever been kissed?" The little voice in my head began to question.

My eagerness caused Brooke to slowly withdraw, which broke my heart. But she tolerated me because I was interesting and mysterious.

Being around Brooke was the only thing that made me happy. She was my hope, the inspiration that kept me getting up every morning.

I even remember riding my bike to the McNamara flower shop at the back of our apartment complex to buy her a rose. I had saved my lunch money so I could surprise her. Anonymously, I slipped it into her mailbox.

When I saw Brooke the next day, she never brought it up. Not knowing if she got my rose drove me crazy! So I decided to sit down and write her a letter. I poured my heart out with emotion, pulling words from my head I didn't even know I knew. I wrote out everything I wanted to say. It was pure poetry.

The next morning before school I gave Brooke the letter. She didn't open it right away. I wanted her to open my letter and read it as I watched from across the hall. I could picture her soft face blush as she took in my words. Instead, Brooke put the letter in the back pocket of her

blue jeans. She stood with her friends, laughing and enjoying the few moments they had left before the school began rang. My anxiety grew with every tick of the clock. The anticipation was killing me.

"Jack, are you alright?" Ms. Richardson asked as she tapped me on the shoulder.

Startled, I replied, "Oh yeah, it's time for our reading session."

When the school bell rang I realized I was out of time. Brooke still hadn't opened the letter.

This next part of the story was told to me by Brooke years after we were married. She explained that she hadn't realized what I had given her. When she finally pulled my letter out of her pocket she opened it and began to read ("My dearest Brooke..."). She couldn't help but laugh because my letter was so over the top. We were only ten years old. I was already talking about marriage!

When Brooke's friends heard her belly laughs they wanted in on the joke. Like a good friend Brooke showed them the letter. My love note was passed from kid to kid. The laughter grew louder and louder in the classroom. Some of the kids even started quoting me and acting it out.

"Oh, Brooke, I love you! One day I want to marry you and have a family! Hahahaha!"

When Mrs. Trident heard the commotion she marched down the aisle, like a dope-sniffing dog to find out what was going on.

"Brooke, we don't pass notes in class, young lady. You should know better. Because it is obvious you don't, I'm going to post this note on the bulletin board for all the kids to see. That should teach you a lesson!"

As you can imagine, I was mortified! The next morning there were kids gathered at the main bulletin board reading all about my feelings for Brooke. There was nothing I could do. Kids pointed, laughed, and called me Romeo. I was so embarrassed.I wished for the floor to

open, dropping me into another universe.

That's when I felt Brooke's eyes on me from down the hall. When I looked up she flashed me a shy smile, making everything instantly better. Later in life, she told me that she found it very attractive that I was so crazy about her.

CINDY

CHAPTER EIGHT

"Children begin by loving their parents; as they grow older they judge them; sometimes they forgive them."
~ Oscar Wilde

Cindy Napier's Diary

November 14, 1987

Jack is 8 years old now and I'm struggling to keep him from running wild. I work at the Knights of Columbus as a cocktail waitress and Jack is home alone. My mother has offered to keep Jack, but I'm not about to let her dig her claws in him. He's my son, not hers.

I'm very upset that my father cannot stay sober enough to watch him for a few hours at night. He says he loves me, but I can never rely on him. All he does is drink now that he's unemployed. When his friends come over he gets so drunk he asks me to flash my tits for them. I only do it to shut him up. What kind of father does that? His friends are starting to notice. I overheard one of them say, "I think Bob's got a thing for his daughter." If they only knew.

My father hasn't paid the rent in months. Now, the landlord is threatening to evict us. I don't know what we are going to do.

November 20, 1987

Jack brought home a live turkey the other day and was storing it in our basement without telling me. I know this because I found the damn thing at 6 am when it started gobbling. The sound was so loud! When I woke I

had a wicked hangover. I'm pretty sure my father did too. Actually, I'm surprised he made it home from the Alley Cat last night.

At first we had no idea what was making the noise. Then my father looked in the basement and sure enough there it was, a full sized turkey in a cage. Jack ran downstairs claiming he won it in some kind of art contest. That kid sure has a wild imagination! I have no idea where he got such a pet, but it's not the first time he has brought home a stray. Although, a turkey is a new one for me.

Jack gets so attached to his stray pets it makes it hard for me to get rid of them. I'm struggling to take care of him, let alone a bunch of wild animals.

March 1, 1988

Jack really did it this time. He befriended a stray cat that's been hanging around the back door. He named him Tom, probably after the cat in the cartoon "Tom & Jerry". Jack's been feeding and giving it milk every day. I even caught the damn thing in bed with him. When I threw the Tom out the back door Jack begged and pleaded with me to let him keep him.

He was so sincere and those little tear-soaked blue eyes tugged at my heart. I agreed to let him keep feeding the cat as long as he didn't bring him into the house anymore. This arrangement was working well until the Tom came up missing. Jack was beside himself. He was starting to panic. I didn't understand it, but I truly felt bad for him. He was clearly in love with Tom.

Then one morning two police officers stopped by to question me about a stolen cat. When I went up to Jack's room to ask him about it, Tom was in bed with him. I was furious!

Then all hell broke loose. Molly, one of the neighbors, accused Jack of breaking into her apartment and stealing

her cat. First of all, the cat was a stray and not hers. But Jack did open her window and take it back. I know he didn't know what he was doing, but it was still considered breaking and entering. When the police questioned my father things went from bad to worse. Next thing you know, Child Protective Services was taking Jack into custody. I wanted to fight it but we are on our way to being evicted anyway. I'm not about to let my mother take him. So Jack going to a foster home is not such a bad thing. This will give me time to figure out how to pay the rent. Maybe I can even get a roommate now.

JACK

CHAPTER NINE

"Until one has loved an animal a part of one's soul remains unawakened."
~Anatole France

Jack Napier - Day 20

As a child I held little trust for adults - kids either, for that matter. I found the most loyal and honest friends to be animals. So I brought home a lot of stray pets.

Tom was my first cat. He was a black and white billicat that had mostly white fur, dotted with irregular black spots. There was even one on his neck that resembled a bow tie. Combined with the big spot on his back, he looked like he was wearing a tuxedo. I thought that was so cool.

Tom was always looking for a little kindness, a handout, a bit of food he could pull out of the garbage. The night I found him I snuck him into my room so he could sleep with me. When my mom found out she tossed him out the back door.

I could relate to his lonely howling as my mother shut the door, abandoning him into the lonely darkness.

Tom craved affection and so did I. My furry friend loved to sit on my lap purring as I tickled the black spot on his tiny head. Hearing him purr, I felt a ray of heat fill my chest. We spent hours sitting on the side of the railroad bank looking up at the stars. Though I was an outgoing kid, I was very much a loner. Tom was my only real friend at the time.

My mom had no problem with me adopting a neighborhood cat as long as I didn't bring him into the house. I could live with that rule for a while. I fed Tom Star-Kist tuna from a small can and poured him a bowl of milk every morning. The more I fed him, the more he came around. I loved seeing his eager little face in the morning when he walked into our yard. I knew he was looking for me, and that made me feel loved. I guess it was a bond between two loners. He needed me and I needed him.

I liked all the neighbors with the exception of one person, Molly Baker. Molly was the same age as my mother and carried a thick black book that was bound by worn leather. She would read from it out loud to herself as she walked through the neighborhood at night. Molly had frizzy black hair the color of charcoal with a large, irregular mole on her nose. Draped in black clothes she resembled the wicked witch of the west. Being eleven years old, I truly believed she was casting spells as she read out loud from her book.

Molly was not fond of me. I could never figure out why. I think she was envious of my popularity in our small apartment complex. She would intently watch everything from her apartment window where I suspect she kept a diary, recording everyone's actions. How else would she have known our business so well? It was rumored that Molly (a widow) was never able to have children. I imagine that's why she was so bitter.

One day Tom didn't show up for his usual meal of tuna and milk. I waited, and waited, getting more and

more worried. Something felt very wrong to me. Desperate to find my friend I took off looking for him. I searched all over town, checking everywhere we had ever been. I couldn't find him anywhere! Thoughts of Jim entered my mind. I couldn't stand to lose another friend.

After a week of searching I was starting to wonder if Tom got hit by a train or a car. Maybe he had been attacked by a dog and was lying in some alley suffering. These thoughts kept me awake at night. I couldn't concentrate in school, and I didn't feel hungry at all. I kept looking with more intensity and determination than ever, but still, no Tom.

Then, on my way home from school one day, I happened to hear a scratching noise as I passed one of the apartment buildings that sat in the very back of our complex. My heart filled with excitement when I saw my long lost friend. Tom was just as excited to see me, scratching at the window like he was trying to open it. I checked to see if it was unlocked, and to my surprise it was. I opened it and let my friend out. We made a quick getaway. When I got Tom home I snuck him into my room. I held him tight all night.

The next morning, I awoke to my mother standing over my bed.

"Why is this cat in your room?"

"Because it's mine! You told me I could have him."

"I told you it was a neighborhood cat. That you could play with it as long as it stayed outside."

"But Tom is mine. He wants to be with me!" I pleaded.

"Explain that to the two police officers downstairs who want to question you about a breaking and entering charge!"

I looked up at her. "Breaking and entering? I just opened a window to let Tom get away from Molly. She stole him and kept him prisoner! "

"Well, get your ass downstairs and start explaining this shit. This is a bad day to have the police at the

house."

There was never a good day to have the police at our house. It always ended badly. I cautiously walked down the steps, feeling the weight of what I had done growing. It made my knees buckle and my heart race.

The officers' demeanor was pleasant when I first walked into the kitchen.

"Are you Jack?" asked the really tall officer.

"Yes, yes sir," I answered.

"We received a call from Ms. Baker about her cat being stolen."

I looked at the officer and, in a respectful tone I said, "It's not her cat. She stole Tom from me."

"She stole the cat from you?" the tall officer questioned with a puzzled look on his face.

My mom tried to stay out of the conversation, but his stocky partner asked, "Is this true, ma'am?"

My mom probably thought it was no big deal. It was a matter of a little boy and a stray cat. How much trouble could anyone get into really?"

"Well, it's a stray cat. It doesn't belong to anyone. Jack has been taking care of it and he thinks of it as his cat."

"Oh, I see," the tall officer responded. "Well, here's the thing, we're going to talk to Ms. Baker to see if she'll let it go. Technically, however, its breaking and entering since the cat was in her home and Jack opened the window and took the cat out of her apartment. If she'll drop the charges, then we can chalk this up as a big misunderstanding and move on."

My mother gave me a sad look, and then shook her head as the officers left to speak with Molly.

"What have you gotten yourself into now?" she said in a condescending voice.

I didn't know. I had no idea what could happen. By this time, Grandpa Bob was starting to stir.

It didn't take long for the officers to return. Their

demeanor had changed as they walked stridently through the back door. Both turned their attention toward the bony man stumbling down the steps with bloodshot eyes.

“What the hell are the police doing here?” Grandpa Bob asked in a scratchy voice, the kind you get from a long night of drinking and smoking.

“They’re here because Jack is being accused of breaking into Molly’s apartment and stealing her cat,” my mother explained.

The tall officer with dark sunglasses perched on top his head asked, "You're Sam's ex-wife aren’t you?" Then he looked at his partner, pressing his bottom teeth against his upper lip.

"That was a long time ago," my mother replied.

"Well, I am sorry to inform you that Ms. Baker would like to press charges. This is a very serious crime, Mrs. O’Malley.”

“Breaking and entering!” my grandfather slurred interrupting the officers. Then he looked at me. “Jack, when did you start breaking into places? You’re not that kind of boy!”

“Grandpa Bob, I didn’t, I just opened the window to let Tom out!”

He waved his hands in the air as he shuffled across the kitchen, finally finding the table and chairs on the other side. Plopping himself down in one of the old Windsor spindle back chairs he shook his head and cried out, “I can’t believe it! Why in the world would you do that?”

The stocky officer interrupted. “Ms. Baker had a few other things to mention as well,” he stopped to sip on his coffee, his stubby little fingers barely gripping the Styrofoam cup. “She said that Jack runs wild throughout the neighborhood doing whatever he wants. That he is not being properly supervised. She said that Grandpa Bob here is the neighborhood drunk and you parade men in and out of the apartment all hours of the day and night.

After reviewing both of your criminal records as well as what we've observed today, I'd be inclined to believe her."

My grandfather and mother looked at the officers, wondering where they were going with all of this. Then they heard the words they were dreading.

"Ma'am, Child Protective Services is on their way. They should be here any minute."

When they arrived they consulted with the officers, then interviewed Ms. Baker, as well as some of the other neighbors. I was then told to start packing my bags. Grandpa Bob was stunned. He just shook his head while he sat at the kitchen table staring at an empty cup of coffee.

My mother didn't even protest. I think she felt this was a great opportunity to get me out of her hair. The Child Protective Services Officer tried to tell her how she could go about getting me back, but I could tell she had stopped listening way before the officer finished talking.

Everyone from the neighborhood saw the officers walk me to the Child Protective Services van. From the corner of my eye, I could see Molly standing there, black book in hand, with a satisfied look on her face.

I glared at her, shooting an angry grin as she held Tom in her arms.

"You fucking bitch!" I screamed inside my head. "I will make you pay for this you stupid cunt! I will fucking destroy you!"

Molly and Tom's figures became smaller and smaller until they eventually disappeared from sight, I lowered my head and daydreamed about the evil things I wanted to do to Molly Baker.

BROOKE

CHAPTER TEN

"When you love someone, truly love them, you lay your heart open to them. You give them a part of yourself that you give to no one else, and you let them inside a part of you that only they can hurt-you literally hand them the razor with a map of where to cut deepest and most painfully on your heart and soul. And when they do strike, it's crippling-like having your heart carved out."
~ Sherrilyn Kenyon

Facebook Message from Brooklyn Page Napier 8/2/2014 at 11:35 pm:

I'm sorry, Tyler, but I can't do this anymore. It's too hard. I can't separate my feelings for you from helping you with your book.

Facebook Message from Tyler Ward 8/2/2014 at 11:37 pm:

What do you mean? I don't understand.

Facebook Message from Brooklyn Page Napier 8/2/2014 at 11:38 pm:

I have fallen in love with you.

Facebook Message from Tyler Ward 8/2/2014 at 11:40 pm:

That's ridiculous. You have fallen in love with the idea because you know it can never happen.

Facebook Message from Brooklyn Page Napier

8/2/2014 at 11:42 pm:

You're an asshole, Tyler! I am done with you! You are a poison!

Facebook Message from Tyler Ward 8/2/2014 at 11:45 pm:

Brooke we are both married. There is nothing I can do about that right now.

Facebook Message from Brooklyn Page Napier 8/2/2014 at 11:48 pm:

I can't do this anymore!

Facebook Message from Tyler Ward 8/9/2014 at 9:40 am:

WTF, did you really unfriend me on Facebook! I have done nothing but been a good friend to you. And you do this and call me a poison! I thought you were my friend.

Facebook Message from Brooklyn Page Napier 8/9/2014 at 9:48 am:

I am. You hurt me, Tyler! You hurt me bad. I have shared things with you that I have not shared with anyone. You know me better than anyone.

It's hard for me to be this close to you. I love you, Tyler. The thought of not being with you is too painful. And every time I see one of your Facebook posts it brings back the painful feelings.

Facebook Message from Tyler Ward 8/9/2014

at 9:50 am:

Brooklyn, you are my best friend. I need your help to finish my book. You are the only one who can help me. You know my story inside and out.

Facebook Message from Brooklyn Page Napier 8/9/2014 at 9:58 am:

I have an appointment with a therapist to try and work through my feelings for you. I want to see what she has to say about this.

Facebook Message from Tyler Ward 8/16/2014 at 9:12 pm:

I've made some changes to the last chapter and I need your input bad :-)

Facebook Message from Tyler Ward 8/19/2014 at 9:14 pm:

Why aren't you answering my messages!

Facebook Message from Brooklyn Page Napier 8/19/2014 at 9:16 pm:

My therapist has instructed me to distance myself from you. She said that I have a tendency to let people use me. I'm sorry.

Facebook Message from Tyler Ward 8/19/2014 at 9:18 pm:

Brooke, this is crazy! This therapist doesn't know me. I'm not using you!

Facebook Message from Brooklyn Page Napier 8/19/2014 at 9:20 pm:

All you ever want to talk about is the book. My life with Jack is falling apart and all you care about it your stupid book. You never ask about me or how I'm doing.

Facebook Message from Tyler Ward 8/19/2014 at 9:23 pm:

I'm so sorry :-(you're right. I'm just so wrapped up in this story. It's my way of validating my existence. To matter.

Facebook Message from Brooklyn Page Napier 8/19/2014 at 9:24 pm:

You do matter, Tyler!

Facebook Message from Tyler Ward 8/19/2014 at 9:26 pm:

If I died tomorrow I don't think anyone would really ever know I existed.

Facebook Message from Brooklyn Page Napier 8/19/2014 at 9:28 pm:

What are you talking about! Your girls will remember you and I will remember you!

Facebook Message from Tyler Ward 8/19/2014 at 9:30 pm:

I know, but I'm talking about a greater purpose. I want the world to remember me when I gone.

Facebook Message from Brooklyn Page Napier 8/19/2014 at 9:33 pm:

That's a shallow way to think, Tyler. It's more important to be loved deeply by those

who are closest to you than to be remembered by people who don't even know you. Focus on making a lasting impression on your daughters.

Facebook Message from Tyler Ward 8/19/2014 at 9:35 pm:

I know :-) You're right, but I want both. I want to leave something behind that people will remember me by. Something that keeps my memory alive.

Facebook Message from Brooklyn Page Napier 8/19/2014 at 9:36 pm:

I don't need that, but I guess I understand.

Facebook Message from Tyler Ward 8/19/2014 at 9:39 pm:

That's why I need your help, Brooke. I need you to help me. I can't do it without you. Please help me.

Facebook Message from Brooklyn Page Napier 8/19/2014 at 9:42 pm:

I will help you, but I just need some time to work through my feelings. I have to disconnect my feelings for you from the book. I need to make it impersonal.

Facebook Message from Tyler Ward 8/19/2014 at 9:44 pm:

Okay deal! I'm so happy that you will be helping me finish the book :-)

Facebook Message from Brooklyn Page Napier 8/26/2014 at 10:09 pm:

I looked at the new version of your ending and I'm not sure I buy it. It needs more development. It feels rushed.

Facebook Message from Tyler Ward 8/26/2014 at 10:11 pm:

What didn't you like specifically? I need details so I know what to rework.

Facebook Message from Brooklyn Page Napier 8/26/2014 at 10:13 pm:

Let me re-read it tonight while my boys are at baseball practice.

Facebook Message from Tyler Ward 8/26/2014 at 10:14 pm:

By the way how are you doing?

Facebook Message from Brooklyn Page Napier 8/26/2014 at 10:15 pm:

I'm alright, I met an old friend from high school for a drink. I think he's got a thing for me lol

Facebook Message from Tyler Ward 8/26/2014 at 10:16 pm:

What! Brooklyn, you're playing with fire.

Facebook Message from Brooklyn Page Napier 8/26/2014 at 10:18 pm:

I know, but he's so nice to me. He genuinely wants to know how I'm doing. He

makes me feel happy.

Facebook Message from Tyler Ward 8/26/2014 at 10:19 pm:

Have you messed around with him?

Facebook Message from Brooklyn Page Napier 8/26/2014 at 10:20 pm:

We kissed.

Facebook Message from Tyler Ward 8/26/2014 at 10:21 pm:

WTF! What about Jack!

Facebook Message from Brooklyn Page Napier 8/26/2014 at 10:23 pm:

Jack and I are over. I'm going to file for divorce. I'm going to ask him to move out of the house this weekend.

Facebook Message from Tyler Ward 8/26/2014 at 10:24 pm:

Are you sure you want to do this? What about your boys?

Facebook Message from Brooklyn Page Napier 8/26/2014 at 10:26 pm:

I'm tired of being lonely! I think it's more important for my boys to see a real loving relationship. What they see now is poison.

Facebook Message from Tyler Ward 8/26/2014 at 10:27 pm:

BROOKE

True, but be careful. Don't do anything stupid

JACK

CHAPTER ELEVEN

"Betrayal is the only truth that sticks."
~Arthur Miller

Jack Napier - Day 22

It was evening by the time my day had finally settled. First, I was processed at the Child Protective Services office, then two off-duty police officers transported me to an old farmhouse on the outskirts of town.

The local kids knew this place as "The Legacy Farm." Smack dab in the center of the property sat a big two-story house covered in lap siding. There was a huge wraparound porch with white spindles. There was a porch swing hanging from the ceiling.

The officers escorted me up a set of wooden steps to the front door. From the arched window I could see a group of kids playing inside.

When we knocked, a young woman with remarkable eyes answered the door. They were a shade of green I had never seen before.

"Ma'am, we were instructed to bring Jack here to stay

with you. Tina from Child Protective Services should have called to inform you of our arrival," the officer explained.

"Of course," she answered. "Tina called about an hour ago."

The beautiful woman smiled at me, welcoming me into her home. She told me how happy she was to have me there.

The officers set my belongings down by the front door, said their goodbyes, and left. The mysterious eyes that captivated me earlier were now fixated on mine.

"My name is Elise. Would you like some cookies and milk?"

I nodded enthusiastically. I had only eaten lunch at the CPS office and it wasn't much.

Elise guided me through the quintessential farmhouse. There was a living room on my left that showcased a crystal chandelier. On the right, the room opened to a den with mahogany paneled walls surrounding a limestone fireplace. In the formal dining room located towards the back of the house there was a cherry grove pedestal table with matching pierced back chairs. Everything was immaculate.

In the kitchen Elise offered me a seat at the breakfast bar. She set a tall glass of cold milk and a plate of warm chocolate chip cookies in front of me.

I dipped the cookies in the milk before I ate them. The chocolate melted in my mouth. It was impossible to eat then slowly. When I finished Elise asked if I wanted more. I quickly nodded yes.

I heard the front door creak open followed by a heavy set of footsteps. I saw the faint image of a man with two young kids by his side. When they became visible the man smiled at me, which was calming to a kid who was afraid of strange men. He introduced himself as Andrew and instructed his two boys, Alex and Travis, to do the same. Andrew was a petite man with soft features. When he spoke is voice floated like a feather, the total opposite of

Elise's voice. It was clear from the start that Elise was in charge.

"I know there has to be a lot going on in your mind right now, but try not to worry too much. We are going to take good care of you while you are here," he assured me.

After filling my belly with cookies and milk, Elise took me to a private room upstairs. Passing Travis's room, I saw racecar posters on the walls. In the corner of his room was a bed shaped like a racecar. When I would daydream about having my own room, this was exactly what I imagined. It was perfect!

Elise directed me past the hall bath to the guest room where I was going to sleep. On the top of my bed sat a pair of brand new pajamas. Elise instructed me to put them on.

"I will come back to tuck you in later," she said, looking at me with a big smile.

Stepping over to the twin bed, I picked up the pajamas. I looked around the room as I sat on the bed and planted my face into the palms of my hands. It was the first time I had gotten a chance to be alone, to really think about what happened. Suddenly, I was overcome with fear. Nothing was familiar to me. The thought of never seeing Brooke again invaded my mind. Anxiety paralyzed my thoughts. I was struggling to breathe. I could feel my heart pounding in my temples.

Lying down, I closed my eyes and took slow, shallow breaths. Eventually, I fell asleep.

When Elise came back to tuck me in, she sat beside me and gently rubbed my back. She spoke in the most soothing voice.

"Everything's going to be okay. You're safe. We love you, Jack."

She then kissed my forehead and said goodnight…

I woke in the morning to the smell of heaven. Feeling like I could already taste the bacon, eggs, and sausage, I raised onto my elbows. I breathed in all the wonderful

scents wafting through the old farmhouse. My stomach was growling.

I popped out of bed and saw a handwritten note sitting neatly on a stack of clothes that Elise left for me.

Jack,

These are for you. Jump in the shower, get dressed, and join us for breakfast.

Love,
Elise

In a flash I was finished with my shower, dressed, and followed the heavenly smells to the kitchen. Walking into the room I was welcomed to breakfast by the whole family. It felt like I was in one of those cheesy 1980s sitcoms, only this was real.

Elise brought me a hot plate of food filled with juicy sausage, sizzling bacon, and scrambled eggs. My fork was ready before the food hit the table. Elise poured me a cold glass of milk and set it next to the half-eaten food. I couldn't believe these people could be so nice to someone they just met. At my mother's house I was the only one out of bed in the morning. I had to pinch myself to make sure this wasn't a dream. I wolfed down my food. I am sure they had never seen anyone eat like it was their last meal on Earth.

Elise giggled, then asked if I wanted more.

Remembering what Grandma had taught me I said, "Yes, ma'am."

She laughed, turned, and began filling my plate again. Eventually, my stomach was so full I had to unbutton my pants. After drinking the rest of my milk, I

sat back in my chair and grunted in satisfaction.

“Wow, that was great,” I murmured.

Alex, who was 11 just like me, asked I liked Star Wars.

"Yes!" I replied wondering to myself if there was any kid on the planet who didn’t love Star Wars.

“Cool! Let’s go check out my Star Wars collection!" he shouted.

Noticing Alex getting up from the table, Mr. Howard looked at us from behind his newspaper. Its crackling sound filled the room. Alex froze in place, realizing t he had not asked to be excused.

“Can we, Dad?" he asked.

Mr. Howard went back to reading the newspaper. With his face hidden he replied, “Yes, you can go.”

Pushing away from the old table in the kitchen I got up and followed Alex to his bedroom. Travis, who was two years younger and the spitting image of Alex, wasn’t far behind. When we got to Alex’s room, we flew into the galaxy, transforming into Hans Solo, Darth Vader, Chewbacca. It wasn’t long before we were acting out the battle scenes.

“Zoooooooom, zoooooom ...”

“Traveling through hyperspace ain't like dusting crops, farm boy.”

“Without precise calculations we could fly right through a star or bounce too close to a supernova, and that'd end your trip real quick, wouldn't it?” I quoted as I pretended to fly the Millennium Falcon throughout Alex’s bedroom.

After we were done playing Star Wars, Alex took me to their treehouse in the back yard. It was the greatest thing I had ever seen. The wood was cedar and masterfully constructed with a molded metal roof on top.

Following Alex through the narrow front door I froze. It was unbelievable! There were armchairs, bookshelves, and even a small kitchen table where we ate our lunch.

Alex was surprised I was so impressed. He told me he and his father had built the tree house together, like it was no big deal. Hearing this put a giant lump in my throat…

The next morning was my first day at Alex's school which was a little peculiar. Unlike my classes in Indianapolis, everyone looked the same. I didn't like it. Most of the kids had known each other a long time, so I definitely felt like an outsider. I had been to so many different schools by the time I was in the fourth grade, I had become a master of change. I could adapt and make friends no matter where I was.

When the school bell rang, I waited with Elise while kids raced past us on their way to class. One by one the doors were closed and the hallway fell silent. I could hear The Pledge of Allegiance leaking into the hallway from underneath each door as we made our way to the principal's office.

I was welcomed by a slender, Scandinavian looking man, with Nordic blond hair and blue eyes. Greeting us with a huge smile, he introduced himself as Principal Becker. He gestured to some chairs in front of his mahogany desk. Elise and I sat. I noticed its wide top was almost bare, except for an inbox that held a few papers, a blotter that protected the beautiful wood, and a single folder. My name was on the tab. It held my school records.

Picking up the folder, Principal Becker started to read, his eyes growing wider and wider as he studied its contents.

"Twelve schools in two years!" he said in disbelief.

I slid down into my seat, wishing I was invisible. I had no idea what the official count was, but I knew twelve was a lot.

"I think your placement at the Howard's is going to be a great thing for you Jack," he said. "I know you have been through a lot. If you have any problems whatsoever,

I want you to feel comfortable to come to me no matter what. Okay?"

I nodded in agreement as Elise gazed at me with a warm smile.

We better get you to class, Jack," Principal Becker started. "Mrs. Howard, thanks for coming in and bringing Jack to us. I think he'll get along great. In fact, he's going to be in Alex's class."

"Isn't that wonderful!" Elise remarked.

I nodded again, feeling like my tongue had sort of stopped working. Looking up at Elise I couldn't help but grin ear to ear. Principal Becker walked me to my new class.

Things were off to a great start. Living with the Howards was like a dream come true. But like all dreams – you eventually wake up.

After being there a couple of months, I noticed a change in Alex. He was obedient around his father, but wild everywhere else. At school he got in trouble for shooting spitballs in the cafeteria. No one bothered to tell his parents; instead, the lunch lady made him sit at the reflection table in the corner of the cafeteria.

It became obvious very quickly there was much more to Alex than I initially thought. He was a kleptomaniac; however, he wasn't very good at it. Every time something came up missing at school, Alex's name was the first one on everyone's lips. When confronted, he denied everything. He made up tall tales trying to get himself out of trouble. Stories only an idiot would take seriously. I didn't think much of anything about Alex's bad behavior. I had seen much worse things than spitballs and missing pencils in my lifetime.

That all changed one Saturday morning after Mr. Howard left the house to go golfing. Elise was going to take us to see the new Batman movie with Michael Keaton. We all jumped in her minivan and headed to get lunch before the movie started.

Alex and Travis were wrestling around in the back, which was starting to drive Elise crazy. In fact, Alex and Travis had a way of driving her crazy a lot of the time. When Mr. Howard wasn't around, which was nearly always, they were the worst kids anyone could ever imagine. Looking back through the rear view mirror Elise saw Alex and Travis fighting.

"Boys, stop it!" she shouted. "STOP IT!"

They acted as if they couldn't hear her and continued to fight. When the brawl was over Alex thought up a wicked brainstorm. He wrote, "Help Us!" on a sheet of paper then stuck it in the back window of the minivan.

Within five minutes I heard sirens then saw flashing lights. A police officer pulled us over then approached our vehicle. He wasn't happy. He instructed Elise to get out of the car, then looked back at the three of us. Fright was written across our faces, but why wouldn't we be afraid? He was a policeman!

Alex realized his prank had gone too far. Never being in this kind of situation before, Alex and Travis had no idea what could happen. I knew all too well. I sat quietly in fear, my knees shaking.

The police officer had Elise put her hands against the minivan. Then he signaled for her to spread her legs by gently kicking the inside of her right foot. She cried as he patted her down. It got worse. He handcuffed her. Then he walked her to his squad car and put her in the back seat.

When the police officer ran a background check on Elise, it showed that she had two kids named Alex and Travis. However, the officer saw three kids, which must have set off a huge red flag. I couldn't hear what was being said, but I'd been through this before with my mother. I was sure he was interrogating Elise about my identity.

The policeman held us hostage for over an hour before he confirmed Elise's story. The officer then ordered all of

us out of the car. The questioning began.

“Which one of you put the sign in the back window of the car?”

We were speechless, motionless. Then Alex stepped forward.

Thank you God, I thought.

Looking at the officer with the saddest eyes ever, he said, “Jack did it...”

I let out a swoosh of air, my mouth hanging open.

“What! No, I didn’t! You did!”

Unfortunately for me, Travis was very jealous of my relationship with his brother so he validated Alex’s story. It was all over for me. Neither the officer nor Elise would believe anything I had to say at this point. After all, I was a foster child from a broken home who was in Elise’s custody because I had gotten in trouble with the law. I fit the profile. Now I had to bear the burden of a crime I did not commit.

After the police officer scolded me for about twenty minutes, he let us go.

Elise started in on me. “How could you do this? I am trying to help you, Jack. You should be ashamed of yourself!”

Elise was so upset we went straight home. Batman was now out of the question. By this time Mr. Howard was back from golfing. Elise told him about the whole incident, how she was handcuffed and put in the back of the police car.

“Why would you do such a horrible thing?” Mr. Howard asked.

“I didn’t make the sign! Alex did, and he’s trying to blame it on me!”

"Jack, you may have never been taught about the consequences of lying. But that's all going to change right now.” Mr. Howard glared right into my eyes.

“I’m going to ask you again! Did you put the sign in the back window?"

"I am telling you the truth! Alex made the sign and put it in the back window."

Anger blazed out of the blue in Mr. Howard's eyes. I felt like I was going to throw up. I didn't know how to convince him that I didn't make the sign.

"Go to your room! Think about what you did and don't come out until I tell you!"

Walking up the steps, I glanced back at Mr. Howard, who was looking endearingly at Alex.

That piece of shit, I thought to myself.

Shrugging his shoulders, Alex looked up at his father as if he was the victim.

The next morning Mr. Howard came to my room with a stack of pancakes. I think he was feeling guilty about not letting me have dinner the night before. Sitting next to me on the twin bed, he asked me if I was ready to tell the truth.

I had no idea what to say. I was telling the truth! I was so confused. Had they even asked Alex if he was telling the truth? Were they even considering that maybe Alex was lying?

In my head I could hear Grandpa Bob quoting his sobriety coin, "To thine own self be true!"

I pleaded with him once again. "I'm telling the truth Mr. Howard. I swear."

With a furrowed brow he explained that he was going to have to do something he didn't like. That it was for my own good.

Like a Pentecostal minister, he threw up his hands. "Spare the rod and spoil the child says the Lord!"

Grabbing the wooden chair from under the desk, he placed it in the center of the room. He then sat down. The old wood making a creaking-cracking sound. He commanded me to come over to him.

I knew too well where this was going. Mr. Howard ordered me to take down my pants and bend over his lap. Remembering what Grandpa Bob used to do to me, I

started to panic. I could feel my lungs collapsing. My chest felt crushed like a gorilla was sitting on me.

Grabbing my arm, Mr. Howard again told me to take down my pants. When I didn't respond he shook me. With my hands shaking, I undid my belt then unzipped my pants. I pulled them down to my ankles. Yanking me onto his lap, Mr. Howard began spanking me with an open hand.

“Thou shalt not lie! Thou shalt not lie!” He repeated as he spanked me harder and harder.

Then the strangest thing happened. See, I was expecting the belt like all the times before. This was nothing. This was a joke! It was almost comical to me. Spanking me a few more times for effect, he stopped. Standing up, he slid the chair back under the desk. I stood tall in the middle of the room with a look that I am sure said, "You can't hurt me, asshole."

Disheveled, Mr. Howard combed his messy hair with this slender fingers.

"I hope by dinner you change your attitude and tell the truth." He commanded as he left the room.

I was once again alone like a prisoner in solitary confinement. Curling myself up in a ball I thought about being back in Broad Ripple, walking along the railroad tracks.

After a long nap I woke to a growling stomach that smelled Elise's cooking, I was starving! If I wanted to eat I was going to have to admit to something I didn’t do.

Walking down the back staircase that led to the kitchen I saw everyone sitting at the table. Before I had a chance to sit down, Mr. Howard confronted me.

“What do you have to say for yourself, Jack?”

Feeling defeated, I looked slowly around the room at my accusers. They were waiting for me to tell them what they wanted to hear. I am sure Alex was wondering how far was I was going to push it before I gave in.

I silently weighing all of my options. I could stand my

ground and fight this all the way, knowing full well I was right. But what good would it do? It would only make my time at the Howards' harder. I decided to suck it up and make my life easier.

My throat was dry as I tried to swallow my pride. "I made the sign and put it in the window," I confessed.

Looking at everyone at the table, I apologized. But every fiber in my body wanted to reach across the table and choke the life out of Alex.

Elise smiled as Mr. Howard's face went soft with relief. In unison, they said, “We forgive you, Jack!”

I looked at Alex with vengeance in my eyes. The smirk he wore made me want to scratch his eyes out.

Taking a seat at the table next to Elise I began to eat. I imagined Alex dancing and celebrating a win of wills. All I could think was, "I may have lost the battle, but I am not going to lose the war."

For my remaining time at the Howards' I tried to stay away from Alex as much possible. When he would enter a room I would quickly exit. I had to stay on my toes to keep out of trouble. It was hard though, always being on guard.

I did well until one day, weeks later when I let my guard down. Some friends from school came over to play in the Howards' treehouse. The first thing Alex suggested was a game of Spin the Bottle. None of other kids knew what it was, so Alex explained the rules.

"The bottle gets spun and whoever the top of the bottle lands on has to say either Truth or Dare."

I had no idea where this was going to go, but it sounded like fun. Plus, I had a huge crush on one of the girls that came over. Alex spun the bottle with force. It landed on Lisa, the girl both Alex and I were gaga over.

“Truth or dare?” Alex asked.

“Dare,” Lisa said, after hesitating.

Alex thought for a moment then he giggled out the words, “I dare you to kiss Jack.”

“NO WAY!” Lisa protested.

"You have to," Alex urged. "That's how the game is played, Lisa!"

Lisa leaned into me, looked into my eyes, and then gently kissed my lips. We held the moment as electricity went down my body. I had never kissed a girl before! Her lips were so soft.

As Lisa pulled away we gazed at each other. Suddenly, I thought about Brooke. My stomach filled with guilt. When Alex saw what was going on he became jealous. Without wasting any time he spun the bottle again. This time it landed on me.

"Truth or dare?" Alex asked.

"Um, dare."

I wasn't going to give Alex the opportunity to embarrass me in front of Lisa with one of his made up stories that made me look like an idiot.

"Okay," Alex thought for a second then continued. "I dare you to say the F word."

"What?"

"You have to say the F word," Alex repeated.

"No!" I replied.

"That's the game, Jack! Say it!"

Looked at Lisa for her approval, she simply smiled back and shrugged he shoulders.

"Fuck!" I blurted.

As fast as I could I grabbed the bottle and spun it. We all watched it spin, the glass clinking against the concrete.

Please let it land on Alex! I sang to myself over and over again in my head.

My prayers were answered. I could now confront Alex about the incident with the sign, if he said truth. And if he said dare, I could really mess with him since he wanted to impress Lisa. Either way, this was going to be fun.

"Truth or dare Alex?"

"Dare," Alex answered.

I thought long and hard about something I could do to get him back for what he pulled a few weeks ago.

“I dare you to take your clothes off and run around the house,” I instructed.

Lisa laughed at the thought of Alex running around naked. With laser eyes fixed on me, Alex cocked his head side. Without the slightest hesitation he took off his clothes and ran around the house like a wiry little chicken with curly blond hair. Lisa and I thought it was the funniest thing. We couldn't stop laughing!

Elise, however, didn’t find it funny at all when she saw her oldest son through the kitchen window above the sink running around with no clothes on. Like a bolt of lightning, she ran out of the kitchen and down off the back porch. She yelled at Alex as she chased him around the yard. He ignored her because he was on a mission to impress Lisa. Watching this reminded me of an episode of Tom and Jerry. Alex was running through bushes and trees that Elise couldn’t fit through.

When Mr. Howard saw what was going on, he ran across the yard like a helmetless linebacker with pulsating veins protruding from his temples. He finally caught up to Alex and grabbed him by his scrawny arm.

“Get your clothes and get into the house." He then pointed at me. "Jack, you as well!”

Seeing the seriousness in Mr. Howard's demeanor, I walked quickly toward the old farmhouse. I stepped carefully around Elise, who stood with her arms crossed, then up the back porch and into the kitchen.

Mr. Howard ordered both Alex and I to sit down on the living room couch. He glared at us for a moment, and then asked.

"What the hell was that all about?"

I sat patiently waiting to hear how Alex was going to try and get out of this one. But when he began, there was no stopping it.

“Dad, Jack told us about this game that we were

playing. It's called Truth or Dare and he dared me to run around the house with no clothes on."

I was dumbfounded. How in the world had I let this happen to me again?

"Mr. Howard!" I protested. "That is not how it happened at all!"

"I don't want to hear it!" Mr. Howard fired back. "I gave you a chance to speak and Alex was the one that came clean. Go ahead, son."

"Well, we were playing this game and the bottle landed on Lisa. Jack dared her to kiss me. So we did. Then the bottle landed on me and he dared me to run around the house with no clothes on. I didn't want to, Dad. The only reason I did was because Jack said he was going to tell you about Lisa kissing me."

With a clenched jaw Mr. Howard looked at me.

"What kind of things go through your head, Jack? Why in the world would you bring this stuff into my house?"

Alex cut in. "And there's something else, Dad."

"There's more?"

"Yeah, Jack said the F word."

My chest deflated, leaving me breathless. I couldn't believe what I was hearing. No one was going to listen to my side of the story. Things were about to get bad for me very quickly. Mr. Howard stomped out of the room. He was so upset he couldn't speak.

Elise was at the dining room table and heard everything. She started to cry hysterically.

"You are poison! You brought your sickness into our home and infecting my boys! I want you out of here!"

She picked up the phone and started dialing.

"Never again! Never, ever again! No more. I can't do this anymore!" she cried.

Mr. Howard rushed back into the room with my toothbrush. He was rubbing soap all over the bristles.

"You want to cuss in my house? You want to bring

cuss words into my home? I'll show what we do to kids who cuss in my home!"

I thought my mother was nuts, but these people were fucking crazy. Mr. Howard handed me the toothbrush.

"Brush your teeth with it. Brush out your dirty mouth!"

I looked at the brush then up at Mr. Howard. "What?"

"You heard me! Brush out your mouth, boy!"

Putting the toothbrush in my mouth I started brushing. It tasted awful! I kept brushing though. I wasn't going to give him the satisfaction of breaking me.

When Elise got off the phone, she started to lecture me.

"I will pray for you, Jack. I will. You're a troubled little boy. I can't have you in my home anymore. I can't do it. Alex, go outside and play. I have to deal with this situation."

Alex quickly left the room, not bothering to look back. Letting out a gigantic swoosh of air, Elise explained that she had called Child Protective Services to come get me. She then walked out of the room. I never saw or heard from her ever again.

Yet I would hear her hurtful words in my head for the rest of my life.

CINDY

CHAPTER TWELVE

"These are the stories that we tell ourselves and only ourselves, and they are better left unshared."
~ Jim Crace

Cindy Napier's Diary

September 11, 1989

I am so ashamed of myself. When I woke this morning I was naked, lying in the shower next to a pile of my own feces. I turned off the water and wrapped myself in a towel then went looking for my clothes.

Nothing looked familiar. I was scared. I walked through the unfamiliar, its walls covered with family portraits. I knew no one in the pictures.

My head was pounding. I was feeling sick to my stomach. Stumbling into a bedroom I looked through one of its dressers. I found a pair of girl sized sweat pants and a tee shirt. I put them on. They were about three sizes too small, but I worked my way into them anyway.

I searched and found my purse which had my keys inside. When I reached for the door to leave, it opened by itself. In walked a short, fat man with a chest hairs showing through his half unbuttoned shirt.

"Hey, Cindy! How you feeling? I got you some coffee," he said. I literally had to gulp back my own vomit. I didn't say a word. He started to laugh.

"You don't remember me, do you?"

"I don't remember much. How did we meet?"

"We met at the bar last night then we came back to my place to snort a little coke. The next thing I knew you were all over me," he explained, winking at me like I

was a little kid.

I then realized the he was the father in all the portraits. I wanted nothing more than to get the hell out of there. When he noticed me looking at the portraits he told me there was nothing to worry about. No one would ever know what happened. How it would be our little secret.

I didn't see my car when I walked outside. So, I asked the stranger where it was. I don't even know his name. Smirking at me ,he answered, "Where the party began. Don't worry I will give you a ride back to your car."

Every mile was more terrible than the one before. I was disgusted with myself. I literally wanted to kill myself.

How had I fallen so far, waking up in a stranger's house with his wife and children's pictures plastered over all the walls?

I'm hoping that journaling about this will help me cope with what I did. I need to make a change. Maybe, it's time to let God into my life. My father has stopped drinking and is getting it together. Maybe I need to do the same.....

JACK

CHAPTER THIRTEEN

"Man is born broken. He lives by mending. The grace of God is glue."
~ Eugene O'Neill

Jack Napier- Day 24

I have come to the realization that my family is gone. That I will never see them again. All I want is to not be awake. But, sleep is like a cat; it only comes to you if you ignore it.

DREAM:

I'm at the beach house in Florida that Brooke and I rented back when our kids were young. It was a beautiful three-story home with a wraparound porch on each level except the third, which was just a tiny room that led to a deck overlooking the ocean. The view was gorgeous. The kind that leaves a permanent image in your memory bank of beautiful things.

I am on the deck. I can hear the ocean mixed with the wheezy sound of the summer wind. The sky is perfectly

blue. I have never felt so calm and relaxed in my entire life. In the distance I see my boys playing on the beach. They remind me of how innocent we are as children, unbroken and pure. Then I hear the gentle sound of wind chimes.

Dylan notices me standing on the porch and yells, "Daddy, come play with us!" He motions with his hand as he runs, signaling me to come play.

I stand there admiring my children. Nothing has ever felt so perfect. The only word I could use to describe the moment is "complete". I think to myself, If there is a heaven this would be it.

I wake to the indescribable pain of true loss. If there is a hell, this would be it.

All I want is to stay forever present in my dream, to never wake to the nightmare that has become of my life.

Like my dream, I once saw the world through hopeful eyes, only to have my heart shattered into a million pieces.

After my stay at the Legacy farm, Child Protective Services sent me back with my mother and grandfather. I never thought I would ever say this but what I thought was hell now felt like heaven.

While I was gone, Grandpa Bob had hit a low point in his life. His drinking was so out of control it caused him to lose the business he worked so hard to build. He was at the bottom, holding onto the very last rung of the ladder that descended into ruin. So he did the only thing he thought might save him.

My grandfather went to his first AA meeting.

When I got back from the Legacy Farm he was well on his way to sobriety. I sometimes even went to the AA meetings with him. I would play in the lobby while everyone told their crazy stories.

It seemed to work. When my grandfather got his six-month token - the one with the Unity, Service, and

Recovery triangle on it - he took me go to the meeting with him. My grandfather was so proud of his accomplishment. Once he accepted his coin, he stood in front of his metal folding chair. Behind him were five matching rows that made up a total of fifty chairs. There was not an empty seat in the large recreation room of the small church where my grandfather was telling his story to a sober group of men and women.

"When I was a kid," he said to the group, "my brother, who was two years older than me, became very ill. I was only five at the time, but I remember all of the doctors and hospital visits."

My grandfather cleared his throat and continued.

"He eventually died of leukemia and I lost my best friend."

Looking down Grandpa Bob closed his eyes as if he was watching a movie on the back of his eyelids.

"It was very hard on my mother. Her response to losing Jimmy was to control every move I made. She never allowed me to do anything that was even remotely dangerous. Yes, I sort of understood why, but I loved to play sports. I loved to take risks!" He said pounding his fist on the podium.

"I wanted to play football in high school, so I snuck around my mother's back and went to tryouts. I made the team! My mother was furious when she found out. She told me I was selfish, that I didn't care about how much I hurt her."

Grandpa stopped to take a breath and wipe the sweat that was starting to form along the top of his forehead.

"When I was picked to be quarterback there was a showdown. I'm sure the neighbors heard that one. I threatened to run away if my mother didn't let me play. So she conceded out of fear of losing me.

My father worked a lot. If he was home he took no part in arguments that centered on me. After all, he had lost his firstborn, the one with all the potential. He had

little interest in anything I did. I always felt like he resented me simply because I was alive. I was pretty much invisible to him."

My grandfather again wiped the sweat from his forehead that quickly returned. His face was gradually turning red like he was sun burnt.

"This made me want to show him I was someone. That I was alive, visible. I worked my way up to starting quarterback for my high school football team, I wanted more than anything to get my father's attention. But he thought football was a waste of time. Still, I always looked in the stands during the games in hope of seeing him. It never happened."

Grandpa Bob's eyes fulling with sadness and his voice started to crack. Quickly recovering he continued.

"I lead my team to a state championship, which was the first in Owen Valley High School history. You would think my father would be impressed but he wasn't. This led me to my first shot of whiskey. I loved how it made me feel despite its taste. I really began drinking heavily after the war. I wanted to forget everything; my brother's death, my father's utter dismissal of me, and what I saw in the war. I am here today to pick up the broken pieces. I want to get my life back together and stay away from the bottle. I am scared as hell because now, sober, I have to face the demons that have haunted me since my brother's death."

The 12-step program worked for my grandfather. After sobering up, he was able to get a job as a used car salesman. Morris, one of his old drinking buddies, was the sales manager at Bud Wolf Chevrolet and got him the job. It turned out, my grandfather was a natural.

While he was attending his AA meetings he met a very charismatic man named Adam. Adam was a local minster who was a frequent speaker at my grandfather's meetings. Grandpa Bob was so impressed with Adam he thought he was exactly what my mother needed in her

life. So, he brought Adam home to meet her. My mother fell for him instantly.

Seeing her father get his life together for the first time, my mother decided it was time for her to do the same. She started going to the small church groups and bible studies that Adam would organize. Within weeks she was fully integrated into his small church.

I had no idea what brought it on, but both my mother and grandfather were acting differently. I even overheard my grandfather talking about the steps he was taking to live a sober life. My mother was talking about Christ and forgiveness. This was definitely a new experience for me. I was unsure if this was just a temporary phase they were in or if it was going to stick.

Grandpa Bob wasn't hanging out at the Alley Cat anymore. He was putting in long days at the used car lot and he was going to his AA meetings every day at lunch. My mother, on the other hand, was talking a foreign language as far as I was concerned. I picked up on a few expressions like "Praise the Lord" from what I had heard Grandma say when she had taken me to her church.

Grandma Daisy's church was disciplined, organized, and everything was perfectly orchestrated. When I went with her, we stood, sat down, kneeled, stood up again, sang, sat down again, and waited in line for communion.

As usual, my mother had gone out of her way to find the most wacko church possible. She couldn't just find a normal church. No. My mother found the door to a religion that was the exact opposite of what I experienced with Grandma Daisy. Extreme was an understatement! People jumped up and down, waved their arms in the air, and shouted, "Praise the Lord!"

They yelled out words I wasn't even sure were words. Some of them ran up and down the aisles then fell to the ground, shaking like they were having seizures.

Compared to grandma Daisy's church, this new religious experience was quite peculiar. They quoted

scripture every time they made a point then shouted, "Praise the Lord! Something about the whole thing didn't seem genuine to me.

Running around in Broad Ripple, I had met my share of characters, but this church seemed to be the epicenter of crazies. The congregation was comprised of former drug users, hookers, and convicted felons.

My mother started taking me on Sundays. I would go to Sunday school, which was something else I hadn't ever experienced. When I went with my grandma Daisy, I sat with her and worshipped with the adults. This was a non-traditional church that was located in a strip mall. The sign above the front door said "THE NEW CHURCH OF CHRIST" in big black letters. As soon as you stepped through the glass double doors in front, your attention fell on a crucifix on the far wall. Underneath it was an old wooden podium for the minister.

It wasn't long before my mother had me attending church on Saturday nights as well. It seemed every time the church was open, she wanted to be there. Everyone carried Bibles, quoted scriptures, and talked about salvation. There was an air of arrogance as they pontificated to one another.

I thought it was all pretty much "out there." However, I liked a good adventure and this looked very interesting. After all, they did play fun games on Saturday nights. Plus, something felt pleasantly different about my mother and I liked it. Wonder of wonders, she stopped cussing! She actually began acting a little bit like a mom.

Unlike at home, the church felt safe. There were no drunken boyfriends smacking me around or telling me to go away. On the contrary, I was treated with respect. I was actually welcomed when I walked in the door.

Despite the churches peculiarity, it was getting easier and easier for me to accept the situation. Plus, Adam was a hard guy not to like. He had a gift for saying the perfect

thing at the right time. He even handled the hard questions with flair.

I remember asking him so many questions. "In school we were learning about the big bang theory, but in Sunday school we were learning about Adam and Eve. I'm really confused. I didn't know what to believe," I pointed out to him.

Adam explained that the big bang theory supposed that two molecules found each other in this vast universe. When they collided, it caused a reaction that spawned another reaction. The entire phenomena created what we call the universe.

He said that it takes a large leap of faith to believe that two molecules found each other in such a vast open space rather than to believe God created it all by design. He told me to imagine two people standing on either end of a football field, each armed with a BB gun. He challenged me to consider the odds that they could point those BB guns at an angle that intersects, and then when they fire, the BBs would actually hit in midair. That made a lot of sense to me.

Later that week Adam took me to one of the parishioner's farms to witness the birth of a colt. I was blown away! There was no doubt in my mind that God had created the universe after seeing that.

I understood what Adam was saying. Seeing that baby colt start walking within an hour of being born was an overwhelming experience. There was no way that was random. There had to be something behind all of this.

Adam had the answers I was looking for and I was starting to like him. He was unlike anyone I had ever met before. I was starting to look up to him as a role model, something I'd always been missing in my life.

Although Adam's church was a little strange, my mother was treating me very differently. She was actually showing me some attention. She was actually listening to what I had to say. For the first time in my life, I had a

mother. This change made me like pretty much everything about the church.

After few months of Sunday school and Bible studies Adam invited my mother and I to go on a church campout. I was so excited! I had never been camping before. We were going to fish, swim, and hike, then at night we would have a campfire and cook S'mores.

When the time finally came, everyone met in the church's parking lot that was adjacent to the Dollar General. We then loaded up the black and yellow bus that Adam borrowed from the Boys & Girls Club of Indianapolis.

My mother and I sat together in the first row of faded green seats. Under her breath she told me all the gossip about everyone as they climbed on the bus.

"Diane has been doing real well. She gets her oldest son back later this month. She's so excited. Oh, and there's Betty, she had a bout with Satan again. Every time she gets herself together, Satan comes along to take it all away. We have to remember to pray for her tonight. Okay, Jack?"

It certainly was weird to hear my mother talk like that, but she was showing me attention and that's all that mattered to me at the time.

It wasn't long before we arrived. Turkey Run State Park was only a few hours from Indianapolis and well known for its beautiful sandstone gorges. Exiting the bus, Adam and a few of the other males directed the adults to set up their tents. Then sent the kids to collect wood for the campfire.

After the camp site was all setup, Adam took me and a few of the other boys fishing. Walking up the river, we found a nice spot where Adam taught us how to hook a worm and cast our line. Of course, I had already learned about fishing from Jim. I didn't want to ruin the moment so I sat in silence listening to Adam's every instruction.

Later that evening, everyone sat around the campfire

while Adam said a prayer. Then we sang Christian camp songs. I looked around with my mother by my side taking it all in. This was the happiest moment in my life. For the first time in my life, I felt like I had a family.

After a long evening by the campfire, people began drifting off to their tents. My mother and I snuggled deep in our sleeping bags and talked about how much fun we were having. It wasn't long before my eyes grew heavy and started to close. I was asleep within minutes.

When I awoke a short time later I had an eerie feeling in my stomach. Looking around the tent I noticed my mother was not in her sleeping bag. I unzipped the front and looked outside. It was still night.

In the distance, I could hear voices but couldn't make out what they were saying. Following the sounds led me to Adam's tent. I hesitated before I unzipped the front of the tent. When I did I found my mother, bare naked, on top of Adam. I felt my heart stop, then it started to race.

When Adam saw me, paralyzed in front of them, he yelled,"Get the hell out of here!"

I was shocked. I couldn't believe what I had seen. And my mother! I felt like I was going to throw up. Once again, she had betrayed my trust. Even worse, I felt lied to by Adam, a man who professed to adhere to God's word. Well, God would not like what I just saw.

Maybe there was something to BBs colliding on a football field. Every time something good happened to me, it ended in sadness. I told myself I would never, ever, trust anyone again.

When I returned to my tent I buried myself in my sleeping bag, got out my flashlight, and began to read my comic book. With my eyes wide open I waited for my mother to come back. She didn't, nor did I sleep at all that night. I wanted so badly to be back home with Brooke, to escape to the railroad tracks I loved so much.

The next morning when my mother returned I couldn't look at her. No matter how hard I tried there was

no getting the pictures of what I saw out of my head. It ate me up inside, making me deeply resent her...

While we were on our camping trip, Grandpa Bob had tumbled from the wagon of sobriety into the abyss of alcoholism.

It all started after a long day of working on the car lot. Morris and my Grandpa Bob came back to our townhouse just behind the Peaches Record Store. They started talking politics. Jimmy Carter was president and the Iran hostage crisis was on the minds of most Americans. Grandpa Bob knew he could work out a better plan to free the hostages than the government.

It was the middle of July which meant it was hot and sticky. The air was so thick it left a musty aftertaste in your mouth when you swallowed. Morris had a brown paper sack that contained six Pabst Blue Ribbon beers. He pulled one from the bag. The moisture from the can left its imprint on Morris's shirt when he pulled the can to his chest. My grandfather's mouth started to water when he saw this.

As Morris pulled off the top tab on the can my grandfather heard the familiar "Fizzzzzz" sound. It was music to his ears. A light mist sprayed from the top of the can as a little bit of foam slowly erupted from the opening. Morris read the look on my grandfather's face.

"Here, have one," he said, reaching into the brown sack.

When my grandfather caught the beer his face wrinkled up like a Walnut shell.

"I don't think this is a good idea," he said. "I haven't had a drink in six months."

"One beer isn't going to hurt. You did a hard day's work, you deserve it. Just have one and relax," Morris explained as he sipped on his beer.

My grandfather cracked open what he had fought so hard to give up. The familiar taste was a sweet reminder to his dry, cracked lips. This first beer that "wasn't going

to hurt" was the start of one of his biggest drinking binges. One that he would talk about many times in his Alcoholics Anonymous meetings later in life.

When my mother and I returned from our awkward bus trip home, we spoke nothing of what happened. We simply grabbed our things from the bus and headed home. At home we found Grandpa Bob sitting in the dark with a bottle of whisky in his hand. I could smell the alcohol on him as soon as we stepped into the room.

My mother nodded as he looked up at her in shame. Walking over she grabbed the bottle and took a pull. She then swallowed loudly as if she was trying to drown out the thoughts in her mind.

Looking at the two of them sitting in the dark I knew things were about to get bad.

CINDY

CHAPTER FOURTEEN

"There are those whose primary ability is to spin wheels of manipulation. It is their second skin, and without these spinning wheels, they simply do not know how to function. They are like toys on wheels of manipulation and control. If you remove one of the wheels, they'll never be able to feel secure, be whole." ~ C. Joybell C

Cindy Napier's Diary

August 21, 1991

It's been a year since I was with Adam. I'm now in Fairbanks, thirty days sober. This has been the hardest thing I have ever done. There is no escaping my past. I'm no longer able to numb myself with drugs and alcohol. The memories of all the horrible things I have done are now free to haunt me.

After Jack walked in on me having sex with Adam I totally fell apart. I was dead inside. I didn't care about anything. I was popping pills and drinking every day. Eventually, I was arrested for child neglect. I was so high I had no idea where my son was.

This was the moment when I finally recognized that I need help. I was under court order to commit myself to Fairbanks, a rehabilitation center, on the east side of Indianapolis.

It's a co-residential rehabilitation program that only segregates men and women by rooms. Common areas and group therapy are shared space. On my first day in the center, the doctors put me on Antabuse and methadone so I could start my detoxification.

Sobriety is a scary thing. It's forcing me to see myself

for who I am, which is the very thing I am running from. I have to look at, and accept, the destruction I left behind. Worse, I have to remember all of the people I have hurt: Sam, his parents, my mother, and most of all, my son.

I am reliving my mistakes, lies, tricks, and deceits, over and over again as I sit alone in my room at night. I'm unable to sleep. I hate myself even more than I thought was possible. My craving for alcohol and drugs gets worse and worse every day I'm sober.

I am looking at life from the bottom up, with no money, and no place to live. My mother has cut me off and I cannot count on my father. So, I fell back on what I know best, finding someone else to prop me up.

I met my meal ticket during a group counseling session. Sy was older man with very little hair and a good-sized beer gut. Fraternizing with the opposite sex is prohibited, but I see Sy quite a bit in the common areas. I learned all that I could about him. He has a good paying job as a master welder at Amtrak, and he is single.

A costly mistake on the job while intoxicated had landed him with the choice of going to rehab or being fired.

Sy is a good 'ol' boy from the Appalachian Mountains in Tennessee. His family migrated to a Southern part of Indianapolis when he was a young boy. They were extremely poor and uneducated. However, Sy is unusually smart. His intelligence enabled him to get high marks on his welder's test and get a good paying job.

Sy came from a huge family, a tree with branches growing every which way. Every single one of his siblings and cousins had children with multiple partners. Sy is the only one who hasn't had any kids yet. I hear he is sterol from all the drinking.

The more I get to know about him, the more I like the idea of being with him. It's not complicated. Sy will be easy to manipulate. If I am going to get my life back on track after rehab, the fastest way to do it will be to make

something happen with him.

In our group therapy sessions, I glance his way a lot, trying to get him to notice me. I have to literally convince myself to like him. He is a large man with intimidating features that make me feel safe. He has a strong jaw, but he is balding. What hair is left grows around his head like a horseshoe. His face is pocked with burn marks from welding sparks, which make his face red and rough like and old piece of leather. When I think of making love to him, I cringe.

JACK

CHAPTER FIFTEEN

"Some, they didn't make it. The temptation just too strong.
How can darkness cloud the mind to what I know as wrong?"
— Kimberly Nalen

Jack Napier - Day 29

I have been in the hospital for almost a month now. My nightmares are getting worse. Last night I had a dream about Sy.

DREAM:

I hear footsteps from underneath my door. They are slow and deliberate. I feel my heart thump against my ribcage as I anticipate of the evil that's making its way to my room. Suddenly, the door flings open and I can see the silhouette of a large man with a belt in his hand. The white light behind him is blinding. As the beast approaches me I lose my breath. I am so scared! The angry man grabs a handful of my hair and pulls me off the bed.

Just the memory of Sy paralyzes my thoughts. I didn't want to but Harleen insisted that I journal about him. She told me that I need to confront my past so I can be free in the present. Actually, writing about my life has not been as bad as I thought. It's helping me relax.

After my mother's fevered dance with the "Devil" and The New Church of Christ, she went completely off the rails. She popped pills and chased after sex in her need to forget about her past. She had dug a hole so deep she gave up on the idea that she would ever get out.

I was being neglected like never before. There was never any food in the house and I was left all alone for days at a time. In a two-week period, Grandpa Bob hadn't seen one sober day. At this point his drinking was no longer a party, it was a sickness. He was now drinking to avoid the painful crash.

He would wake up late in the morning and take a couple of shots of whisky to get rid of his hangover. Every day started the same: No breakfast, no hello, just booze. Eventually, he lost track of the days and was missing work on a regular basis. Morris at the used car lot couldn't take it anymore.

Grandpa Bob didn't bother telling my mother that he got fired. Maybe he was embarrassed, or just so sick from his need to drink that he couldn't. He would dress for work then sneak off to the Alley Cat in the morning. My mother, who was lost in her own depraved party, didn't suspect a thing.

At one point Grandpa Bob was nowhere to be found. He was late again on rent. I knew this because I had found a handwritten note on the front door that said "EVICTION WARNING NOTICE." I knew from experience that soon our keys would no longer work. This also meant I would have to spend a few days in the same clothes looking for a place to sleep while my grandfather got his shit together. Hopefully, this wouldn't be with one of my mom's loser boyfriends.

I decided I was going to find him and straighten things out sooner rather than later. So, I rode my bike down a few blocks then over several streets until I saw the Alley Cat. It was tucked behind the Broad Ripple Auto Body Shop. I parked my bike outside the entrance, then opened the heavy metal door. As soon as I walked through the door, I could smell cigarette smoke mixed with stale beer and bad breath. It was packed. All the voices sounded like one giant screeching noise.

"What if I can't find him?" I murmured to myself.

Then I heard the laugh that identified my Grandpa Bob no matter where he was.

"MMAAAAH, MMAAAAH, MMAAAAH!" he belted, throwing back a shot of Irish whisky.

He was sitting close to a young lady with a fair complexion and dirty-blonde hair. The kind of blonde you get when you bleach your hair with peroxide. She was wearing a really tight V-neck tee shirt that showed off her boobs.

Pointing at me, Grandpa Bob shouted, "That's my boy! Come give me a hug knucklehead!" Then he looked over his shoulder to big tits. "Tina, show my boy your tits." He busted out laughing "MMAAAAH, MMAAAAH!"

Without the slightest hesitation, Tina lifted her tight T-shirt and gave me more than an eyeful. I had seen women's breasts in the magazines I found while dumpster diving with my friends, but never in real life.

My heart was racing like I was being chased by a pack of wild dogs. I started to sweat profusely and unwilling blinked my eyes. Finally, she put her shirt down. I just stood there frozen in place as everyone in the bar laughed.

"What do you need kid?" Grandpa Bob asked.

"What I have to say is private, Grandpa Bob."

"Oh come on, kid! You can tell me now. What is it?" he said, clearly an effort to impress his friend.

"I don't want to say," I said with a "please go outside with me" expression.

"Don't you have friends to go play with?" he asked, now irritated with our exchange.

"Yes. This is important, Grandpa Bob."

"Then say it, son!"

Feeling I had no choice, I shouted, "We're being evicted again!"

My grandfather glared at me, grinding his teeth. He was angry with me for embarrassing him in front of Tina.

"Go on, kid! That's an adult matter. I'll take care of it!" He glanced over at Tina. "He has no idea what's going on. My landlord is a real asshole and never fixes anything, so I withhold my rent until the work gets done. In return, he threatens to evict us. It's just a game I have to play to get stuff done."

Looking back at me, he shouted, "Hey, kid, don't look at me like I stole your candy. It'll be fine. Now go play."

It was an impossible situation. I had nowhere to go and no one to look out for me.

As I suspected we were evicted and I was on the streets of Broad Ripple. Eventually, Child Protective Services was called and took me in while they looked for my mother. When they found her she was arrested and charged with child neglect. By court order she had to check into the Fairbanks and get clean. This time grandma Daisy got involved and was able to get temporary custody of me.

When my mother got out of Fairbanks, she married Sy and they had two kids. I would visit them over summer break and one weekend a month during the school year. My mother wasn't happy about the situation because she felt Grandma Daisy got exactly what she wanted.

At first my mother and Sy were able to control their drinking. But my mother, being her reckless self, got restless. The stress of having two young kids started to get to her. A casual glass of wine turned into several, which triggered her need for the pleasures of something

stronger. It was straight downhill from there. Sy, trying to escape the humiliation of her actions, also started drinking heavily. They had unconsciously formed a bond that enabled each other's addictions.

Sy was having violent mood swings on a daily basis. His frustration would grow when we didn't understand his delusions. When this happened Sy and my mother would screaming at each other for hours. My brother and sister would hide under the covers. My mother would storm out of the house, leaving Sy alone with my brother and sister, knowing he couldn't leave. What Sy didn't realize was that she planned the whole thing so she could go out and party with her new friends in Beech Grove.

Sy started hearing rumors that my mother was cheating on him. People were even questioning whether little Mikey was even Sy's. The rumors undid him. He was infuriated and embarrassed. The louder the gossip got, the more violent his mood swings grew. He became so paranoid that my mother stayed away from him out of fear that he would hurt her.

Sy would hang out in the detached garage in the back of the house and develop conspiracy theories. He would write down license plate numbers on small pieces of paper and taped them all over the walls of the garage. Then he would pin lines of string between the numbers in random patterns that only he understood.

Sy was definitely very different than anyone else in his family. Though he had only gone to grade school for two years as a child, he was remarkably intelligent. This made him stand out from the rest of his illiterate siblings. And when I say they were illiterate, I mean they couldn't even write their names on a piece of paper.

When Sy's family migrated to Indianapolis he got a job at Muller Welding on the maintenance crew. His curiosities led him to learn all about welding. He soon asked the master welders to let him give it a try. When they saw how quickly he picked up the techniques, they

made him an apprentice. From there he quickly became a master welder. When Amtrak got wind of his abilities they offered him a good paying job with benefits.

I remember walked in on Sy one morning while he was in the garage. He started asking me lots of questions about the project he was working on.

"What does this look like to you, Jack?" he asked.

I knew from past experiences if I didn't answer, he would become very suspicious, frustrated, and start yelling. He would even whack me in the back of the head sometimes, asking me the same question again. I quickly learned how to placate him by answering his question with a question of my own.

For example, one day Sy asked me a question once about a problem he was working on.

"Jack, what do you see within these two numbers?" he said as he pointed them out on the wall.

I quickly responded, "Um, I actually think there might be some kind of math connection. Why is there a string between them?"

"I see. Yes. Yes. I see," Sy repeated over and over, thinking about my answer. "I find a difference divisible by seventeen. Yes. Yes. I find by seventeen. I see. Yes. Yes."

While Sy was talking to himself, staring at the numbers on the wall, I slipped out of the garage. I promised myself to never go back in there.

Despite my promise to myself, I stumbled into the garage one evening when I thought Sy wasn't home. All I needed was a bike pump for five minutes. This time Sy was working on a funny looking metal box with the words "Commodore 64" on the front. I was afraid to ask what the metal box was for. When Sy saw me looking at it he explained it was a personal computer, and he was disassembling it to see how it worked.

Sy was wearing a pair of magnifying glasses on his head that made him look like his eyes made up half of his face. I couldn't help but laugh. Looking up at me with his

magnified eyes, he stared for a moment, then said, "Do you want to know what I really think this is?"

I didn't want to know, but being nice to Sy was always advantageous.

"What is it?"

"This is how the government is going to spy on us in the future. See, we plug this into our televisions and then they can watch what we do. They have rooms full of mainframe computers collecting all this data. I'm finding out how it works because I can reverse engineer it. I can then possibly figure out a way to watch them! All I need to do is follow their connection, track the relays back, and learn where their control center is located."

At this point he was talking to the computer console. I grabbed the bike pump and got the hell out of there as fast as I could!

There were times when Sy's mood turned so sour that he was truly evil. It normally came after he started drinking, or when he had a fight with my mother. In her usual manipulative pattern, she would frustrate him then storm out of the house, leaving me to deal with the aftermath.

My mother was a master manipulator. She knew how to work people, and Sy was one of her favorite victims. If she wanted the house to herself she would pick a fight, then kick Sy out. If he refused to leave she would threaten to call the police. While he was gone, she would throw all of his stuff on the front lawn. My mother would go on a rampage destroying Sy's things, throwing dishes and glasses, shattering them on the walls. It was a mess.

During one of her fits of rage I joined her. she was drunk and I was on an adrenaline high. My mother was throwing dishes at the wall and tuning over furniture. At first I was discussed because my brother and sister we in their cribs crying at the top of their lungs. They were scared and that really pissed me off. But there was nothing I could do about it. My mother was like a tornado

destroying everything in her path. If got in the way I would just become part of her destruction.

So, I let go. When I say let go I mean I lost it. I started hammered holes into my bedroom walls. It felt so good! Every whack of the hammer made me feel better. Before I knew it the room was filled with a fog of drywall dust.

When my mother saw the damage the next morning, she nearly flipped her lid. She knew if Sy saw this he would go crazy. She was afraid he would hurt me badly. Not knowing how to fix drywall, she went to K-Mart and bought as many posters as she could find. Before Sy returned home she had the walls of my room completely covered. Not one hole could be seen.

CINDY

CHAPTER SIXTEEN

"The chains of habit are generally too small to be felt until they are too strong to be broken."
~Samuel Johnson

Cindy Napier's Diary

November 13, 1993

Here I am again two years after Fairbanks reinventing myself. I have moved in with my father, who now lives in Bloomington in an effort to get away from Sy. It wasn't long after Sy and I were out of rehab that we started living together. Within a few months on the outside, I realized I needed Sy's income to survive. So, I gave him subtle hints. Eventually, he asked me to marry him.

We went to the local Justice of the Peace where we tied the knot. Then it was straight to a place where neither of us should have gone, the Not Here Bar and Lounge to celebrate. After a few stiff drinks, a niggling bit of dread invaded my mind. I stopped myself and concentrated on all of the benefits of being married to Sy.

We moved to Beech Grove which is very similar to Broad Ripple and its era of architecture. Amtrak is the main employer. The mostly Irish population loves to drink their native whiskey after a hard day of work. Never the less there's never a dull moment! The gossip lines are like telepathic vibes from person to person where no one is left out.

A few months after we were married I got really sick. When I went to the doctor he said I was pregnant! How could this have happened? I was on birth control! I

considered having an abortion, but I decided that maybe a baby would be good for me. It would secure my financial future by tying me to Sy. Nine months later, Danielle was born.

A month after that I was pregnant again! When the neighbors found out they would joke, saying, "Welcome to the Irish twins club." This time I was determined to have an abortion, but Sy found my pregnancy test in the trashcan. When he questioned me about it I was forced to confirm what he already knew. There was no way Sy would agree to an abortion and I was afraid to do it behind his back. So, I gave birth to my second son Michael. I was now trapped in another loveless marriage. I turned to my old friends, sex, drugs, and partying for relief.

While I was drowning in self-destruction, Sy was in freefall of his own. He was drinking every day and his mental condition was getting worse. Sy's paranoia had grown to the point where he was hearing voices. He actually thought Russian spies were watching him through video cameras that were planted in our house and at work. He was talking to himself and seeing things that weren't there. He tried to convince me he was seeing patterns in his work orders, in the numbers themselves, which gave the Russians the location of U.S. nuclear missiles.

Sy had become extremely violent. I was afraid he was going to hurt me. His mood swings were happening every day now and when he drank they were even worse.

When I noticed bruises all over Jack's body, I had a bad feeling that Sy was responsible. When I asked Jack about it he got really anxious. He told me he had gotten into a really bad bike wreck. I could see in his eyes he was lying to me.

I decided to take him to the park for a picnic to try and get some answers. I could see that he was in a lot of pain. When I tried to touch him he would flinch. Pushing

for answers got me nowhere. So I just rubbed his back as he slept on my lap. I have not been a good mother to him, but I love him very much.

Despite my feelings for my mother the best thing I can do for Jack at this point is let him go. I need to let my mother keep him 100% of the time. I am trying hard not to mess up his brother and sister's life like I did his. He needs so much more than I can ever give him. My mother absolutely adores him and will care for him like I never could. It breaks my heart, but I need to let him go...

Sy started talking about his conspiracy theories at work and important people were noticing. They tolerated it for a while but when it started distracting other workers Sy's manager finally confronted him. He immediately got defensive, yelling that everyone was conspiring against him.

His boss had to call security. By the time they arrived Sy was completely out of control. He fought them while they tried to get him to calm down. So, they called the Beech Grove police who took Sy into custody.

At his bail hearing Sy stepped clear over the line into crazy world. He didn't understand the legal procedures and wanted to represent himself. When he spoke to the judge he started babbling about conspiracies, making absolutely no sense. So, the judge remanded Sy to the local mental institution for an evaluation. What was only supposed to be a few days turned into a few weeks. Eventually the commitment was for an indefinite period of time.

Sy was diagnosed as "schizophrenic" and deemed a danger to society. I divorced him as quickly as I could say his two-letter name.

While all this was going on with Sy, my father had found a way to get himself clean again. This time, he took his Alcoholics Anonymous meetings and his sobriety seriously. He moved from Broad Ripple to Bloomington in an effort to separate himself from his old drinking

buddies, favorite haunts, and bad habits. Plus, Bloomington is only thirty minutes from his hometown of Spencer.

My father found a job working as a maintenance man for the Boys and Girls Club of Bloomington. In only a few months he worked his way up to the head of maintenance.

Life for my father was easy and simple, just like the hotel room he lived in. The Gaslight Inn was a dive on the south side of Bloomington. It was a place where people who had hit rock bottom came to make a new start. It was a pay by the day, week, or month hotel. The majority of the people that lived there were long-term residents. Most were recovering alcoholics like my father.

Each room had a small kitchen just off the sleeping area. The bathroom was tiny, with just a standup shower and small sink. But that's all my father needed. He went to work during the day then to his AA meetings at night. When he was done, it was back to the Gas Light to sleep, and do it all over again.

It's the perfect place for me and the kids to make a new start. I know it will be hard on my father but I can't help it, I'm in financial trouble with nowhere else to go.

JACK

CHAPTER SEVENTEEN

"Many abused children cling to the hope that growing up will bring escape and freedom. But the personality formed in the environment of coercive control is not well adapted to adult life. The survivor is left with fundamental problems in basic trust, autonomy, and initiative. She approaches the task of early adulthood establishing independence and intimacy burdened by major impairments in self-care, in cognition and in memory, in identity, and in the capacity to form stable relationships. She is still a prisoner of her childhood: attempting to create a new life, she reencounters the trauma."

~ Judith Lewis Herman

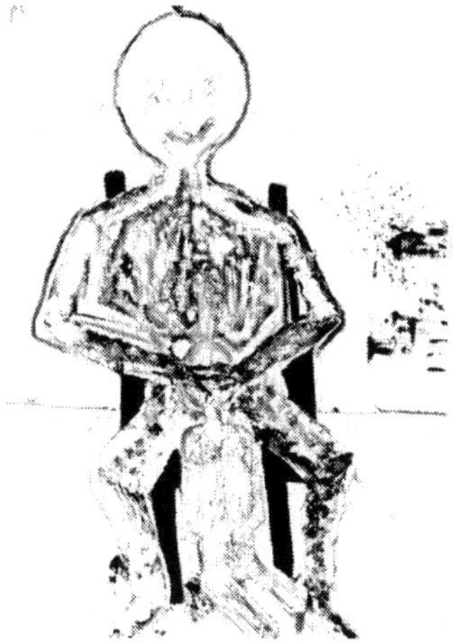

Jack Napier - Day 34

Unfortunately for me, it wasn't long before Sy discovered the holes in my bedroom walls. What followed would kill any self-esteem I ever had, leaving in its place a terminal fear of the night.

It all started one Sunday morning when I was visiting my mother in Beech Grove. My mom had done a good job

of keeping Sy out of my room and the holes in my walls a secret. But I made a careless mistake. My friend Tim was waiting for me to go dirt bike riding at the park and I was in such a hurry to have a good time I left one of the wrenches in the driveway. It rained that night, and by Sunday morning it was rusty. When Sy found it, he confronted me immediately.

Before he had a chance to interrogate me my mother started in on him about not helping enough with the babies. He tried his best not to argue, but he let loose when she picked his last nerve. All their screaming and fighting roared throughout the house like thunder, making Danielle and Michael afraid. Crying kids soon accompanied the adult screaming. I quickly retreated to my room, hoping to become invisible.

That set the tone for the whole day. I took quiet steps everywhere I went in the house, avoiding both my mother and Sy. After hours of arguing with Sy, my mother took my brother and sister and left the house for the night. I'm not sure why she didn't take me. I was so elusive that day she must have forgotten that I was there. Nonetheless, I was left alone with a ticking time bomb.

When my mother frustrated Sy past his breaking point, he went straight to the kitchen, plopped down at the table, and crawled into a bottle of booze. Then he erupted into a rage. Things that he might have overlook on another day became a personal crime against him. I was always the first outlet for his madness.

Suddenly, Sy remembered finding the rusty wrench. Hiding in my room I could hear his rage building.

"G-GOD DAAAAMN IT! Every f-f-fucking time...."

Then I heard his heavy footsteps approaching my room. My light was off. I had made sure of that. Hopefully he would think I was asleep and just go away. The sound of his movements paused, then I heard then move closer, becoming louder. I could feel my gut wrench as each of Sy's footsteps pounded like a bass drum in my

chest. While I lay still, squeezing my eyes shut, I willed him to leave. Then the door flew open! Sy blinded me with a click of the light. I opened my eyes, just a slit, enough to track his movements. He staggered around. Then I felt his stare burn a hole into me as I lay on the dirty mattress on the floor.

“Whaaat the f-f-fucks’s your proooobIem boy?”

I pretended I was asleep and didn't hear him.

“How maaany times have I tooold you to t-t-take care of m-my tools?"

I was breathing so heavy I couldn’t answer.

"I k-know you caaaan hear m-m-me! You beeeeetter anssswer me or I will give yoooou an ass whipping you’ll n-never fooorget!”

Catching my breath, I begged him for forgiveness. “I’m sorry. I didn’t mean to forget the wrench. I will never do it again!”

“Yeah, yooou saaay that e-e-every time. Yooou’re sorry. Do yooou think I’m f-f-fucking stupid?! Yooou need to take b-b-better care of m-my tools. I shouldn’t let yooou use them at a-all!”

“I'm sorry, Sy! It was an accident!”

All of a sudden the posters in the room caught his attention.

“Whaaat’s this s-s-shit? Why the h-hell wooould yooou bring this s-shit into my hoooouse?”

Sy squinted his eyes at one of the posters that was starting to peel off the wall. I saw it at the same time.

“Whaaat the f-f-fuck is this!” Sy yelled as he walked toward the poster and pulled it off the wall.

He was stunned when he saw the holes that it covered. He exploded into a fury of craziness, real craziness. Moving like a bull moose, he crossed the room, jerking me off the mattress by my hair and dragged me to the wall.

He smashed my head in and out of the drywall over and over again. A cloud of dust filled the room. I choked

on the debris. Dropping me to the floor, he stomped on my face, then pulled down more of the posters. Seeing more holes, he went right over the edge of sanity.

"Whaaat the f-f-fuck is your problem? What maaakes yoooou think yoooou have the right p-p-put holes in my waaaalls? Yooou doooon't live h-here. This isn't yoooour f-f-fucking hoooouse!"

He then picked me up by my shirt collar and threw me across the room. I was in a daze, my ears ringing from the blow to my head. He continued to pull down posters until the bare, broken walls were totally revealed.

He grabbed me again by the hair and smashed my face into the wall. The drywall dust mingled with the blood that was running down my face. I gasped for air, fighting to get away. I think this excited him.

Turning me toward him, he punched me in the face with his huge fist. My nose exploded, blood flying in all directions. He hit me again in the mouth, splitting both corners wide open. Suddenly, with tornado-like force, Sy threw me on the mattress. There was a look of satisfaction on his face as he flipped off the light and walked out.

He hadn't knocked me out, but I couldn't think. My whole body was numb. I relived everything in slow motion. Gradually, I regained my senses and started shaking uncontrollably. I tried to push myself up, but my arms were too weak.

It wasn't long before Sy was back. This time, he didn't even bother to turn on the light. Walking slowly to the end of the dirty mattress where I lay, he stood in silence. I could smell the stench of distilled spirits oozing from his pores. I closed my eyes tightly, expecting another beating. When it didn't come, I opened them with trepidation. That's when I saw him doing the unthinkable: he started to unzip his pants like he was going to take a piss.

"Yooou're a-a worthless p-p-piece of shittt!"

Grabbing me by the back of my head he pulled me up on my knees. Shaking me violently, he yelled, “Y-You pieeece of s-shit!”

He smacked my face with his other hand. Looking up at him in a daze I couldn’t believe what I was seeing. He reached into his pocket and removed a quarter-moon welding knife and held it to my throat.

“I s-should fuucking k-kill you!”

Sy’s eyes were as dark as coal cinders. I remember thinking to myself this was the end. I didn’t care, I was ready to leave this fucking hell.

“Kill me!” I screamed.

I was no longer afraid. I didn't give a fuck. A part of me wanted to die. I think my sudden confidence startled Sy as common sense caught the best of him. He put his knife away and let me go. I fell to the floor.

I could feel his sweat drip on my leg. Breathing heavily, he paused to catch his breath. He then pulled off his belt. Creating a loop with the worn leather he pulled it together with force, making a loud popping sound.

"SMACK, SMACK!"

He did this several times, I think in an effort to intensify the moment. Picking me up from the floor he throw me face down on the bed. Then he pulled down my pajama pants and beat me with his belt. I could feel him losing control.

Then Sy did the worst thing I could ever imagine. He unbuttoned his pants and removed his penis. I had no idea what was about to happen. I begged God to take make it stop, but He wasn’t listening. I was too weak to fight. Looking at the wall in front of me I saw Sy’s silhouette from the light of the moon. I heard him spit into his hand. Then I blacked out.

When I woke, I felt a warm liquid zigzagging all over my body. It randomly made its way from my toes to my head. The smell was sour and made me want to gag.

When I looked up, I saw Sy pissing on me. Finishing

he stumbled back, wiping the sweat off his face. The hair that outlined his head like a horseshoe was disheveled. I lay motionless on the mattress, now covered in dried blood and drywall dust. My body seemed to float above me. I couldn't move. I felt nothing, nothing but shame. I eventually fell asleep.

DREAM:

I am walking down the hall to Sy's room. Every step, my hatred for him building. When I enter the kitchen I find him hunched over, his head in his hands, sitting at the table.

I make myself sit down across from him, drywall dust and blood cover my face. With no expression or emotion whatsoever, I stare at him.

Sick from the night before, he doesn't notice me. When he does, he notices my unwavering stare. He grows restless, twitching in his chair. Looking at my distorted face, I can tell he feels uncomfortable.

"What the fuck are you looking at boy?" he mumbles.

I don't say a word. I can tell he doesn't know what to think.

I start to speak very slowly, very deliberately.

"One day when I grow up…"

I stop and hold my breath for a moment. Sy doesn't say a word during this awkward moment, his eyes anxiously lock on me.

"One night, you are going to wake in a cold sweat and when you look up, you are going to see me standing over you holding this rusty hook blade knife."

As I say these words, I hold the knife in front of me.

"When you wake, you will realize what feels like sweat is actually a puddle of your own blood."

Sy looks at me, his bloodshot eyes flashing with memories of what he had done to me. Finally, I see fear. Exactly what I wanted. He now knows he will have to

sleep with one eye open for the rest of his miserable life.

CINDY

CHAPTER EIGHTTEEN

"For last year's words belong to last year's language. And next year's words await another voice. And to make an end is to make a beginning."
T.S. Eliot

Cindy Napier's Diary

March 29th 1994

When I arrived in Bloomington with Michael and Danielle, my father welcomed us with open arms. All I wanted was get the hell out of Indianapolis and far away from Sy. With no job and no money, I had no choice but to show up at my father's doorstep.

To say he had no room for us was an understatement. A full sized bed and an old black and white TV on top of a dresser took up most of the room. There was a dingy smell that filled the air and the only source of light was an old ceiling fan above the bed that made a constant clanking sound. When Danielle and Michael fell asleep, my father and I sat at the small wooden table where he ate his meals. We talked until the sun started to rise. He told me about his recovery and his new job at Boys and Girls Club.

I broke down and cried when I told my father how I was going to make a fresh start, get off the booze, and create a decent life for my children. I had a plan to get sober, go back to school, and become a paralegal. I was going to apply for government assistance so I could get a place for my own to live.

He listened intently until his eyes grew red-rimmed. I could see him struggling to keep them open.

"I need to get a little rest so I can make it through the day tomorrow. How about I make a bed for myself on the floor and you take the bed?" he asked.

That night, I slept in the bed with my babies, one on each side of me. I whispered to them while they were asleep, that we were safe.

We lived like this for several months while I applied to as many housing programs as I could. I even applied for food stamps and cash assistance, which wasn't difficult to get with two kids and no job.

While I waited to see if I got into any of the housing programs, I faithfully attended AA meetings with my father. That's when I met Leo, an ex-Indiana University football player, whom my father was sponsoring.

Our acquaintance started as a friendship that soon became more. Dating other people in the program was frowned upon so we had to hide our relationship from the others.

Leo was a large black guy who was awarded a football scholarship, then lost it when he stopped going to class. Eventually he was cut from the team, which led him to drop out of school. He then drifted from job to job, nothing sticking. Desperate for money he started stealing to curb his cravings. When he got arrested a condition of his probation was to attend AA, which led him to me.

Life was getting so boring! Our coffee meets turned from cream and sugar to sex. Neither of us had a place of our own, so we would do it wherever it was convenient, the back seat of the car, a gas station bathroom, and once in the public library restroom. Every once in a while, I would sneak out of the room at the Gas Light late at night when everyone was asleep. I would find Leo in the woods beside the Inn. I knew what I was doing was not good for me, but I was struggling with sobriety. There was no outlet for me, so instead of taking a drink or popping pills, I had sex.

Then everything change. I received a notice in the

mail that I was approved for one of the housing programs! I was going to have a place of my own for the first time in my life! It didn't take me long to sign the contract and get moved in. I was so proud of myself. I made it happen.

My new place was a nice A-frame style house with the master bedroom on the first floor and two bedrooms on the second floor. Of course, Leo practically moved in with me, which turned out to be a disaster. When our AA group found out it didn't go over well. Leo and I soon fell off the wagon and right onto skid road. We began drinking and using again. Sober, we sort of worked. Drunk or high was a different story.

When Jack came to visit for the summer he begged me to let him live with me permanently. I refused at first, but he was so persistent. I could see how much he loved his brother and sister, so I conceded.

I was surprised when my mother agreed to let him live with me. At first things worked out well, but soon Jack was getting into it with Leo. Then he started running with the wrong crowd. He was only 15 years old! I could see the slippery slope he was on. I was struggling with sobriety myself. So I called my mother to come get him.

Jack was blindsided when she showed up.

JACK

CHAPTER NINETEEN

"Childhood should be carefree, playing in the sun; not living a nightmare in the darkness of the soul."
~Dave Pelzer

Jack Napier - Day 39

When my mother saw the bruises on my arms she knew better than to make me come back and visit. Hell, she was as scared of Sy as I was.

I lived with my grandmother for almost a year before I saw my mother again. That's when I learned she left Sy and moved to Bloomington. I immediately wanted to visit so I could see my brother and sister. Having them in my life made me feel a sense of family, which I desperately longed for. But what I really wanted was to be back in my mother's life. I desperately wanted her affection, for her to love me.

So, I spent the summer before eighth grade with my mother in Bloomington. The attic where she lived had been converted into an extra-large bedroom. It was

perfect! My brother and sister along with me turned it into a small apartment with a TV and a couch.

It wasn't long before I made friends with the kids in trailer park adjacent to our house. Unlike my friends in Broad Ripple, these kids were wild. We would meet at an old abandoned house at the end of our street to smoke, drink, and tell funny stories.

I was unsupervised and having the time of my life. It got even more interesting when my new friend Rich introduced me to a thirty-something woman named Cathy Colletti, who had five-year-old son. Cathy had a thing for high school boys like Rich and myself. When we weren't at the abandoned house, we were at Cathy's. She would buy us beer and let us party at her house all night long. When her son Danny would go to bed things would get crazy.

I actually hated going over there because Cathy reminded me of my mother. Rich had a thing for her, though, so I went along with it for him. When we were there I had to get drunk to deal with the situation. It made me sick to see Cathy, who was my mother's age, all over my friend. Rich was only fifteen - half her age! She would make out with him right in front of me, doing everything but actually have sex.

This went on for weeks. When Rich became more comfortable going over there he would invite others to join us. These visits now became full-blown underage drinking parties. Cathy was buying us all alcohol and word was getting out that this was the place to be.

At one of the parties Cathy got on the coffee table and started dancing like a stripper for a group of boys. She flirting with one who, ironically, looked a lot like Rich. Pulling up her top she flashed him her breasts. When the song was over she found Rich. She grabbed him by the hand and led him to her bedroom.

That's when Amy, one of the girls that lived in the trailer park, waved at me to come over and talk to her. Amy had a younger sister the same age as my brother

who were friends, so I saw Amy a lot.

We talked for hours about school, music, and all kinds of other meaningless stuff. It got so late it was only her and I. We started to kiss. I could taste the sprits on her lips.

Grabbing my hand, she put it under her shirt. My pulse started to race. Laying on the floor we covering ourselves with an old army blanket. I got on top of her and started to grind. I was so nervous I started to shake inside. Grabbing my hand she moved it down to her panties. Moving my hand downward, I could feel a patch of hair. My heart was now beating so fast it felt like it was skipping beats.

Suddenly I was overtaken with the feeling that I was doing something wrong. Amy unbuttoned my pants and started to push them down. I guess this was my signal to take them off. I wanted to stop, but something inside wouldn't allow me. So, I took off my pants. Then I removed her panties. I was so used to things in my life moving in slow motion but at that moment it was in fast forward. Before I knew it I was inside her. It should have felt amazing to a kid who had never had sex. Instead I felt a deep emptiness. I pictured my mother as a kid. Was Amy doing this because she was trying to fill a hole? Was I doing the same thing?

I immediately pulled out, put on my pants, and got the hell out of there. I am sure I made her feel like a whore, which was not my intent. When I got home I took a shower. I scrubbed myself over and over, desperately trying to clean the memory off me. I was riddled with the guilt for months.

A few days later Rich and I were on our way to Cathy's. We were later than usual. When we got to her house no one was there, which I thought was odd. We opened her door and walked inside. I heard the familiar grunting sounds I grew up with. Rich was clueless, but I knew right away what was happening. I tried to stop him

from going into Cathy's room. When he opened the door he stood frozen. Noticing Rich at the door, Cathy rolled over and covered herself with the bed sheet.

"It's not what it looks like!" Cathy shouted.

Rich didn't say a word, instead he took off running. He was never the same after that.

After all the drama with Cathy, Rich and I were ready to have some fun and forget about the whole ordeal. That summer break was a blast. By far the best up to that point in my life.

The summer seemed to end almost as fast as it began. Before I knew it my grandmother was there to pick me up. She was in for a big surprise because I hadn't packed. I wasn't planning on leaving.

"What's going on, honey?" she asked noticing is wasn't ready. "Didn't you know I was coming today?"

"W-w-well, Grandma," I stuttered. "Um, I wanted to ask you something."

"What is it, Jack?"

"I was wondering. I want to know... I want to ask, if, well..."

"Come out with it," she demanded.

"I want to live here with my brother and sister," I quickly blurted out.

She glared at me in utter bewilderment. I could tell she didn't know what to say.

"What about football? You have worked so hard."

"Grandma, I have thought about it. I really don't want to play anymore."

"You're so good. You love football. You've been playing ever since you were old enough to run!" The wrinkles on Grandma Daisy face told me she was struggling with my decision. Finally, she let out a sigh.

"Your mother finally has a place of her own and it looks like she has got her act together," she conceded.

I'm sure my decision came as a shock to Grandma Daisy but I know she didn't want me to resent her for not

letting me stay.

"Is that a yes, Grandma?"

"That's a yes, Jack. You know I love you more than anything in this world. I want you to be happy."

She ran her fingers through my hair, then she gave me a big hug. Slinging her purse over her shoulder, she plodded towards the door. There was a sadness in her heart that I can still feel to this day. She had fought so hard to save me from her daughter, only to lose me by my own accord. But I was chasing my mother's love and there was nothing I could do to stop.

CINDY

CHAPTER TWENTY

"Young girls are like helpless children in the hands of amorous men, whatever is said to them is true and whatever manipulation on their bodies seems like love to them, sooner or later, they come back to their senses. but the scars are not dead inasmuch as her spoiler lives."
~Michael Bassey Johnson

Cindy Napier's Diary

May 26th 1995

There are memories that are so horrific to us, we have to try and suppress them by any means necessary. They consume the space where self-esteem struggles to grow. Their sole purpose is to deprive us of happiness.

When I was a child, I was burdened with a heavy blanket of bad memories. It's not until now that I have been able to confront them. My concern has never been for my own wellbeing, it has been for the benefit of Jack's. The evil that is done to us as children is like a virus that infiltrates our DNA; it becomes a part of who we are. If we are not carful it can be passed on to our children.

As much as I want to, I can never tell Jack the truth. I just hope that writing about it will somehow set me free.

When I was a child, I was my father's little princess. He absolutely adored me. I would sleep in his arms at night and he would curl himself around me. This made me feel protected and loved. We had a special bond that I never felt with my mother.

Then things changed when I got into middle school. My father had become a fulltime drunk. When he would hug me I could smell the booze on his breath. He would

whisper in my ear how much he loved me. Then he would kiss me on the lips like he did when I was a kid. At 13 years old, it was extremely awkward. It made me so uncomfortable. I tolerated it because I loved him, which was a big mistake.

As I grew older, my father fell deeper into his alcoholism and things got worse. What started off as inappropriate, crossed the line. One night on our way home from Spencer, my father pulled me over from the passenger side of the car so I was sitting next to him. He then put his arm around me and kissed my forehead. His eyes were glossy and he reeked of whiskey.

He started rubbing my shoulders which at first felt good, then became uncomfortable when he made his was to my chest. When I pulled away and he protested.

"What's wrong, sweetie! You know how much I love you. Don't be afraid, I would never hurt you."

Obviously, he was drunk, but there was a sincerity in his eyes that I couldn't resist. I loved him more than anything it the world.

Taking my hand, he placed it on his thigh. He was breathing heavily. Then he moved my hand over until I felt his hardness. He ran his fingers though the back of my hair like he did when I was a child. Then I saw his eyes close! We started swerving all over the road! Quickly, I pulled away as the car swerved into the oncoming traffic. Opening his eyes, my father grabbed the steering wheel and pulled over to the side of the road. Then he passed out. I was so scared, I didn't know what to do.

Pushing him over to the passenger side I got behind the steering wheel and contemplated what I was going to do. My father had let me drive the car in the country before, but we were in the city. I wasn't comfortable driving but I had no choice. If I didn't my father would surely be arrested. I wasn't about to let that happen. So, I sucked it up and drove home.

When we got to the house I left him in the car. In the morning when my mother found him I told her he drove me home then went out to meet some friends. My mother didn't suspect a thing.

JACK

CHAPTER TWENTY-ONE

"Killing is not so easy as the innocent believe."
~J.K. Rowling

Jack Napier - Day 41

Like a broken record that repeats itself, my life in Bloomington turned into a mess. Yes, I was having a blast with my new friends - but things at home were not good. My mother and her new boyfriend Leo would have sex in the living room at night while my brother, sister, and I were upstairs in bed. I guess they thought we were asleep. I could hear every detail which would send me into an internal rage. For one thing, if I could hear it, so could Danielle and Michael. My mother had no shame. No pride. No love, for anyone but herself.

Needing to release the anger that was building within me, I started cutting myself with a knife. I remember seeing cuts on the arm of one of the kids I met when I was in the Child Protective Services center. When I asked him about it he described how it made him feel better. I thought he was crazy. Why would anyone do that? But there it was, a pocketknife pushed against my arm, slowly cutting into my skin. And it felt good!

I put on my headphones and cranked up the music to drown out the disgusting sounds my mother and Leo made. Then I would start cutting myself. Each cut made me feel better. I can't explain why but it did.

I tried to stay away from the house as much as possible, but I would break down with hunger and go home. My mother fell off the wagon before she was in the new house for even three months. She was back to being the drunk I grew up with, and Leo was along for the ride. The two of them together were like wild teenagers on spring break.

I knew it was only the beginning, but this time I would be wiser. I wasn't going to let Leo do to me what Sy did.

I overheard Leo and my mom having sex in the living room one night. I had to do something to get the sound out of my head. So, I crammed my headphones over my ears, turned my Ratt album up as high as the volume would go, and started to cut myself.

Then I heard my mother yell. I ripped off my headphones.

“Come on, bitch! I’m going to fuck you in the ass!”

“No you’re not!” she screamed.

“The fuck I’m not!”

I heard my mother struggling. She was crying, begging, demanding Leo to stop.

“Please, Leo, stop! Stop it!”

Then, I heard a loud, painful moan

"AHHHHHHH!" There was a gasp then another moan "AHHHHHHH!"

I didn't know what to do. This went on for several minutes. I could hear my brother and sister crying. I went to brother’s room first, picked him up, then got my sister. I put them in bed with me so I could keep an eye on them.

“I am scared, Jack, why is Mommy crying?” Danielle asked.

“Mommy and Leo are fighting. Don’t worry, you are

safe with me. It will be over soon." I whispered.

I was so upset I started shaking inside. Then there was an eerie silence in the house. I could hear my mother sobbing while Leo was breathing heavy.

After a few seconds, I heard someone turn on the television. The sounds of "The Tonight Show" drifted up the stairs. I felt helpless. All I could do was stare at the ceiling. I didn't sleep a wink that night.

When I came out of my room the next morning, Leo was walking around the house naked like he was the king. Suddenly I was emboldened, angry, and absolutely pissed off.

"My brother and sister don't need to see you walking around the house naked. Please have some respect and put some clothes on," I demanded.

"Fuck you!" he fired back. "You don't tell me what to do!"

I couldn't believe what my mother had invited into our home. I loathed the hateful feeling I had in the pit of my stomach. I wanted to kill him.

Grabbing a beer out of the refrigerator, I could see Leo's bare ass as he stood facing the fridge.

Turning around he saw me looking at him.

"What the fuck are you looking at? Don't tell me you're one of those queer boys."

I glared at him standing there with his dick in his hand and screamed, "You fucking ASSHOLE!"

Then I turned and ran up to my bedroom, forgetting what I wanted from the kitchen in the first place. My anger was growing like a volcano, ready to erupt. My thoughts circled back to the only idea that made sense, I had to kill the son-of-a-bitch.

The next day at the old abandoned house, I told Rich about my plan to kill Leo.

"Are you kidding?" Rich said in complete shock.

Grabbing the bottle of whiskey Rich was holding, I took a giant pull.

"You're kidding, right?" he said again.

"No, I'm not," I answered. "He's an asshole! He's smacking my brother and sister around and fucking my mom in the living room right in our faces. My mom doesn't even give a shit, she just lets it happen! He's going to end up killing one of us one day, and it's most likely going to be me."

"Holy shit! He is fucking your mother right in front of you? That's fucked up, man!"

"Yes it is. I need your help to take him out so he doesn't kill one of us."

"What? I'm not helping you kill someone!" Rich cried.

"You won't do anything that will get you in trouble," I slurred. "I won't let you get in trouble. You're my best friend. I just need some help executing my plan."

Rich studied me hard. When I didn't back down, he knew I was serious.

"What do you have in mind?"

"Come with me and I'll show you."

The first part of the plan was to find the right weapon. So, Rich and I got on the transit and headed to the Walmart on the southwest side of Bloomington. When we got there we checked out the shotguns in the Sporting Goods Department.

"I am going deer hunting and I am looking for just the right shotgun, what do you recommend?" I asked the clerk.

"You look awful young to be buying a shotgun," the clerk replied.

"We're just looking. My friend here is going hunting with his dad and is thinking about asking him to buy him one," I quickly replied.

"Well, I would recommend this one right here." The clerk pulled an all-black shotgun off the rack behind him and started explaining all of its features.

This was exactly what I needed. We put it on hold

under Rich's name until we could find an adult to buy it for him. This part of the plan turned out to be easier than I thought.

I asked Rich to get his uncle Tim to buy him the shotgun. I explained that I was the only one with a motive, if the cops found it after the murder it wouldn't be traceable back to me because it would be in Tim's name. And it wouldn't be a problem for him because he didn't even know Leo. I explained to him that he could give me the shotgun a couple of days before the murder then immediately report it stolen to the police. This way it was on record that the shotgun was stolen. It made the whole deal sound okay to Rich, so he agreed to do his part.

Asking Rich's uncle to buy the shotgun wasn't hard at all. Tim was an avid hunter and all for it. In fact, he told Rich it was about time he learned how to hunt. Tim even paid for the shotgun out of his own pocket!

Several days later, I came home from school and snuck into my mother's bedroom before anyone else got home. I unlocked the window so I could later enter the bedroom from the outside.

The evening went along as usual. Leo slugged down a few beers; around midnight, he and my mother went to bed. I could hear the sound of the TV float upstairs to the attic as I started to nod off to sleep.

At exactly two in the morning, my watch alarm beeped. I tiptoed over to my bedroom window. Slowly, and very quietly I opened it and stepped out onto the asphalt-shingled roof over the front porch. Like cat, I found the lattice and climbed down to the banister. As soon as my feet hit the ground, I took off running through the backyard to graveyard just beyond our house.

It was so cold I could see my breath in the air when I exhaled. I had to jog pretty far, but I eventually found Old Man Kregen's tombstone. This is where I told Rich to hide the shotgun. Looking around, I could see many of the names on the graves were Kregen. One grave was new. I

envisioned one just like it for Leo. The shotgun was right where we had planned.

Grabbing the instrument of death, or as Jim called it, “The Devil’s Right Hand”, I started back toward the house. A part of me was feeling uncertain if this was the right thing to do. If I got caught I would spend my life in jail. Was Leo’s life worth it?

When I finally got to my mother’s bedroom window I squatted down, waiting for the right moment. My heart was racing and my legs were shaking. I wasn't ready to kill someone. The act of planning it out felt so good, but right then and there I was scared.

I don't know if it was divine intervention or what but my little sister saved me by opening the door to my mother’s bedroom at just the right moment. I could see her silhouette swimming in the light behind her. She was crying, telling my mother about a horrible nightmare she’d just had. My mother picked her up and put her in the bed.

My body went limp with relief. There was no way I could go through with my plan now. I sat against the house watching my breath as I exhaled into the bitter cold. Although I was relieved, I felt like a coward.

I put the shotgun back under the pile of sticks and leaves behind the tombstone in the graveyard. then I went back to the house, climbed up the lattice, and through my window. Although I was back in bed, my eyes never closed.

When Rich went to the cemetery at five in the morning, he found the shotgun right where I had told him I would leave it. Rich’s part of the plan was to get rid of the evidence.

After discarding several other ideas he came up with an ingenious plan. If he broke down the shotgun in to pieces, hiding parts in different areas of the lake. No one would ever figure it out even if they found one part. So piece-by-piece, barrel, trigger, butt, chamber, bolt, sling

and site, he divided the pieces into three different plastic bags.

At six thirty sharp, Rich hefted his backpack onto his shoulders and left for school. He wanted to drop the parts into the lake before anyone's prying eyes would be awake to see him.

Rich threw the pieces of the first bag into the main part of lake. Then he walked to the opposite side and with sweaty hands despite the cold, he undid the top of the second bag, scanned the lake for walkers, and threw the pieces into the water. He then took the last bag to a dense stand of cattails in a sort of swampy area and threw the rest of the pieces into the mud. Each piece sunk like the lake was eating them for breakfast.

After that, Rich ran to school, breathing more easily when he joined a group of kids all trying to avoid the tardy bell.

I was already in class, sitting at my desk yawning, when Rich walked in. He approached me with a look that said, "Tell me what happened right now, or I will punch you in the face."

"I couldn't do it," I whispered.

"What!?" Rich replied with a stunned look on his face that quickly melted into a look of relief. After a few seconds he continued, "Are you kidding me?"

"No, my sister walked into the room just as I was opening the window. I couldn't go through with it with her in the room."

"Well, guess what?"

"What?" I said as I looked at Rich and suddenly realized that he had gotten rid of the evidence.

"Yeah, my uncle is going to go ape shit when I tell him I lost it."

"SHIT!" I shouted, which turned all eyes on me.

"SHHHHHHH! What did you expect?" Rich fired back. "I thought you went through with it."

I was secretly happy the plan fell through but I felt

bad for putting Rich in this position with his uncle....

Weeks went by and Leo remained the asshole that he was. It was event getting worse. I was starting to regret my decision to not kill him.

The only pleasure I had was my secret, knowing that Leo had no idea how close he came to dying. I visualized killing him over and over again. Even though I knew I could never do it, it helped me get through the day.

I was now spending a lot of time at the old abandoned house. I was even spending the night there. I would drink myself to sleep.

I remember waking up at the abandoned house one morning to the faint sound of crying. I stumbled around the house until I found where it was coming from. It was a cat. I found it curled up in a ball in one of the broken-down closets. It didn't look like it felt very well. Not sick, just not well. It was a billicat like Tom which made me smile.

Sitting down next to my new friend, I started petting it. I noticed she had a tight, swollen belly.

"Are you pregnant, girl? You look like you are ready to give birth soon," I murmured. "Don't worry girl, I will take care of you."

I had to leave soon because it was getting very late and I wanted to sleep in my own bed for a change. Maybe I could sneak into the house, grab something to eat, and go to bed without anyone knowing I was home, I thought.

Two days later when I returned to the abandoned house, mama cat had given birth. I was the first to meet the fuzzy little furballs that lay beside her. In fact, I was the only one that even knew these little critters existed. The abandoned house had become my second home. I spent more time there than any of my friends.

This next part of the story is something that I am very ashamed of. A few weeks after the kittens were born I got drunk and something invaded my brain. I cannot fully explain why I did what I did, but it's something I relive in

my dreams to this day.

DREAM:

There is a stray cat in my house. I throw it out but It keeps coming back. When I close the door it just appears back in the house. I become angry and strangle it. It won't stop so I try and kill it. It won't die. It just keeps coming at me until I wake.

I bet I have had this dream a hundred times over the years.

At the abandoned house I was playing with one of the kittens when the image of Leo entered my head. He was forcing my mother to have sex with him. The images rushed at me like cars colliding. The sounds of moans, groans, and crying rang loud in my ears. I wanted to kill him.

That's when I realized I was gripping the kitten's neck with my left hand and slapping it with my right. It was frantically trying to get away, but I held it tight. I slapped it again and again, each blow making me feel better. It released something inside me I knew was wrong, but it felt good. I had control! The slapping soon turned into punches.

"You motherfucker, I will fucking kill you!" I screamed.

I wanted the kitten to feel my pain. I wanted it to suffer just like I did. Putting both my hands around its neck I started choking the life out of the kitten. It tried to climb my arm with its back paws, leaving deep scratches. It thrashed to get free. The more it fought the harder I squeezed. I could see the fear in its eyes. It was so scared it shit itself. Only then did I come to my senses.

Controlling the monster that was struggling to get out, I started shaking. I put the kitten down.

I was mortified by what I had done. The look of terror

in the kitten's eyes scribbled a haunting picture on my brain that would torment me for the rest of my life. I couldn't believe what I had done. Worse, I couldn't believe what I had become.

I was Sy.

Depressed, ashamed, and sobbing, I took another swig of whiskey. I looked out the broken window in the front of the abandoned house. The glass was so old parts of it were sagging from its own weight. The objects seen through it were obscured. The gravel driveway in front, lined with overgrown mulberry bushes, looked blurry. The houses just beyond them were oblong and wavy. The whole thing reminded me of the House of Mirrors at the county fair. Over the past few months I had stood at the window admiring the surrounding homes. Looking across the street, I could see the flickering lights from the television sets in their living rooms. I imagined a mother and father snuggling together with their kids on the couch. I pretended I was with them. These innocent daydreams turned into a new life for me. I wasn't sleeping at night; instead I was watching a life I could dream about.

I couldn't help but think how lonely the abandoned house must have felt. Sitting there all day watching the homes around it filled with families while it sat abandoned with no one to love it but a broken down teenager.

I felt a drop of sadness slowly roll down my cheek, leaving a cold trail of helplessness. Stumbling across the room, I finished off the bottle of whiskey, then struggled home to try and sleep it off.

To my surprise, Grandma Daisy was in the living room when I got home. She had been waiting on me for several hours. When I saw the shock on her face it stunned me.

"Oh my God, what has happened to you, Jack?" She asked.

She hadn't seen me in months. I am sure she smelled the booze on my breath. I knew I looked like crap. Even Rich told me I looked sick a few weeks back. I had lost so much weight, I was frail and weak.

"Jack, you are so pale and you have dark rings under your eyes. What has happened to you?" she asked again with concern.

"What are you doing here, Grandma?"

"Your grandfather called me. He found out you haven't been going to school."

Taking a long look at me, she said, "I went through this with your grandfather for many years, and then with your mother. I'm not going to lose you like I lost them. You are too good for this! I'm going to take you home with me and take care of you. You need help, Jack."

The way she said these words in her soft-spoken voice left me no other option but to go home with her. I didn't want to fight it. I was tired, hungry, and I was ready to go back to sanity.

CINDY

CHAPTER TWENTY-TWO

"Your perspective on life comes from the cage you were held captive in."
~Shannon L. Alder

Cindy Napier's Diary

May 28th 1995

After the car incident with my father, things were very awkward for me. I don't know if he had any memory of what he did or not. He never spoke of it and I sure wasn't going to say anything.

Up until the end of my junior year my father was never around. When he was I did my best to stay clear of him. On rare occasions he would stumble up to me and whisper in my ear like he did when I was a child. Like then, I could smell the booze on his breath. When he looked at me it was extremely uncomfortable. I couldn't get the memory of what he did out of my head. I wanted nothing to do with the one person I once loved so much.

When he picked up on my feelings he started drinking even more. One night he stumbled into my room, drunk and crying. He asked me why I was being so cold to him. I don't think he had a clue about what happened that night in the car. He must have blacked out. He was so sincere, it broke my heart. I love him so much and I want to forgive him. So I did.

BROOKE

CHAPTER TWENTY-THREE

"Sometimes it takes a heartbreak to shake us awake and help us see we are worth so much more than we're settling for."
~ Mandy Hale

Facebook Message from Brooklyn Page Napier 8/28/2014 at 12:09 am:

Nick called me the other night drunk. He begged me to come over to his house.

Facebook Message from Tyler Ward 8/28/2014 at 12:10 am:

Did you?

Facebook Message from Brooklyn Page Napier 8/28/2014 at 12:11 am:

No, but a part of me wanted to.

Facebook Message from Tyler Ward 8/28/2014 at 12:12 am:

That's not good, Brooke. It sounds like he just wants to have sex with you.

Facebook Message from Brooklyn Page Napier 8/28/2014 at 12:13 am:

What's wrong with that?

Facebook Message from Tyler Ward 8/28/2014 at 12:15 am:

He just going to use you. Don't let

yourself be taken advantage of. You don't want to be that kind of girl.

Facebook Message from Brooklyn Page Napier 8/28/2014 at 12:16 am:

I know. I'm just lonely. I'm asking Jack to move out this weekend? Wish me luck!

Facebook Message from Tyler Ward 8/28/2014 at 12:17 am:

Good luck I guess. Are you sure you want to do that?

Facebook Message from Brooklyn Page Napier 8/28/2014 at 12:18 am:

I'm done. I need to move on with my life.

Facebook Message from Tyler Ward 8/28/2014 at 12:19 am:

Okay, I'll be praying for you.

Facebook Message from Brooklyn Page Napier 8/28/2014 at 12:20 am:

Thanks :-)

Facebook Message from Tyler Ward 8/30/2014 at 8:07 am:

So, what happened?

Facebook Message from Brooklyn Page Napier 8/30/2014 at 8:09 am:

I didn't go through with it :-(I chickened out and got drunk instead lol

Facebook Message from Tyler Ward 8/30/2014 at 8:10 am:

This is a big decision so take your time. It's important you make the right decision for you and your boys.

Facebook Message from Brooklyn Page Napier 8/30/2014 at 8:11 am:

I did something bad.

Facebook Message from Tyler Ward 8/30/2014 at 8:12 am:

What did you do, Brooke?

Facebook Message from Brooklyn Page Napier 8/30/2014 at 8:13 am:

I went over to Nick's house last night…

Facebook Message from Tyler Ward 8/30/2014 at 8:14 am:

And?

Facebook Message from Brooklyn Page Napier 8/30/2014 at 8:15 am:

He was so sweet to me. We stayed up all night talking. He's so sincere.

Facebook Message from Tyler Ward 8/30/2014 at 8:16 am:

Did you have sex with him?

Facebook Message from Brooklyn Page Napier 8/30/2014 at 8:20 am:

Yes

Facebook Message from Tyler Ward 8/30/2014 at 8:21 am:

You're a married woman. That's not right.

Facebook Message from Brooklyn Page Napier 8/30/2014 at 8:23 am:

I'm lonely, Tyler :-(

I need affection. I feel like I have wasted the last 10 years of life, time I will never get back. I want to live again! I want to explore my sexuality. I want to have fun!

Facebook Message from Tyler Ward 8/30/2014 at 8:24 am:

Then get divorced!

Facebook Message from Brooklyn Page Napier 8/30/2014 at 8:28 am:

I don't want to hurt my kids. They are so young. It would break my heart to destroy our family. I just can't do it.

Facebook Message from Tyler Ward 8/30/2014 at 8:29 am:

Cheating on your husband is not the way to do it.

Facebook Message from Brooklyn Page Napier 8/30/2014 at 8:30 am:

I know, but I don't see any other way.

Facebook Message from Tyler Ward 8/30/2014 at 8:31 am:

Suck it up and file for divorce.

Facebook Message from Brooklyn Page Napier 8/30/2014 at 8:33 am:

That's easy to say, Tyler! You're not happy, so why don't you file for divorce?

Facebook Message from Tyler Ward 8/30/2014 at 8:35 am:

I'm not ready to give up just yet. Marriage is hard and it takes lots of work. You don't just throw it all away because the sex gets old or things aren't perfect.

Facebook Message from Brooklyn Page Napier 8/30/2014 at 8:38 am:

That's the thing, if two people were meant to be together it wouldn't be hard. If they spoke the same love language it would be natural. Jack and I speak completely different love languages.

My grandparents spoke the same love language and they were married for over 60 years.

Facebook Message from Tyler Ward 8/30/2014 at 8:40 am:

I think people were different back then. They didn't have the Internet and dating apps on their cell phones. Our society is all about instant gratification. When

things get hard it's too easy to move on.

Facebook Message from Brooklyn Page Napier 8/30/2014 at 8:42 am:

I agree but I have fought for our marriage for 13 years. I can't take it anymore. I'm missing out on life.

Facebook Message from Tyler Ward 8/30/2014 at 8:44 am:

So what are you going to do? Stay married and have flings? That's not the kind of life you want your kids to emulate.

Facebook Message from Brooklyn Page Napier 8/30/2014 at 8:45 am:

They won't know

Facebook Message from Tyler Ward 8/30/2014 at 8:47 am:

Our kids are smarter than you think. I feel it's better for them to see what a good relationship looks like even if that means their parent have to get divorced.

Facebook Message from Brooklyn Page Napier 8/30/2014 at 8:48 am:

I'm not sure I was meant to be married.

Facebook Message from Tyler Ward 8/30/2014 at 8:49 am:

Just be careful, Brooke.

Facebook Message from Brooklyn Page Napier 9/2/2014 at 10:37 pm:

Nick keeps calling me when he is drunk, begging me to come over. All we do is have sex and then he passes out. When I leave I feel like shit about myself.

Facebook Message from Tyler Ward 9/2/2014 at 10:38 pm:

I told you he was going to use you for sex. You need to stop it now or it's going to destroy your self-esteem.

Facebook Message from Brooklyn Page Napier 9/2/2014 at 10:39 pm:

I know :-(I just get so lonely and Nick is easy.

Facebook Message from Tyler Ward 9/2/2014 at 10:40 pm:

You need to stop.

Facebook Message from Brooklyn Page Napier 9/2/2014 at 10:42 pm:

I told my therapist and she agrees with you. She is encouraging me to seek marriage counseling with Jack. If he knew about Nick I don't know what he would do. I'm afraid he would snap.

Facebook Message from Tyler Ward 9/2/2014 at 10:44 pm:

You need to cut it off with Nick. When you feel lonely just call me. I will help you work through it.

Facebook Message from Brooklyn Page Napier

9/2/2014 at 10:45 pm:

Okay

Facebook Message from Tyler Ward 9/5/2014 at 7:49 am:

What are you getting into this weekend?

Facebook Message from Brooklyn Page Napier 9/5/2014 at 7:51 am:

Jack is taking the boys camping this weekend so I'm home alone. This will be a good test for me.

Facebook Message from Tyler Ward 9/5/2014 at 7:52 am:

I'm here if you need me, Brooke.

Facebook Message from Brooklyn Page Napier 9/6/2014 at 8:22 am:

I was good last night :-)

Facebook Message from Tyler Ward 9/6/2014 at 8:23 am:

That's awesome! Don't you feel good about yourself?

Facebook Message from Brooklyn Page Napier 9/6/2014 at 8:24 am:

I do! I want to thank you. You have really been my best friend these last few months.

Facebook Message from Tyler Ward 9/6/2014 at 8:25 am:

<3

Facebook Message from Brooklyn Page Napier 9/7/2014 at 8:00 am:

OMG, Nick wouldn't stop calling me last night. When I didn't answer his calls or text messages he got hostile. Look at this message:

Where the fuck are you, Brooke!! Why aren't you answering my calls or text messages? This is bullshit! Are you fucking someone else?

You better hope you're not with some other guy!

Facebook Message from Tyler Ward 9/4/2014 at 8:01 am:

That's not good, Brooke!

Facebook Message from Brooklyn Page Napier 9/4/2014 at 8:03 am:

I know, then this morning he sent me a message apologizing. He said he was drunk and worried about me. I think he's bipolar!

Facebook Message from Tyler Ward 9/4/2014 at 8:04 am:

This is not a good situation! You need to stay far away from him.

CINDY

CHAPTER TWENTY-FOUR

"In the end one needs more courage to live than to kill himself."
~ Albert Camus

Cindy Napier's Diary

May 31 1995

My life is filled with nothing but emptiness and regret. I have dug a hole so deep there is no getting out. All I can do is self-medicate to cope with the hatred I have for myself.

I had so much potential before my senior year in high school. My modeling career was starting to take off, I had professional pictures taken, and my mother and I were talking to an agent in New York City. My life was so exciting.

Then came Jack. I have never come to grips with the circumstances that caused my pregnancy. In fact, I have tried to block it out of my memory my entire life. But it has caught up to me in the wake of my father's death.

Jack's father is... my father.

Even writing this makes my stomach feel like it's filled with razorblades.

It happened my junior year in high school. My father was buying me and my friend's alcohol and our house had become the place to party. In my father's warped brain, having the party at the house was his way of being a part of my life. He would get so drunk he would completely black out. His relationship with my mother was completely falling apart. She was working three jobs to keep the bills paid which left me alone with my father

most of the time.

When my father would get really drunk he would crawl in bed with me and try cuddle. At first it was innocent, like when I was a child. But, then it became inappropriate. I was drinking myself and would barely remember the night before.

On carbonation day at the Indy 500 my life changed forever. The sad thing is I don't even remember. My friends and I skipped school to go to the track. It was an all day party followed by an all-night party back at my house. That's when I blacked out.

I woke up the next morning in bed with my father! I didn't have any clothes on and neither did he. I was shocked. I immediately got dressed. My father was passed out. Even in death he has no idea what happened. As far as he knows he woke up alone.

At first, I just thought we were drunk, that I had fallen asleep in my father's bed like I did when I was a kid. But when my period was late I became concerned. I really didn't think anything happened between my father and me. But when Jack was born I just knew in my gut my father was responsible. A mother has an intuition about these things. I never said anything to anyone about this. My father was clueless and I left it that way.

In a weird way I needed him to be close to Jack. In the process of doing this I became dependent on him. When he died all of this came back to haunt me. I don't want to fuck up Jack's life like my father fucked up mine. Despite the resentment I have for my mother, I asked her to raise him. I asked her to make sure he has a chance at life. Now it's time for me to rest.

My Wishes for My Death:

1. *No keeping me alive on tubes, cutting off of anything.*

2. *Celebration of life after I am cremated.*
3. *Ashes are to be given to my daughter & she can decide how to handle this.*
4. *Do not weep for me, for I am a woman of faith and have made my peace and have been forgiven by Christ & my love of Mary, St. Dympha, St. Rita, and St. Michael.*
5. *My wishes are that you love one another as Christ has loved us.*
6. *Replace anger with forgiving your enemies, because you only hurt yourself by being angry.*
7. *The world is the opposite of the spiritual world. The Jewish Bible is read from back to front.*
8. *My body may have died, but my spirit lives on forever, and I will always be in your heart.*
9. *I loved all of you very much, and like the song 'Purple Rain', I never meant to cause you any sorrow, I only wanted to see you laughing in the purple rain.*
10. *May God in the name of Jesus, Mary & all the saints & angels bless you & all of the future generations in our family always.*
11. *I will always be with you in spirit.*
12. *A quote from Wayne Dyer: "Goodbye my past, I kissed it, hey kids, I wouldn't have missed it."*
13. *Do not cry for me because I have gone back to the one that created me. I am in the arms of Christ, & with those that have just stepped over to another realm.*

See you all on the other side.

Love & Peace Always
Mom

JACK

CHAPTER TWENTY-FIVE

"Here, from her ashes you lay. A broken girl so lost in despondency that you know that even if she does find her way out of this labyrinth in hell, that she will never see, feel, taste, or touch life the same again."
~ Amanda Steele

Jack Napier - Day 49

After I got settled in with Grandma Daisy, I was greeted with bad news. Grandpa Bob had a massive heart attack and died unexpectedly. I immediately remembered the turkey in the basement, sitting on his lap while he told me his war stories, and the times we spent together at his AA meetings.

Grandpa Bob had been sober for many years. But loneliness eventually snuck up on him. He didn't jump of a bridge like Jim. Instead, he put a whiskey bottle in his mouth and like pulling the trigger of a gun, he let it kill him. My mother was now left with no one to take care of her.

My head filled with regret because once I left Bloomington I never went back. Which meant I didn't

have a chance to see Grandpa Bob before he died. I felt horrible.

I was starting to withdraw, becoming invisible to those around me. I tried to reconnect with Brooke but things were so different between us now. It was nothing like it was when we were in grade school.

I remember having a brief exchange with her that put things in perspective. As usual when I saw her my face lit up like a Christmas tree. When she told me all about how she got accepted to Indiana University the lights flicker off. I would be lucky to even graduate high school at that point, I thought to myself. She didn't have to say it, I could see it in her expression when she asked me what colleges I applied to.

"I'm thinking about taking a year off before I start college," I replied, trying to cover up the fact I wasn't sure I was going to even graduate high school. She told me she thought that was great. But what I heard was, "You're a loser, Jack."

I was sure Brooke would move on and I would never see her again. The spark we had between us was now fading into the shadows of my broken heart. Then came the knockout blow.

Grandma was sitting at the dining room table with her head in her hands when I got home. I could immediately feel her sorrow as soon as I walked through the door. I saw pain written across the wrinkles in her face. There were dark bags under her eyes. I knew something was seriously wrong.

"What is it, Grandma?" I asked.

"Jack, you better sit down..." she murmured.

Sitting down in the chair across from her I thought, *What could be so bad that I need to sit down?* Then it dawned on me. There was only one person in the world that could cause my grandmother that much grief. It couldn't be anyone else.

"It's your mother, Jack. She has been burning her

candle at both ends for years. It's finally caught up with her."

"Is she..." My eyes grew large and my stomach began to sour.

She gazed at me, years of pain and disappointment rolling down her cheeks, smearing mascara all the way to her chin. She slowly nodded her head, as if in slow motion. I sat in disbelief.

"How? How, Grandma?"

Grandma Daisy curled her chin into her chest and looked down at the table.

"They believe she overdosed on methadone. However, it could have been a combination of a lot of different drugs. Whatever it was, it caused her heart to stop. When the paramedics tried to revive her, it was just too late. Her brain was deprived of oxygen for too long. She is brain dead and they want us to take her off of life support."

Grandma Daisy reached across the table and held my hand. The two of us just sat there as the sun sank into the Earth, casting a blanket of darkness upon us.

I wasn't sad at this point. I was shocked. There were a thousand emotions running through my head. I was angry, disappointed, and distressed that she couldn't have just been a regular mother.

Over the next couple of days, I spent a lot of time at the hospital, talking with the doctors and reliving my life with her.

There was nothing we could do to save her at this point. My mother was brain dead. Grandma Daisy, my siblings, and I all agreed the best thing to do was to take her off of life support. We each took a turn alone in the room with her for a private moment.

At first I didn't want to say goodbye. She was the cause of so many bad things that happened to me. What I couldn't understand is why I cared so much?

At the last minute, I changed my mind. I entered the

room and looked at her lying lifeless in the tiny hospital bed. She was on a breathing machine, with tubes and wires on every part of her body. There was even one down her throat. All at once, feelings that I did not even know I felt came flooding out. I gently took her hand, then like a child I cried.

"I love you, Mom. I always have, but sometimes you are a hard woman to love back. All I ever wanted was to feel like you loved me. I'm sorry this has happened to you."

I sat on the bed beside my mother and held her hand. I ran my fingers through her dark hair, remembering all of the good things about her. The times we'd had together that I'd totally forgotten about. Like how she would take me to the Indianapolis Museum of Art and walk the grounds with me. I could vividly remember holding her hand, skipping around signing Jiminy Cricket's version of "Zip-a-Dee-Doo-Dah." I leaned over and kissed her on the cheek. I told her I loved her.

Walking out of the room, I stopped at the doorway to look back. My emotions were at war. I avoided the rest of my family and hid in the restroom long enough to wash my face with cold water, trying to regain some kind of composure.

When I returned to my mother's room, everyone was present and there was a nurse standing over her, preparing to remove the respirator. The nurse explained that once removed, she would only have a few minutes before her heart would stop beating and she would be gone from us. She asked each of us if we understood what was about to happen. We nodded in turn. She then removed the respirator. We were all startled when Mother gasped for air! Her face contorted in pain. Then there was a horrible, bone-chilling moan.

"Is she in pain?!" I screamed at the nurse. "Somebody do something! She is still alive!"

"No, no she is not alive, nor does she feel any pain.

This is just how the body reacts. It is very natural. She left us days ago," the nurse explained.

I then looked at the monitor. My mother's heart rate was quickly slowing, then eventually it flat lined. The room was uncomfortably silent, but you could hear the roar of muted grief and sadness that consumed each of us. We were all remembering her in our own way.

It took me several months to get over the loss of my mother. I felt very lonely. Even after her death I was desperately seeking her love.

It almost seemed like time was moving backward for me. The closer I got to the end of my senior year in high school, the more slowly the clock ticked.

Losing my mother made me want to know who my father was. When I asked Grandma Daisy about it, she tried to tell me to leave it alone. She explained that some things are better left unknown. That was not an answer I could accept. I wanted to know that part of my past and I was determined to get answers. Grandma Daisy knew she couldn't stop me, so eventually she conceded.

The only phone number she had was John O'Malley's, Sam's father. Giving me the number, she explained that John O'Malley was my grandfather. It suddenly struck me as odd that I didn't know any of this. Why didn't I know this part of my life?

Grandma Daisy's lips trembled as she dialed the number and handed me the phone. I could hear the vibrating sound of the ring. Eventually there was a voice on the other end.

"Hello?"

"Are you John, I mean John O'Malley," I asked, my voice cracking with fear.

"Yes I am. Who is this?"

"Um, Jack, Jack O'Malley."

There was silence on the other end for an awkward moment.

"Jack?" John finally said. "Cindy's son?"

"Yes," I answered. "Cindy is my mother."

"Can I ask why you are calling?" the scratchy voice asked.

"Well, I was hoping to speak to my father, Sam."

It was dead silent. I wanted to go on asking questions, but I made myself wait for him to speak.

"Jack, first of all, my son Sam is in the FBI. It's hard enough for me to reach him, let alone to tell you how to get a hold of him. But that's a different point. I hate to be the one to tell you this, but Sam is not your father. You're going to have to search somewhere else for whatever it is you are trying to find."

I was flabbergasted, stunned into silence. The phone seemed to simply hang from my head until the man who I thought was my grandfather continued.

"Jack, please don't call here again." With that, the line went dead.

My hands shook as I slowly put the phone back on its receiver. It felt like someone had stuck a knife into my heart. I had no idea what to think. I was immobilized and humiliated. Had my mother lied to me? Or was John lying to me?

It then occurred to me that it didn't really matter. I didn't know the man anyway, and Sam never bothered to reach out to me. Screw him! I didn't need that son of a bitch anyway.

A part of me always questioned whether Sam was my father. Now that my mother was dead I would never know the truth.

I decided to remove all traces of Sam O'Malley from my life. I would take my grandmother's last name. Jake Napier had a good ring to it and Grandma Daisy was more of a father to me than anyone.

As soon as I turned eighteen I went to the courthouse and changed my name officially. From that day forward I would be known as Jack Napier.

BROOKE

CHAPTER TWENTY-SIX

"Indifference and neglect often do much more damage than outright dislike."
~ J.K. Rowling

Facebook Message from Brooklyn Page Napier 10/1/2014 at 7:34 am:

Good Morning!

Facebook Message from Tyler Ward 10/1/2014 at 7:35 am:

Hey, how's it going?

Facebook Message from Brooklyn Page Napier 10/1/2014 at 7:37 am:

I broke things off with Nick and Jack has agreed to go to counseling with me.

Facebook Message from Tyler Ward 10/1/2014 at 7:39 am:

That's a positive step!

Facebook Message from Brooklyn Page Napier 10/1/2014 at 7:41 am:

I know but when I really think about it I'm not sure I want it to work. I'm so burnt out with the whole thing. When I look at Jack I just don't feel it anymore.

Facebook Message from Tyler Ward 10/1/2014

at 7:43 am:

It's not easy! You have to focus on the good things about him. The things that made you fall in love with him.

Facebook Message from Brooklyn Page Napier 10/1/2014 at 7:44 am:

I guess.

Facebook Message from Tyler Ward 10/1/2014 at 7:45 am:

How did you meet Jack anyway?

Facebook Message from Brooklyn Page Napier 10/1/2014 at 7:48 am:

I actually grew up with him but we lost contact after high school. We re-connected on a summer study abroad trip to Helsinki Finland my junior year of college. He was attending the Indianapolis satellite campus so I was surprised when I saw him when I got there.

Facebook Message from Tyler Ward 10/1/2014 at 7:49 am:

Wow! That's a weird coincidence..

Facebook Message from Brooklyn Page Napier 10/1/2014 at 7:55 am:

It gets even more weird. As a going away gift, our class was invited to a Russian ballet in St. Petersburg. This was our final event before all the American students headed back to the States. When

we got there the girls went shopping and the guys checked out the bars. We didn't see each other until the mandatory ballet we all had to attend.

Here's where it gets really weird. The day of the ballet all the girls were on time and bought our tickets together. Of course the guys were late so they bought their ticket much later than us.

When I looked at my ticket I noticed I was not sitting next to the other girls on the third level. My ticket was on the second level. So I found my seat and waited for the ballet to start. That's when Jack walked up. When I asked him what he was doing he showed me his ticket. It was the seat next to mine. I couldn't believe it! It had to be more than just a coincidence. At time I thought it was fate. But, now I realize that was just the hopeless romantic in me.

Facebook Message from Tyler Ward 10/1/2014 at 7:56 am:

Everything happens for a reason Brooke.

Facebook Message from Brooklyn Page Napier 10/1/2014 at 7:57 am:

I don't believe that shit anymore.

Facebook Message from Tyler Ward 10/1/2014 at 7:58 am:

You got three awesome boys as a result. Could you imagine life without them!!

Facebook Message from Brooklyn Page Napier 10/1/2014 at 8:01 am:

They are as miserable as I am. They see Jack and I fighting all the time. What kind of life is that for a kid to see. All we are doing is fucking them up now and later in life.

Facebook Message from Tyler Ward 10/1/2014 at 8:03 am:

I'm just saying there was a reason you met Jack. Maybe there a reason you are having problems now. Love is not easy Brooke.

Facebook Message from Brooklyn Page Napier 10/1/2014 at 8:08 am:

I love my kids but I should never have dated Jack let alone marry him.

Facebook Message from Tyler Ward 10/1/2014 at 8:11 am:

You shouldn't say things like that Brooke.

Facebook Message from Brooklyn Page Napier 10/1/2014 at 8:12 am:

The first time Jack and I were together he basically raped me.

Facebook Message from Tyler Ward 10/1/2014 at 8:13 am:

What?!!!

Facebook Message from Brooklyn Page Napier 10/1/2014 at 8:15 am:

Yes! We were in Finland and it was my 21st birthday. Our class took a cruise from Helsinki to Stockholm and I got really drunk. I remember doing shots with my economics professor and then I blacked out. When I woke up in the morning I was in my bed and I had little memory of the night before.

When I went to breakfast everyone was staring at me like I was crazy. My best friend Heather started filling me in about all the craziness. Apparently I was wasted and out of control. Then she told me I left the ship's disco with Jack and never returned, although Jack did. It's was rumored that Jack and I had sex. There was also rumor that Jack took pictures!

I was devastated because for one thing I was a virgin. I was so upset I didn't confront Jack about it until we got back to school in Helsinki. He admitted to having sex with me but that I basically pushed myself on him. That was bullshit! Jack's aggressive by nature so I'm sure he took advantage of me. Plus, he felt so guilty about it when I approached him. He was so nice to me the rest of the trip. I'm sure he was afraid I was going to report him. Anyway, from there our fucked up relationship blossomed!

Facebook Message from Tyler Ward 10/1/2014 at 8:09 am:

I don't know what to say. That's really messed up.

Facebook Message from Brooklyn Page Napier

10/1/2014 at 8:10 am:

I know!

JACK

CHAPTER TWENTY-SEVEN

"There's nowhere you can be that isn't where you're meant to be..."
~ John Lennon

Jack Napier - Day 51

After I graduated from North Central I started taking classes at a local community college. Indiana University Purdue University Indianapolis (IUPUI) was the place where kids at the main campuses in Bloomington and West Lafayette fell back on, the ones who couldn't balance school and social life. It was also the place for kids who didn't have good enough grades to get into the main campuses. I was one of the kids in academic purgatory. Even though IUPUI was a top rated school for academics, it had the stigma of being the place kids went to when they couldn't get into a "good college."

I didn't care, I was just glad to be out of high school and in control of what classes I took. For the first three years of college I was focused on getting good grades so I didn't have to struggle after I graduated. I didn't want to end up like my mom and grandpa Bob. I wanted a family, a real family. So, I was focused like never before.

Then at the end of my junior year a flyer outside my advisor's office caught my eye. It was an invitation to spend the summer in Finland at the Helsinki School of Economics and Business Administration on an exchange program. It would also count as credit toward my degree. I was dying for a little adventure, so I applied immediately.

I got into the exchange program, and before I knew it I was getting off a plane at the Helsinki International Airport. Our group was greeted by a beautiful Finnish girl with silky hair that was so blonde it was almost white, and bright blue eyes that looked like two sapphire crystals. She introduced herself as Netta, then explained that she was assigned to chaperone our group during our stay in Mikkeli. After collecting our bags we walked through the airport to a van parked outside. As we drove up to the dorms, I spotted a familiar face. When I got out of the van, I froze in place. *No freaking way,* I thought.

"Hi, Jack! What are you doing here?" Brooke asked, surprised to see me as well.

The butterflies in my stomach started to multiply, sending my nerves into overload. I was at a loss for words.

"I can't believe I didn't notice your name on the student roster," Brooke continued.

"It's because I changed my last name to Napier," I replied.

"That was very nice of you to take your grandmother's last name. I know how important she has been in your life."

"My old last name never really belonged to me, and after my mother died I wanted to make a clean start. I know it may sound weird but my grandma's last name has a lot of meaning to me."

I hadn't seen Brooke since high school. I couldn't believe it took all this time for us to bump into each other.

"You really do look great, Brooke." The feelings I had

for her quickly rushed back to me like a child who has found their lost puppy.

It wasn't long before we sparked up our old friendship. We had morning coffee, then met for lunch almost every day. Sometimes in the evenings we would jog through the pine forest together, and still in running clothes, we would sit and talk for hours. It seemed just like old times, but much better..

Every morning when I woke, I would think, *it's only 45 minutes until I get to see Brooke for coffee.* Then one morning Brooke didn't show. I sat there alone, a million questions whipping through my mind. Was she okay? Was she sick? Had I done something that made her unhappy with me? When the next morning came and she didn't show again, I went looking for her. When I found her she just blew it off like it was no big deal. Over the next few weeks she become more and more distant.

Then one night like a car wreck I was blindsided with the truth. The Finnish students had put together a costume party for all the Americans. It was going to be a real blowout.

No one recognized me when I walked into the party with my face painted like Gene Simmons from Kiss. Brooke knew it was me right away. When we were kids she would watch me draw different versions of the band members.

Brooke was dressed as Pocahontas. Her hair was braided into pigtails, and she was crowned with an Indian style headdress. Hugging her slender body was a revealing light brown skirt with slits on each side, and fig leaves sewn on at the hem. She had the eye of every guy in the room. I couldn't fight the urge to look at her. I loved everything about her.

When Brooke saw me, she smiled. I was sure that was my cue to walk toward her. Halfway through the room, she turned to Mika, one of the Finnish chaperones. Her eyes twinkled as he leaned in and kissed her on the cheek.

What?? My heart didn't just sink, it dropped into the pit of my stomach like a giant bolder. No amount of makeup could cover my sadness.

What was that about? Was Brooklyn dating Mika? *That would explain why she's been so distant,* I thought.

I tried not to look at Brooke, but I couldn't get her out of my line of sight. All night I watched as they talked and flirted, while the empty hole in me grew. Then, Mika took Brooke's hand and they left the bar. She didn't even stop to say goodbye.

Although there wasn't enough alcohol at the bar to dull the pain I was feeling, I tried anyway. Straight shots chased with beer, then hard-cider chased with more shots. I was sure taking another girl home would make me feel better.

At this point, I had no inhibitions. I was the life of the party. By the end of the night I had become friendly with a local Finnish girl. I saw three of her, but was planning on leaving with the one in the middle. I didn't know her name, but it wasn't like I was going to remember it anyway. Even if I did there was no way I could pronounce it in my drunken state.

As we continued to talk it became apparent that we found each other intriguing, maybe because we were so different from one another. Her complexion was almost translucent, draped with flowing blonde hair that accentuated her blue eyes.

When we left I invited myself to her dorm room. I was ready to redeem myself. Peeling off layers of clothes, I haltingly explored her body with my hands. Then I kissed her neck.

Suddenly unbidden images of Brooke ran through my head. Just like all the corny love stories I thought were so cliché, I pulled away. I couldn't do it.

Sliding down onto her bed, I shook my head, wishing Brooke's image would just get out of my head.

"You are in love with the girl at the bar, the one you

kept watching. I saw how you looked at her. I think it's cute," said the Finnish beauty in her sexy accent.

Then she curled up in my arms, pulled the blanket up over both of us, and turned off the lamp. There in the dark, in lonely silence, we lay together, wrapped in each other's arms.

For the next few days, everything was in slow motion for me. The end of the trip was only a few weeks away. I could hardly wait to board the plane for Indiana.

The following week we had our class trip to St. Petersburg to see a Russian Ballet. When we got there the girls went there way and we went ours. Markus, the chaperone for the guys, slyly told us he could get some homemade champagne. We were in! Within an hour Markus was back with enough bubbly to knock every one of us on our ass.

We drank until the sun came up, then drank some more. After all, a bunch of guys going to a ballet sounded pretty unmanly. Later that day, the girls made it to the show hours before it was scheduled to start. They went window shopping, had lunch, and watched Russian people go about their lives. Right on time, they picking up their tickets.

The guys didn't feel like doing much of anything but dying. We were so busy trying to recover from our wicked champagne hangovers that we lost track of time. We had to rush to get to the show before it started. Running up to the will call window at the last minute, we feared our tickets had been given away. We were lucky; they were still there.

Once inside the Mariinsky Theatre, I stopped at the second level, while the rest of the guys continued to the third. My ticket clearly said I was on the second level.

"Hey guys, doesn't your ticket say second level?"

"No," they all replied.

Glancing at my ticket, I confirmed that my seat was on the second level. There was no mistake about it.

When I got to my seat I found Brooklyn sitting in the seat right next to mine.

"What are you doing here?" I asked, completely confused.

You're not going to believe this, but all the girls are on the 3rd floor and I'm the only one on the 2nd."

"You're kidding, me too!" I shouted.

The moment suddenly changed from a strange coincidence to something divine.

"I thought you were mad at me, Brooke." I murmured.

Brooke gazed at me for a moment, her eyes telling me all I needed to know.

The lights slowly dimmed as the curtain went up revealing two dancers swimming in a pool light. It was absolutely stunning. It wasn't just a dance, it was poetry, with a stream of motion that told a story.

I felt Brooke's eyes on me as I marveled at the dancers. Reaching over I slipped my hand into hers. I felt complete.

When we returned to Finland our class was invited to take a cruise to Stockholm as a going away gift.

It just happened to be Brooke's 21st birthday and it was the first time we were intimate. Although, Brooke was so drunk she doesn't remember. It all started at dinner on the ship. Brooke was slowly getting wasted while I was keeping my cool and pacing myself.

The dining room was elegant with crystal chandeliers and round tables dressed in white tablecloths. Brooke sat next to me while I made small talk with one of our economics professors. Under the table, however, her hand had a mind of its own. Firmly gripping my thigh, it massaged its way up my groin. I pulled my legs inward and glared at Brooke to stop. I think this turned her on because next thing I knew she was rubbing her foot against my leg. Then she grabbed my crotch as she bit down on her bottom lip.

What the hell? I had never seen Brooke this way

before. There was a mixture of emotions whirling around inside of me. I was aroused, but something didn't feel right. This was Brooke! She wasn't that kind of girl.

After dinner we went to the ship's disco. Brooke grabbed my hand and guided me through the crowd until we were in the center of the rotating dance floor. Next thing you know she was grinded on me like a stripper.

"Y-y-ou knooow whaaaat I n-n-need?" Brooke slurred as she pulled on my shirt.

"What's that?" I replied.

"I n-n-need my caaaamera! Cooome wiith me to geeet my caaaamera, Jaaack!" Then Brooke whispered in my ear. "Leeet's g-g-go nooow!"

Her warm breath sent chills down my neck. When we got to her room, Brooke was all over me like she was on the dance floor. Then she started taking my shirt off. Next thing I knew we were both naked. I wasn't making love to her like I had always envisioned. Instead, I was fucking her like an animal.

Then I heard a retching sound. Brooke was dry heaving as hung off the side of the bed. I think she was trying to keep the room from spinning. Picking her up I carried her to the bathroom and resting her head on the plastic toilet seat. After sitting with Brooke for a while I cleaned her up then put pajamas on her.

KNOCK! KNOCK! KNOCK!

"Hold on a minute!" I yelled.

Closing the bathroom door I quickly put my clothes back on. When I answered the door I saw the after party standing in front of me. They asked where Brooke was and I explained how she wasn't feeling well.

"Come down the hall to Chris's, we're playing drinking games."

I wasn't sure that was a good idea with Brooke being sick and all. So, I declined at first.

"Come on, she'll be alright!" they pressed.

Regretfully, I agreed.

The next day Brooke looked like she had the stomach flu. Things were definitely awkward between us on the trip back home. Later that week Brooke approached me discreetly. She directed me to a conference room where she started integrating me like she was trying to solve a cold case.

"Did we have sex that night on the cruse?" She asked.

She didn't remember?! I thought.

"Yes," I said, not sure how best to answer the question.

Brooke immediately began to cry. I felt like an asshole but I didn't do anything wrong. Anyone else in my position would have done the same thing. If I would have known how this was going to haunt our relationship I would have never let her talk me into going back to her room. I said the only thing I thought would fix the situation.

"Brooke, I love you!"

"This is not how it was supposed to happen, Jack!"

"We were drunk, Brooke, and you were all over me."

"You should have been a gentleman and done the right thing!"

"Look, I am sorry. I love you." It was all I could say.

BROOKE

CHAPTER TWENTY-EIGHT

"I am living in hell from one day to the next. But there is nothing I can do to escape. I don't know where I would go if I did. I feel utterly powerless, and that feeling is my prison. I entered of my own free will. I locked the door, and I threw away the key."
~ Haruki Murakami

Facebook Message from Tyler Ward 10/7/2014:

What's up?

Facebook Message from Brooklyn Page Napier 10/7/2014:

Just trying to stay away from Jack!

Facebook Message from Tyler Ward 10/7/2014:

Why is that?

Facebook Message from Brooklyn Page Napier 10/7/2014:

He lost his temper the other night and he's being a real asshole.

Facebook Message from Tyler Ward 10/7/2014:

That's not good!

Facebook Message from Brooklyn Page Napier 10/7/2014:

He's not a very likable person. My parents can't stand him and they like everyone LOL! That should have been my first clue not to marry him.

Facebook Message from Tyler Ward 10/7/2014:

So why did you marry him then?

Facebook Message from Brooklyn Page Napier 10/7/2014:

There is something about him I feel connected to. A venerability that attracts me to him. Jack had a rough childhood and I think deep down inside I felt like I could help him. But all he has done is bring me down.

Facebook Message from Tyler Ward 10/7/2014:

That's not good.

Facebook Message from Brooklyn Page Napier 10/7/2014:

I know! Right after we graduated from college we had a big fight that almost end it all. Jack and I met some friends at the Casbah in Broad Ripple and Jack got really drunk. We had been fighting about our wedding plans because my parents were not happy about me marrying him. He wanted me to stand up to my parents but I wasn't ready for that.

After the bar closed Jack and I said goodbye to our friends, then hopped on our bikes and started pedaling our way to my apartment. Jack was so drunk he wrecked his

bike and had to hop on the back of mine.

On the way home Jack starred in about how he was not good enough for me. How he would only complicate my life.

Boy was he right! I should have listened but the way he said it made me more attracted to him.

Facebook Message from Tyler Ward 10/7/2014:

We are always more attracted to the things we cannot have.

Facebook Message from Brooklyn Page Napier 10/7/2014:

Very true! When we got back to my place things got really crazy. Jack had a meltdown. He told me how I couldn't begin to understand what his life was like. Like he was the only person who ever had it bad.

Then he starred punching the wall an throwing furniture. I was so scared I was about to call the police. I'm surprised my neighbors didn't!

When Jack finished his tantrum he fell to the floor and crawled in to a fetal position and began to cry. I sat down beside him and tried to calm him. That's when he told me about the horrible things his step father did to him.

It broke my heart.

Facebook Message from Tyler Ward 10/7/2014:

Wow!

Facebook Message from Brooklyn Page Napier 10/7/2014:

Yeah, WOW is right! That's when we got married.

Facebook Message from Tyler Ward 10/7/2014:

Is there someone in your life Jack reminded you of?

Facebook Message from Brooklyn Page Napier 10/7/2014:

I don't know. Maybe he reminded me of myself.

Facebook Message from Tyler Ward 10/7/2014:

What do you mean?

Facebook Message from Brooklyn Page Napier 10/7/2014:

Maybe I see a reflection of my own sadness in Jack.

Facebook Message from Tyler Ward 10/7/2014:

That's sad Brooke!

Facebook Message from Brooklyn Page Napier 10/7/2014:

Unfortunately, that's life.

Facebook Message from Tyler Ward 10/7/2014:

It doesn't have to be that way. You deserve

to be happy.

Facebook Message from Brooklyn Page Napier 10/7/2014:

I know : (

JACK

CHAPTER TWENTY-NINE

"The sorrow we feel when we lose a loved one is the price we pay to have had them in our lives."
~ Rob Liano

Jack Napier - Day 56

After Brooke and I were married things were rough for the first couple of years. I resented her for not standing up to her parents and she resented me for never wanting to visit her family. We quickly had kids thinking that would help. We even moved Grandma Daisy into the house so she could help with the kids. She was truly a blessing. The boys loved having her with them every day and to me, her presence was like the old familiar pillow I loved as a child.

It wasn't log after Grandma moved it that she was diagnosed with cancer. The diagnosis was a vague explanation of an out-of-control cell growth in Grandma's left kidney. Treatment was "iffy" at best, and might even cause additional complications. We tried chemotherapy for a while, but it was awful. She wanted to stop, and I couldn't blame her. She told me she had reflected on her life, and the legacy she was leaving behind more than satisfied her. So, Grandma Daisy spent her remaining days with me and my three boys. At this point Brooke was

very elusive and I hardly saw her anymore. She was not happy and I really don't know why. She even started taking Prozac.

It was hard for me to watch Grandma Daisy's health deteriorate. One day we were joking and watching a movie, and the next day she was losing her balance and falling. Deep down inside, I knew the end was coming.

A few weeks later, we purchased a wheelchair for her and had a ramp built onto the front porch. It wasn't long before the dining room became her bedroom. The central location made it easier to care for her when she was finally bedridden.

The insurance company provided a part-time nurse who came in the mornings and afternoons. Grandma Daisy would fall into and out of consciousness while I sat at her bedside.

One morning, I remember waking particularly early. I walked to the kitchen, checking on her as I passed. Charlie was sitting by her side, holding her hand. My heart lurched at the sight of this gentle tableau. Grandma Daisy's eyes were open and she was staring at the cracks in ceiling. She knew that Charlie was there but she struggled to turn her head to look at him. When he was in her line of sight, she smiled. I started to tear up. She was in extreme pain, yet she still smiled on those she loved.

I joined Charlie at her side, and kissed her on the forehead. My eyes drifted up to meet hers. For a moment there was that twinkle that I loved so much.

"Jack," she said with a heavy breath and watery eyes, "You've turned out to be a fine, fine man. I couldn't have asked...for anything better."

"Shhh, you need to save your energy," I said, fighting back my tears.

"There is something that is very important that I need to tell you, Jack."

"What is it, Grandma?"

Her face twisted in sorrow then she whispered, "I am sorry you never had a father. I see the father you are to your boys and I am so proud of you. And your mother is proud of you too. I know you had your differences, but she loved you, Jack. She was young and very confused when she had you, but she always loved you. She just didn't know how to show it."

She swallowed and licked her dry lips as I tried to mask the pain that showed on my face. Then Grandma Daisy looked up and studied me, like she was trying to memorize every detail of the moment. She struggled hard to smile.

That was my last memory of her. She died in her sleep that night.

Grandma Daisy wanted to be cremated, and insisted on having a small ceremony with only her immediate family. She requested that her ashes be used while planting a tree in the front yard of our house. I complied with her every wish except for one.

When the day came to let her rest, I stood before my family with Grandma Daisy's ashes in my hands. My voice cracked, my eyes filled with wonderful memories of my guardian angel. This was the first time my kids saw me openly weep. I told her one last time what she meant to me.

"When no one wanted me, you were there to take me in. When I fell, you picked me up. Sometimes you even carried me when I could no longer walk. You were always there. You are my Guardian Angel. Everything that is good in me is because of you and your sacrifices. True success is measured not by what we possess but rather how much we are loved. You are the most successful person I have ever known. I will miss you more that you could ever imagine. Having you in my life has truly been a blessing."

I then poured part of her ashes in the hole I dug the night before, and planted a river birch among them. It

was her favorite tree. She loved the white flaking bark. I kept part of her ashes to be buried with me when I die.

That was not part of her last wish, however, I could not bear the thought of her being alone. I wanted to have her by my side even in death.

I packed the loose dirt around the tree's base with my foot. When I noticed my boys watching me, I dropped the shovel, and held out my arms to them. We hugged each other in one monolithic embrace.

BROOKE

CHAPTER THIRTY

"Sex is the consolation you have when you can't have love."
~ Gabriel Garcia

Facebook Message from Tyler Ward 10/1/2014 at 12:43 am:

Hey : (

Facebook Message from Brooklyn Page Napier 10/1/2014 at 12:44 am:

What's wrong?

Facebook Message from Tyler Ward 10/1/2014 at 12:45 am:

I have writers block!

Facebook Message from Brooklyn Page Napier 10/1/2014 at 12:46 am:

What are you stuck on?

Facebook Message from Tyler Ward 10/1/2014 at 12:48 am:

I'm trying to figure out the underlining theme of my book? Right now it feels like my story has ADHD lol

Facebook Message from Brooklyn Page Napier 10/1/2014 at 12:49 am:

Hahaha! That's funny!

Facebook Message from Brooklyn Page Napier 10/1/2014 at 12:51 am:

Why do you write? What is it about writing that you love?

Facebook Message from Tyler Ward 10/1/2014 at 12:52 am:

It's my escape.

Facebook Message from Brooklyn Page Napier 10/1/2014 at 12:54 am:

My escape is reading. Things are so bad with Jack all I do is read and masturbate lol

Facebook Message from Tyler Ward 10/1/2014 at 12:55 am:

: o

Facebook Message from Brooklyn Page Napier 10/1/2014 at 12:56 am:

How are things with you and Kim?

Facebook Message from Tyler Ward 10/1/2014 at 12:59 am:

Nothing's really changed. I get once a month maintenance sex as usual. I hope she's just going through a phase. I can't imagine spending my 40s like this. I'm at my sexual peak!

Facebook Message from Brooklyn Page Napier 10/1/2014 at 1:01 am:

I don't know about Kim but these last few

years in my 30s, I've been randy as hell.

Facebook Message from Tyler Ward 10/1/2014 at 1:02 am:

Stop! Your killing me!

Facebook Message from Brooklyn Page Napier 10/1/2014 at 1:03 am:

Are you getting excited :--

Facebook Message from Tyler Ward 10/1/2014 at 1:04 am:

Maybe lol

Facebook Message from Brooklyn Page Napier 10/1/2014 at 1:05 am:

Send me a pic!

Facebook Message from Tyler Ward 10/1/2014 at 1:06 am:

What?!! Have you been drinking?

Facebook Message from Brooklyn Page Napier 10/1/2014 at 1:07 am:

Maybe

Facebook Message from Brooklyn Page Napier 10/1/2014 at 1:10 am:

So?

Facebook Message from Tyler Ward 10/1/2014 at 1:11 am:

Send me one first.

Facebook Message from Brooklyn Page Napier 10/1/2014 at 1:13 am:

Ok I'll send it to your cell phone so you can delete it. I don't trust Facebook.

Facebook Message from Tyler Ward 10/1/2014 at 1:14 am:

K

Facebook Message from Tyler Ward 10/1/2014 at 1:18 am:

OMG those are nice!

Facebook Message from Brooklyn Page Napier 10/1/2014 at 1:19 am:

Are you masturbating?

Facebook Message from Tyler Ward 10/1/2014 at 1:20 am:

:)

Facebook Message from Brooklyn Page Napier 10/1/2014 at 1:21 am:

I want to see!

Facebook Message from Tyler Ward 10/1/2014 at 1:22 am:

I don't know ... I've never done that.

Facebook Message from Brooklyn Page Napier 10/1/2014 at 1:23 am:

We had a deal :)

Facebook Message from Tyler Ward 10/1/2014 at 1:28 am:

Okay, check your phone

Facebook Message from Brooklyn Page Napier 10/1/2014 at 1:32 am:

OMG, I want that inside me so bad right now!

Facebook Message from Brooklyn Page Napier 10/1/2014 at 1:40 am:

Hello? You there?

Facebook Message from Tyler Ward 10/2/2014 at 9:04 am:

You deleted my pic right?

Facebook Message from Brooklyn Page Napier 10/2/2014 at 9:06 am:

What happened to you last night?

Facebook Message from Tyler Ward 10/2/2014 at 9:08 am:

I fell asleep. You deleted the pic I sent you right?

Facebook Message from Brooklyn Page Napier 10/2/2014 at 9:09 am:

YES!

Facebook Message from Tyler Ward 10/2/2014 at 9:10 am:

Good!

Facebook Message from Brooklyn Page Napier 10/2/2014 at 9:12 am:

You don't have to be an asshole about it!

Facebook Message from Tyler Ward 10/2/2014 at 9:13 am:

Sorry, I just feel bad about it.

Facebook Message from Brooklyn Page Napier 10/2/2014 at 9:14 am:

Why?

Facebook Message from Tyler Ward 10/2/2014 at 9:16 am:

I shouldn't have sent that pic.

Facebook Message from Brooklyn Page Napier 10/2/2014 at 9:17 am:

We were just having fun, relax!

Facebook Message from Tyler Ward 10/2/2014 at 9:18 am:

I guess.

Facebook Message from Brooklyn Page Napier 10/2/2014 at 9:19 am:

I can see you're in a bad mood so have a nice day!

JACK

CHAPTER THIRTY-ONE

"Revenge, the sweetest morsel to the mouth that ever was cooked in Hell."
- Walter Scott

Jack Napier – Day 59

Brooke became very distant towards me. When we were together she wanted her "space," which meant I was left alone. Eventually, we were sleeping in separate rooms. I felt like we were living separate lives. This went on for 12 years. At first, I toughed it out for the kids, but then I started to suspect that maybe Brooke was having an affair. So, I tried hacking into her Facebook account.

Figuring out her password was easy; it was the name of our first dog, Bailey. She obsessed over that dog like a newborn baby. If we were out to dinner it wouldn't be five minutes before she would start worrying about him, if he had enough food and water, if he was lonely. The whole ordeal would ruin the night.

Once I was in her Facebook account I saw lots of private messages from her sister Amy, then some from

her friend Stacey. There was nothing suggesting an affair, just a lot of backhanded comments about me never being around anymore. After about an hour of surfing through Brooke's picture comments and messages I decided to quit. Right then a message popped up. It was from Tyler Ward.

Facebook Message from Tyler Ward 10/25/2014 at 11:45 pm:

Is everything okay? I haven't heard from you in a while.

"Tyler Ward! You fucking asshole!" I shouted at my laptop. Then I went to check if there were other messages between Brooke and him.

I saw a list of conversations that seemed to go on forever. It was so overwhelming I didn't know where to start. The more I read the more I filled with hate.

Facebook Message from Brooklyn Page Napier 10/11/2014 at 10:49 pm:

I got on Tinder last week.

Facebook Message from Tyler Ward 10/11/2014 at 10:50 pm:

What?! Why???

Facebook Message from Brooklyn Page Napier 10/11/2014 at 10:51 pm:

It's not bad. You should try it :-)

Facebook Message from Tyler Ward 10/11/2014 at 10:52 pm:

Have you been drinking again?

Facebook Message from Brooklyn Page Napier 10/11/2014 at 10:53 pm:

Just a little :-)

Facebook Message from Tyler Ward 10/11/2014 at 10:54 pm:

You need to get off Tinder!

Facebook Message from Brooklyn Page Napier 10/11/2014 at 10:55 pm:

Why do you care!

Facebook Message from Tyler Ward 10/11/2014 at 10:56 pm:

Because you are my friend!

Facebook Message from Brooklyn Page Napier 10/11/2014 at 10:59 pm:

I started thinking last night... This is/has always been a mostly one-sided friendship. I love ya, but you are there when you need something. You are self-centered and self-serving. You RARELY text just to ask "how are you"...

You say you are worried about others using me, but you are the one who uses me the most. You tell me not to cheat on Jack but yet you fucked me! YOU ARE A FUCKING HYPOCRITE!!!

Facebook Message from Tyler Ward 10/11/2014 at 11:02 pm:

I never used you. I have always been upfront with you.

Facebook Message from Brooklyn Page Napier 10/11/2014 at 11:03 pm:

You are the biggest mind fuck I ever met!

Facebook Message from Tyler Ward 10/11/2014 at 11:04 pm:

You're drunk! I'm done talking about this.

Facebook Message from Brooklyn Page Napier 10/11/2014 at 11:05 pm:

Fuck you!

Facebook Message from Brooklyn Page Napier 10/12/2014 at 9:08 am:

Tyler, I'm so sorry! I just saw our conversation from last night. I didn't mean what I said. I was drunk and hurt.

Facebook Message from Tyler Ward 10/12/2014 at 9:10 am:

Brooke, I'm sorry you are going through this stuff with Jack. I really am. I'm also very worried about you.

Facebook Message from Brooklyn Page Napier 10/12/2014 at 9:11 am:

I'm not in a good place right now. I need help.

Facebook Message from Tyler Ward 10/12/2014 at 9:13 am:

Maybe you need to go on a mission trip. That's what I do when I need to rehabilitate my soul.

Facebook Message from Brooklyn Page Napier 10/12/2014 at 9:14 am:

Yes! We should go on one together!

Facebook Message from Tyler Ward 10/12/2014 at 9:15 am:

Let me look into it for you.

Facebook Message from Brooklyn Page Napier 10/12/2014 at 9:17 am:

Awesome! I don't want to lose you as a friend. Let's just forget about what happened between us last night.

Facebook Message from Tyler Ward 10/12/2014 at 9:18 am:

Okay

Facebook Message from Tyler Ward 10/17/2014 at 10:20 am:

I checked into mission trips and the good ones are expensive. You don't want to go on a cheap one your first time.

Facebook Message from Brooklyn Page Napier 10/17/2014 at 10:21 am:

How much?

Facebook Message from Tyler Ward 10/17/2014 at 10:22 am:

The one to South African is $7,000

Facebook Message from Brooklyn Page Napier 10/17/2014 at 10:23 am:

Wow! That is expensive.

Facebook Message from Tyler Ward 10/17/2014 at 10:25 am:

It covers airfare, food, lodging, and materials to build homes. Most people raise the money through sponsors at their church. That's how I did it.

Facebook Message from Brooklyn Page Napier 10/17/2014 at 10:26 am:

I don't go to church :-(

Facebook Message from Tyler Ward 10/17/2014 at 10:27 am:

Maybe that's where you should start :-)

Facebook Message from Brooklyn Page Napier 10/20/2014 at 11:28 pm:

I officially filed for divorce.

Facebook Message from Tyler Ward 10/20/2014 at 11:29 pm:

What?!

Facebook Message from Brooklyn Page Napier 10/20/2014 at 11:30 pm:

I need to see you.

Facebook Message from Tyler Ward 9/20/2014

10/20/2014 at 11:31 pm:

Okay

JACK

CHAPTER THIRTY-TWO

"I didn't want to wake up. I was having a much better time asleep. And that's really sad. It was almost like a reverse nightmare, like when you wake up from a nightmare you're so relieved. I woke up into a nightmare."
~Ned Vizzini

Jack Napier – Day 60

It hasn't been a good morning for me. Asleep, I have been bombarded with nightmares. Awake, I feel nothing but doubt, fear, and anxiety. I'm restless like a caged bird that flutters its wings in hopes of freeing itself.

Harleen has sensed my mood. I can tell she desperately wants to help me find the truth. This has caused her to push me out of my comfort zone by asking questions about the night my family was murdered.

When she came to see me this morning she skipped the small talk and went right into her questioning.

"Jack I read your journals. I have to say it's not what I was expecting. In fact, some of it was very disturbing."

"What did you expect?" I replied.

"You have such an innocent smile. I just can't imagine you doing some of the things you wrote about."

"Well, when life rapes you sometimes all you can do is smile back," I mumbled.

"See that's disturbing, Jack."

"You're misunderstanding me, I'm just saying that some things are out of our control. So why fight it?"

"Rape is a disturbing analogy, Jack!"

"I was making a point and obviously it worked!"

"I worry about you. There's a very dark side to you." Harleen murmured.

"Harleen, we all have a dark side to us. Some of us embrace it while others run from it. I choose to embrace it."

"You have to be careful, Jack."

"I know I'm fucked up but I'm not a bad person. I'm just a good person that had bad stuff happen to me."

Harleen gazed at me as her eyes swelled. She then quickly changed the subject.

“Jack, I would like to talk to you about what happened the night your family was—”

I quickly interrupted, “Do the police think I killed my family?”

Catching Harleen off guard, she was silent. I don’t think she was expecting me to ask that question.

Making it even more awkward I continued, “Do you think I killed my family?”

I could tell she was unsure. She gave me the textbook answer I was expecting.

“Jack, it doesn’t matter what I think. It only matters what the police can prove. They have found no evidence that anyone else was in the house and statistically most people who are murdered in their own home are killed by someone who is close to them.

The only thing that prevents them from charging you with murders is the fact they found you tied to a chair when they arrived at the house," she added.

"I told you, I remembered being tied to the chair and I have been having flashbacks of Brooke being shot. Then it's all a blank. I don't know why I can't remember!" I pleaded.

I began punching myself in the head, over and over again.

Harleen grabbed my arm.

"Jack, you need to keep it together. We are so close to knowing what really happened. I need to ask you some tough questions to see if we can unlock your memory. You may not like what we uncover, but it will be the truth. Is that okay?" She said gazing into my eyes. Willing me to tell the truth.

"Yes." I replied.

"The police interviewed your sister-in-law. She is ready to testify that your were threatening Brooke. She told the police that Brooke said you lost your temper, that she was afraid of you. Is this true, Jack?"

"She cheated on me and now she has become a slut. I don't want my boys to see the things I saw growing up. So, of course I lost my temper but Brooke wasn't afraid of me. She got off on pushing my buttons and messing with my mind."

"Can you tell me about the problems Brooke and you had when you were married?"

"Brooke had become distant to me. I don't know why. At first, I thought she was having an affair. I confronted her about it and she denied it." I stopped and swallowed hard then continued.

"I begged her to tell me what had changed between us. She had a litany of excuses, like how I never held her hand anymore, how she wanted to work, but I wanted her to care for our children. When I told her I thought she cared more about teaching other people's kids than our own, she shouted that I was not her jailer. No, I wasn't, I just wanted our kids to have a mother at home, something I always dreamed of and never had." I explained.

"Her complaints went from silly to crazy. Sometimes she completely lost it. She would tell me that my horrible childhood had followed me into our married life. She said I had become cold and controlling. I know she didn't mean it."

"Was there more, Jack?" Harleen prodded.

"Okay. All right, she cheated on me. Is that what you want to hear? She said she was depression and I was the reason. When I pressed her..." I stopped, looked down, took a deep breath, and then blew it out. "Brooke told me she was no longer 'in love' with me; what I heard was she no longer loved me. She tried to tell me how you can love someone, but not be 'in love' with them. I told her that was bullshit. You either love someone or you don't.

All the loneliness I felt as a child came rushing back to me like a disease. I couldn't eat or sleep for weeks. I thought about my mother and how she too struggled to love me. Maybe I am unlovable."

My voice cracked with emotion. I began sobbing, so much I couldn't draw in enough breath to get my words out. It took me a moment to get myself together.

"Brooke asked what I wanted from her. I told her I wanted her to notice when I wasn't around. To think of me when she woke in the morning and remember me as she fell asleep at night. I wanted to be the air that filled her lungs, the color that brightened her world. Most of all I wanted to feel her love inside my bruised and beaten heart."

The warmth I once saw in Harleen's eyes turned cold. She glared at me.

"Jack, let's cut the bullshit! We both know you killed your family!"

"What?!" I yelled, completely shocked by Harleen's tone.

"There's no other explanation. What I want to know is how you tied yourself to the chair?"

"I DIDN'T KILL MY FAMILY! "

Harleen moved her hand and gripped the bottom of her chin. Her cinnamon eyes wanted the truth.

"Brooke divorced you and took your kids from you. Everything you worked so hard to build collapsed in on itself. So, you snapped. You killed your wife then your children."

I was so angry I lost it. Getting up in Harleen's face, I yelled, "I DIDN'T KILL MY FAMILY!"

I knew I was on dangerous ground. Quickly calming myself down, I asked, "Am I being charged with murdering my family?"

Harleen glared at me. See could see the truth in my eyes. She then leaned in and kissed me. It wasn't a "I feel your pain" kiss either. It was an "I have wanted to kiss you ever since the day we met" kiss.

"Jack, they are going to release you from the hospital. I don't know what will happen next but you need to continue to get help. There is a lot of pain pent up in you that needs to work its way out in therapy. Otherwise it will release itself in another way, a not so good way. I am very concerned about you."

"What doesn't kill us makes us stronger, right?" I whispered.

That is my last memory of Harleen.

EPILOGUE

Surrounded by flames I sit with the barrel of the pistol in my mouth, its metallic shaft resting on my tongue. I want to feel what it's like to kill myself.

Removing the cold steel from my lips, I pull out three photos and a piece of paper from my back pocket. The first photo is of Brooke and I sitting on the couch embracing each other. We were in college. Her head was in my lap and you could see the love we had for each other in our eyes. The picture becomes blurry as my eyes turn into a swimming pool of lost memories.

The next picture is of Sawyer at his baptism. With his bottom and legs exposed, Father Ted is baptizing him. And lastly there is a family picture with Mickey Mouse at Disney Land. It was the last time we were together as a family before Brooke filed for divorce. The expressions on my boys' faces was priceless. Like a dream. They were oblivious to reality, a state of mind I could only wish for.

I then unfolded my final divorce decree, my eyes focusing on the signature date. May 31, 2015, our wedding anniversary. Exactly thirteen years. It was now sixty days after Brooke filed for divorce. In Indiana there is a statutory waiting period for of sixty days before a divorce can be finalized. They do this to slow down the process, to make you really think about your decision. All it really does is prolong the pain.

This provoked me to relive my last memory of Brooke. A memory I wanted to make disappear.

I am sitting in a chair with my arms tied behind my back and my legs strapped to its front legs. Brooke is standing in front of me. Her knees are shaking and she is pointing a handgun at my head. She gulps for air as she cries historically.

"Y-Y-You did this to me!" She starts then stops, interrupted by her need to breath. Mascara is oozing down her cheeks. Her eyes are puffy with dark red circles

around them. "I was never good enough for you! You killed any self-esteem I ever had."

Taking the handle of the pistol she lightly taps the side of her head as she bites down on her bottom lip.

"I know about Tyler!" I shout as the image of him with and Brooke burn a hole in me.

"So what! You pushed me away, what do you expect!"

I want to hurt him.

"I don't love you Jack! I never loved you!"

My voice is paralyzed. My already broken heart shatters. I gaze at Brooke, bagging her to shoot me.

"I want out of this fucking hell! I want my kids out of this fucking hell!!!" she screams.

"What did you do Brooke? Please don't tell me you ..." I whisper.

"I did what was best for them! They belong with me!"

My body collapses in on itself. I'm sitting but I can feel my legs losing their strength. I become light headed.

Glaring at Brooke I yell, "NO!!!"

BANG!

Brooke drops to the floor in front of me. I blackout.

The sound of Riley cowering by my side brings me back to reality. She is scared.

I know I should hate Brooke for what she did but I still love her. I cannot allow the world to know the truth. I must protect her memory.

I can hear the sound of fire trucks as I point my pistol at Riley. My eye sockets become a sea of emotion. My heart sinks in my chest as I pull the trigger.

My ears are ringing from the gun shot. I get up and walk over to the mirror that is now shattered into little pieces like a spider web. I look at my distorted reflection that is blurred by smeared blood. For a split second I see the little boy I once was, a good boy. I am sad to see him go.

My veins become cold as my heart begins to rot. I can

hear a tapping sound in my head. I beg it to stop but it won't. I am overcome with numbness. I no longer want to know what it feels like to kill myself. Instead I want to know what it feels like to kill someone else.

Grabbing a piece of the broken mirror I put it to my cheek. I press hard until I see blood. Then, I slice down to the corner of my mouth exposing my flesh. I then stuck the piece of mirror into the other side of my mouth and do the same.

Throwing the blood stained piece of mirror on the floor, I wipe my mouth smearing blood across my face. I look at the open window at the back of the room that is now my means of escape.

CONFIDENTIAL PHYCHOLOGICAL REPORT

NAME:	JACK NAPIER	**BIRTHDATE:**	11/14/1978
ADDRESS:	555 DARTMOUTH CT.	**AGE:**	41
	INDPLS, IN 46260		
PHONE:	555-555-5555		
EXAMINER	AMANDA WHITE		

ASSESSMENT

JACK NAPIER 06/16/2020

I IDENTIFY JACK NAPIER AS A PSYCHOPATH. MY FILE REVIEW ASSESSMENT USING THE PSYCHOPATHY CHECKLIST-REVISED (PCL-R) PLACES HIM IN THE 91ST PERCENTILE OF OFFENDERS. THE SCORE ON ONE FACTOR (SELFISH, CALLOUS, AND REMORSELESS USE OF OTHERS) PUT HIM IN THE TOP 1 PERCENT OF INMATES. CLEARLY, THIS SCORE MORE THAN EXCEEDS THE CUTOFF FOR PSYCHOPATHY. THE INSTRUMENTAL NATURE OF THE VIOLENT ACTS JACK COMMITTED IS CLEAR. I BELIEVE THAT JACK WAITED FOR AND, LIKELY, FANTASIZED ABOUT THE KILLINGS. IN HIS MIND, THESE CALLOUS ACTS AVENGED ALL OF THE PERCEIVED WRONGS DONE TO HIM AS A CHILD.

I KNOW OF JACK'S DEVIANCE, LEVEL OF PSYCHOPATHY, AND FANTASY ABOUT KILLING

BECAUSE OF OBSERVATIONS I MADE WHILE EVALUATING HIM AND READING THROUGH HIS JOURNALS.

I FEEL JACK ALSO SUFFERS FROM ANTISOCIAL PERSONALITY DISORDER, ASPD. OVER THE COURSE OF MY ASSESSMENT JACK HAS DISPLAYED A PATTERN OF MALADAPTIVE, IMPULSIVE, AND AGGRESSIVE BEHAVIOR. WHEN PUSHED TO CONFORM HE OFTEN BECOMES VIOLENT.

JACK ESCAPES INTO HIS FANTASIES WHEN UNDER DURESS, OFTEN LOSING HIS GRIP ON REALITY. FOR EXAMPLE, DURING OUR INTERVIEWS HE WOULD REFER TO ME AS HARLEEN AND HAVE CONVERSATIONS WITH ME THAT MADE ABSOLUTELY NO SENSE. HIS JOURNALS WERE A RANDOM COLLECTION OF WHAT I SUSPECT WERE RANDOM MEMORIES AND FANTASIES. THERE WERE EVEN FICTIONAL FACEBOOK CONVERSATION BETWEEN JACK'S DECEASED WIFE AND SOMEONE SHE WAS HAVING AN AFFAIR WITH. JACK IS CLEARLY DELUSIONAL.

SEVERAL YEARS AGO JACK'S WIFE AND CHILDREN WERE MURDERED RIGHT IN FRONT OF JACK WHO WAS TIED TO A CHAIR. THE KILLERS WERE NEVER FOUND. BECAUSE OF THIS AND THE FACT THAT JACK WAS SEXUALLY ABUSED AS A CHILD, I BELIEVE JACK SUFFERERS FROM POST TRAUMATIC DISTRESS DISORDER. THIS MAY HAVE TRIGGERED HIS PSYCHOPATHY.

BECAUSE JACK WAS MOLESTED AS A CHILD (VICTIMS OFTEN REPEAT THE ACTS OF THEIR VIOLATOR) WE SEARCHED HIS HOME EXPECTING TO FIND A CACHE OF SEXUALLY EXPLICIT PHOTOS

OF CHILDREN, INITIALLY WE DID NOT. THEN I WALKED OVER TO THE CLOSET, REACHED UP ABOVE THE OPENING, AND TAPPED ON THE PANELING INSIDE THE CLOSET. AFTER A PIECE CAME LOOSE, I REACHED IN AND EXTRACTED A PACKAGE TIGHTLY WRAPPED IN PLASTIC. THIS SEEMED TO BE A TREASURE FOR JACK, ONE THAT HE WOULD NOT LET EVEN A TORNADO OR FLOOD DAMAGE. AFTER UNWRAPPING IT, I HAD APPROXIMATELY A 2-FOOT PILE OF SHRINK WRAP AT MY FEET, AND I HELD A STACK OF SEXUALLY EXPLICIT PHOTOS OF NAKED MEN. AT FIRST I WAS CONFUSED, THEN IT OCCURRED TO ME THESE COULD BE PICTURES OF JACKS VICTIMS. AFTER FURTHER RESEARCH EVERYONE ONE THEM WERE KNOWN AND UNKNOWN PEDOPHILES. ALL OF WHOM JACK KILLED AFTER HIS FAMILY WAS MURDERED.

THE COMBINATION OF PSYCHOPATHY, ANTISOCIAL CHARACTERISTICS, SCHIZOTYPAL TRAITS, PARANOIA, AND A STRONG DESIRE FOR REVENGE IDENTIFIES JACK AS A VERY VOLATILE AND DANGEROUS INDIVIDUAL. ADDING HIS CALLOUS AND AGGRESSIVE PERSONALITY, FASCINATION WITH KILLING, AND HATRED FOR PEDOPHILES HAS MADE HIM A TICKING BOMB. I NOW RECOGNIZE THE APPROACH ONTO HIS PROPERTY AS THE DETONATOR. HIS DEFENSE OF HIS HOME WAS A RAISON D'ETRE FOR HIM, AND HE LIKELY BOTH FANTASIZED AND PLANNED FOR THE DAY.

UNFORTUNATELY, AT THE TIME, THE RCMP MEMBERS DID NOT HAVE THE KNOWLEDGE OF HIS POTENTIAL FOR VIOLENCE AND LEVEL OF DANGEROUSNESS. THIS TRAGIC EVENT

HIGHLIGHTS THE VALUE OF INTELLIGENCE LED POLICING IN DETERMINING THE THREAT TO MEMBERS OF THE CRIMINAL JUSTICE COMMUNITY AND THEIR FAMILIES.

IT IS MY CONCLUSION THAT JACK REMAIN INSTITUTIONALIZED UNTIL HE IS FIT TO STAND TRIAL.

36335433R00130

Made in the USA
Middletown, DE
30 October 2016

Printed in Canada